VISUAL LANGUAGE

FOR DESIGNERS

ROCKPORT PUBLISHERS

PRINCIPLES FOR
CREATING GRAPHICS THAT
PEOPLE UNDERSTAND

CONNIE MALAMED

ACKNOWLEDGMENTS

My heartfelt thanks to the designers around the globe
who contributed their exceptional work to this book
and to all the professors and researchers who happily
answered my stream of questions. Thanks to everyone
at Rockport Publishers for their dedication and
hard work.

DEDICATION

To Tom for untiring support,
Hannah for invaluable help,
and Rebecca and Silas for sweet encouragement.

Jean-Manuel Duvivier
Illustration, Belgium

CONTENTS

ight is swift, comprehensive, simultaneously analytic, and synthetic. It requires so little energy to function, as it does, at the speed of light, that it permits our minds to receive and hold an infinite number of items of information in a fraction of a second."

CALEB GATTENGO, *Towards a Visual Culture*

WE HAVE NO CHOICE but to be drawn to images. Our brains are beautifully wired for the visual experience. For those with intact visual systems, vision is the dominant sense for acquiring perceptual information. We have over one million nerve fibers sending signals from the eye to the brain, and an estimated 20 billion neurons analyzing and integrating visual information at rapid speed.[1] We have a surprisingly large capacity for picture memory, and can remember thousands of images with few errors.[2]

We are also compelled to understand images. Upon viewing a visual, we immediately ask, "What is it?" and "What does it mean?" Our minds need to make sense of the world, and we do so actively. To understand something is to scan and search our memory stores, to call forth associations and emotions, and to use what we already know to interpret and infer meaning on the unknown. As we derive pleasure, satisfaction, and competence from understanding, we seek to understand more.

Acquiring a sense of our innate mental and visual capacities can enable graphic designers and illustrators to express their message with accurate intent. For example, if one's goal is to visually explain a process, then understanding how humans comprehend and learn helps the designer create a well-defined information graphic. If one's purpose is to evoke a passionate response, then an understanding of how emotions are tied to memory enables the designer to create a poster that sizzles. If one's purpose is to visualize data, then understanding the constraints of short-term memory enables the designer to create a graph or chart that is easily grasped.

In the beginning was the dot.

Maziar Zand,
M. Zand Studio, *Iran*

This book explores how the human brain processes visual information. It presents ways to leverage the strengths of our cognitive architecture and to compensate for its limitations. It proposes principles for creating graphics that are comprehensible, memorable, and informative. It examines the unique ways we can provide cognitive and emotional meaning through visual language. Most important, this book is meant to inspire new and creative ways of designing to inform.

We depend on visual language for its efficient and informative value. As the quantity of global information grows exponentially, communicating with visuals allows us to comprehend large quantities of data. We often find that technological and scientific information is so rich and complex, it can only be represented through imagery. Using an informative approach to visual language allows the audience to perceive concepts and relationships that they had not previously realized.

Our neurons seem to be plugged in to the digital stream, having adjusted to the continual barrage of visual information. With multiple windows, scrolling text, personal digital assistants, new media, digital imagery, video on demand, advertising banners, and pop-ups, we have come to appreciate the fact that visuals reduce the time it takes for a viewer to understand and respond to information. The sheer quantity of visual messages relayed through new technology has led some to call imagery "the new public language."

Visual communication is fitting for a multilingual, global culture. Using basic design elements, it's possible to bypass differences in symbol perception and language to convey our message through imagery. Gyorgy Kepes, influential designer and art educator, envisioned this in 1944, when he wrote, "Visual communication is universal and international; it knows no limits of tongue, vocabulary, or grammar, and it can be perceived by the illiterate as well as by the literate."

▲ *Imagery enables us to apprehend concepts that are difficult to explain. By visualizing three layers of the human form as distinct bodies and using blurred doubles to express motion, the artist provides a glimpse of how each interconnected layer of the body performs while running.*

Daniel Muller, *United States*

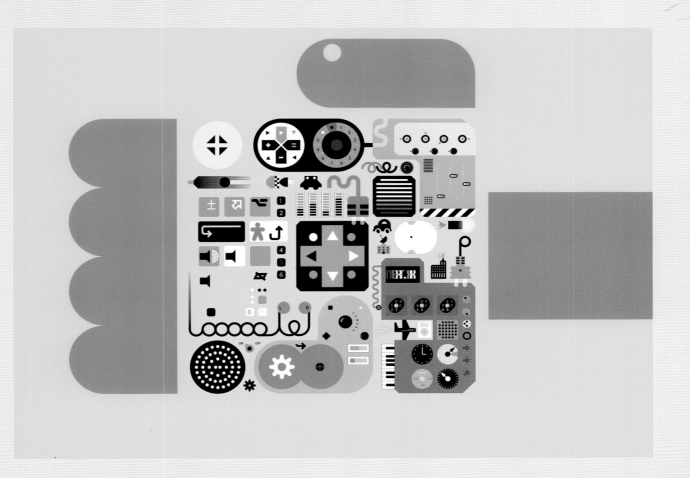

▲ This graphic for Vodafone pairs the complex symbols of technology with the simplicity of iconic forms to effectively convey "technology at your fingertips."

Peter Grundy, Grundini,
United Kingdom

▶ In this graphic depicting the greeting customs of four different cultures, the illustrator uses a minimum of graceful strokes and effective symbols to convey his message.

Nigel Holmes,
United States

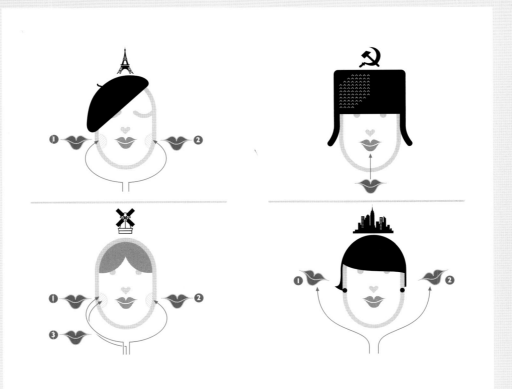

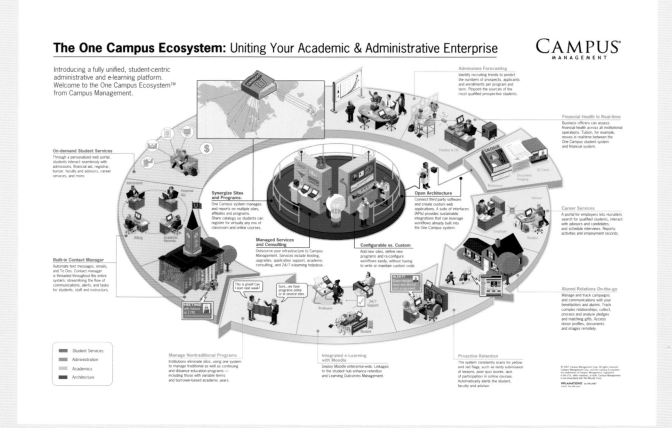

The One Campus Ecosystem: Uniting Your Academic & Administrative Enterprise

CAMPUS
MANAGEMENT

Introducing a fully unified, student-centric administrative and e-learning platform. Welcome to the One Campus Ecosystem™ from Campus Management.

Admissions Forecasting
Identify recruiting trends to predict the numbers of prospects, applicants and enrollments per program and term. Pinpoint the sources of the most qualified prospective students.

Financial Health in Real-time
Business officers can assess financial health across all institutional operations. Tuition, for example, moves in real-time between the One Campus student system and financial system.

On-demand Student Services
Through a personalized web portal, students interact seamlessly with admissions, financial aid, registrar, bursar, faculty and advisors, career services, and more.

Synergize Sites and Programs:
One Campus system manages and reports on multiple sites, affiliates and programs. Share catalogs so students can register for virtually any mix of classroom and online courses.

Open Architecture
Connect third party software and create custom web applications. A suite of interfaces (APIs) provides sustainable integrations that can leverage workflows already built into the One Campus system.

Career Services
A portal for employers lets recruiters search for qualified students, interact with advisors and candidates, and schedule interviews. Reports activities and employment records.

Built-in Contact Manager
Automate text messages, emails, and To Dos. Contact manager is threaded throughout the entire system, streamlining the flow of communications, alerts, and tasks for students, staff and instructors.

Managed Services and Consulting
Outsource your infrastructure to Campus Management. Services include hosting, upgrades, application support, academic consulting, and 24/7 e-learning helpdesk.

Configurable vs. Custom
Add new sites, define new programs and re-configure workflows easily, without having to write or maintain custom code.

Alumni Relations On-the-go
Manage and track campaigns and communications with your benefactors and alumni. Track complex relationships; collect, process and analyze pledges and matching gifts. Access donor profiles, documents and images remotely.

Manage Nontraditional Programs
Institutions eliminate silos, using one system to manage traditional as well as continuing and distance education programs — including those with variable terms and borrower-based academic years.

Integrated e-Learning with Moodle
Deploy Moodle enterprise wide. Linkages to the student hub enhance retention and Learning Outcomes Management.

Proactive Retention
The system constantly scans for yellow and red flags, such as tardy submission of lessons, poor quiz scores, lack of participation in online courses. Automatically alerts the student, faculty and advisor.

- Student Services
- Administration
- Academics
- Architecture

▲ *Visual language enables us to depict processes and systems in their entirety so we can understand the big perspective. This diagram of a campus enterprise system details each component of the system while presenting the global view.*

Taylor Marks, XPLANE,
United States

Communication through imagery has other advantages as well. To explain something hidden from view, such as the mechanics of a machine or the human body, a cross section of the object or a transparent human figure works well. When we need to describe an invisible process, such as how a mobile text message is transmitted, iconic forms interconnected with arrows can be used to represent a system and its events. To communicate a difficult or abstract concept, we may choose to depict it with a visual metaphor to make the idea concrete. Precise charts and tables help to structure information so audiences can easily absorb the facts. When we wish to instigate a call to action, we find that emotionally charged imagery is the most memorable. We see that a graphic with humor or novelty can capture our audience's attention and provide motivation and interest. And when the task calls for an immediate response, we know that a graphic will provide quick comprehension. The power of visual communication is immeasurable.

▶ *This snapshot of social media trends on the Internet was created for* Business Week *magazine. The clear and precise pixel graph provides the coherency we need to make comparisons, find patterns, and appreciate the richness of the data.*

Arno Ghelfi, *United States*

Social Media as a Percentage of Web Traffic

April 2006		April 2007
1%—	**+668%**	— Web Traffic
2%		12%

Percentage of Upload/Edit per visit

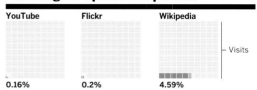

YouTube	Flickr	Wikipedia
		— Visits
0.16%	0.2%	4.59%

Social Technographics Categories

Percent of each generation in each Social Technographics category

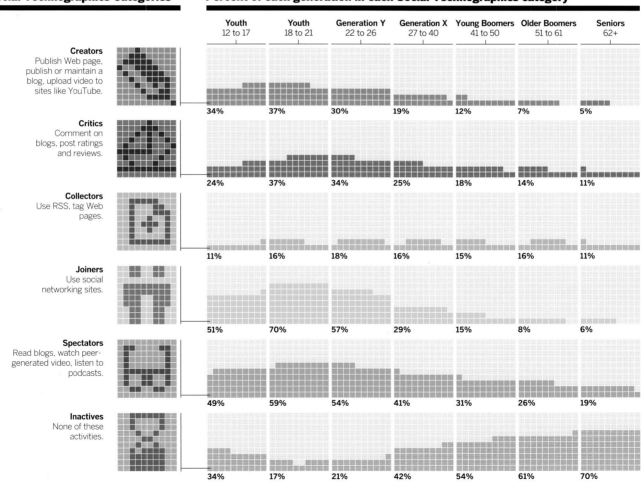

	Youth 12 to 17	Youth 18 to 21	Generation Y 22 to 26	Generation X 27 to 40	Young Boomers 41 to 50	Older Boomers 51 to 61	Seniors 62+
Creators Publish Web page, publish or maintain a blog, upload video to sites like YouTube.	34%	37%	30%	19%	12%	7%	5%
Critics Comment on blogs, post ratings and reviews.	24%	37%	34%	25%	18%	14%	11%
Collectors Use RSS, tag Web pages.	11%	16%	18%	16%	15%	16%	11%
Joiners Use social networking sites.	51%	70%	57%	29%	15%	8%	6%
Spectators Read blogs, watch peer-generated video, listen to podcasts.	49%	59%	54%	41%	31%	26%	19%
Inactives None of these activities.	34%	17%	21%	42%	54%	61%	70%

The Designer's Challenge

The never-ending flood of facts and data in our contemporary world has caused a paradigm shift in how we relate to information. Whereas at one time information was community based, slow to retrieve, and often the domain of experts, information is now global, instantaneous, and often in the public domain. We now want information and content in our own hands and on our own terms. We maintain an underlying belief that it is our fundamental right to have access to well-structured and organized information. As a result, information design is exploding as organizations and individuals scramble to manage an overwhelming quantity of content. Understanding the most effective ways to inform is now a principal concern. According to professor of information design Dino Karabeg, "Informing can make the difference between the technologically advanced culture which wanders aimlessly and often destructively, and a culture with vision and direction."[4]

This has profound implications for graphic communication. There is an increasing demand for the information-packed graphic, greater competition for an audience's visual attention, and ever more complex visual problems requiring original solutions. There are requirements to design for pluralistic cultures and a continuous need to design for the latest technologies.

As part of this new path, visual communicators need a sense of how the mind functions. Effective informative graphics focus on the audience. An increased awareness of how people process visual information can help the designer create meaningful messages that are understood on both a cognitive and emotional level. An informative image is not only well designed; it captures both the feeling of the content and facilitates an understanding of it. The final product affects how the audience perceives, organizes, interprets, and stores the message. The new role of a graphic designer is to direct the cognitive and emotional processes of the audience. In shaping the information space of a visually saturated world, efficient and accurate communication is of primary importance.

Step Inside

Visual Language for Designers is based on research from the interconnected fields of visual communication and graphic design, learning theory and instructional design, cognitive psychology and neuroscience, and information visualization. The imagery incorporates an expansive definition of visual design, exemplifying the diverse fields from which this research is drawn. This type of fusion is natural in a world of collaboration, interrelationships, and blurry delineations, and represents the diverse requests that contemporary designers must often fulfill.

The first section of *Visual Language for Designers* presents an overview of how we perceive, understand, and acquire visual information. The reader will also be introduced to the important concept of cognitive load, which has significant implications in the design of informative graphics.

The second section presents principles for creating graphics that accommodate the human mind and emotions. These principles are intended as a guide—as a space for exploration and discovery rather than hard-and-fast rules. The principles are meant to serve as a catalyst for finding visual solutions and fine-tuning one's work. Most important, this book is meant to inspire new and creative ways of designing to inform.

With a reflective background, this poster captures the museum experience as it receives varying images from the changing surroundings.

Boris Ljubicic, Studio International, *Croatia*

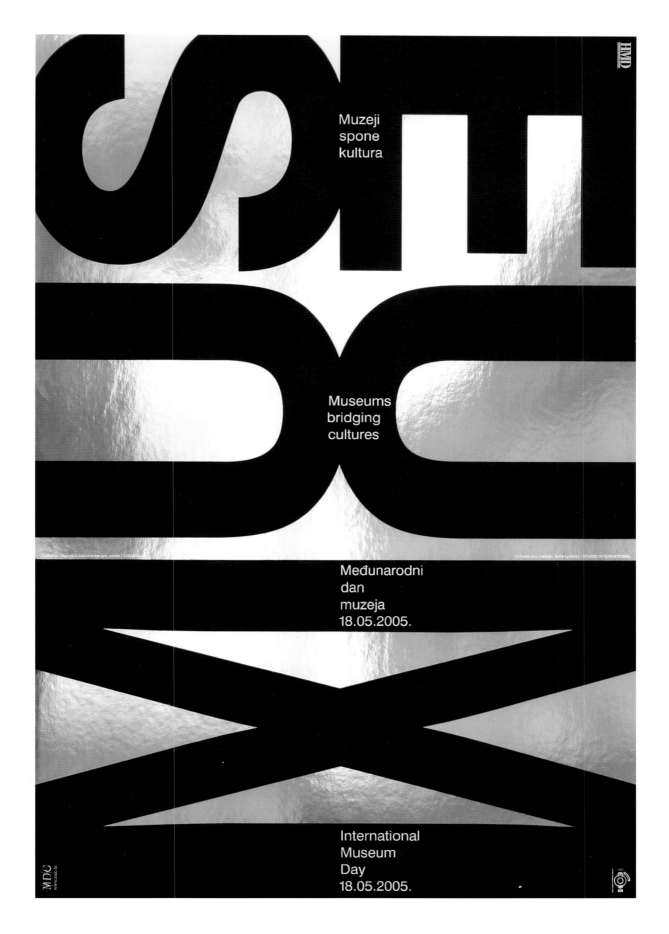

AN Emergent Mosaic OF Wikipedian Activity

Received Honorable Mention in 2007 NetSci Visualizing Network Dynamics Competition
http://vw.indiana.edu/07netsci/

AUTHORS

Bruce W. Herr (Visualization Expert)
Todd M. Holloway, (Data Mining Expert)
Elisha Hardy (Graphic Design)
Katy Börner (Advisor & Sponsor)
Kevin Boyack, Sandia Labs (Node Layout)
School of Library and Information Science
Department of Computer Science
Indiana University
Bloomington, IN 47405, USA
{bherr,tohollow,efhardy,katy}@indiana.edu
kboyack@sandia.gov

INTRODUCTION

This emergent mosaic supplies a macro view of all of the English Wikipedia (http://en.wikipedia.org) and reveals those areas that are currently 'hot', meaning, of late, they are being frequently revised.

ARTICLE NETWORK

The provided dataset [1,2] comprises 659,388 interconnected Wikipedia articles. One article (node) is connected to another if it links to it. There are 16,582,425 links.

POSITIONING

Articles are shown close to one another if they are similar, and far apart if they are different. Two articles are said to be similar if articles that link to one often link to the other.

MOSAIC

The 1,869 images were taken directly from Wikipedia. This represents approximately one image for every 300 articles. The images were selected automatically in a three step process. First, the layout was cut into half inch tiles. Next, the articles in each tile were ranked by their indegree, i.e., the number of articles that link to them. Finally, the first image of the highest ranked article that contains a non-icon image was selected for display. All images of controversial subject matter were kept, making it appropriate for mature audiences.

"The mosaic stunningly illustrates the broad spectrum of what I would call the diffuse focus of the masses. Its value is in its all-encompassing overview, and that it allows one to explore and compare this focus. It would be interesting to see how it changes over time, my faith in humankind would be restored to someday see that Albert Einstein and Muhammad generated more interest than Britney Spears."

Daniel Zeller (Visual Artist)
New York City

"Bruce and Todd have shown a volcanic landscape with lava pools, geysers and crusted-over areas. So far the best representation out there to show what moves mankind's minds. A true mindscape of the public."

Ingo Günther (Journalism & Art)
Tokyo National University for Fine Arts & Music, Japan

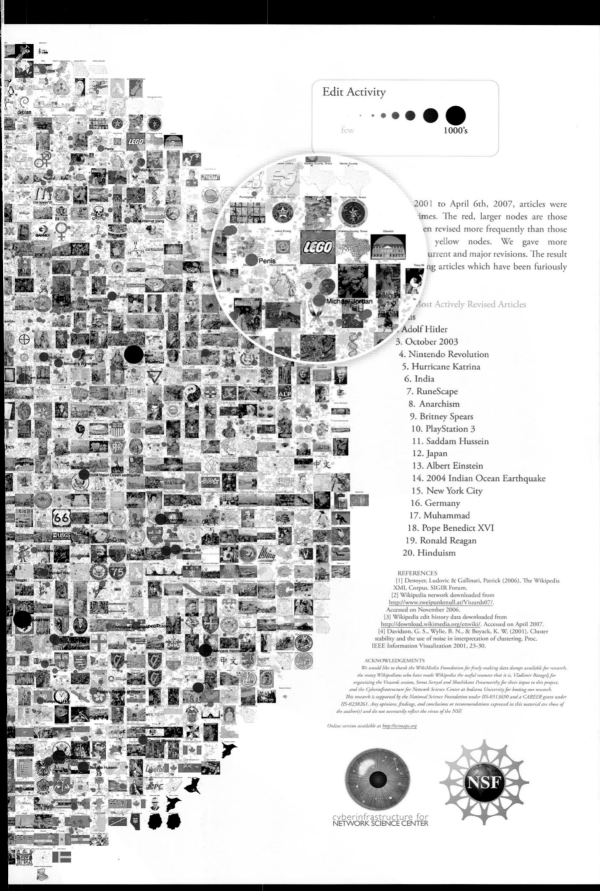

Edit Activity

few   1000's

2001 to April 6th, 2007, articles were
...imes. The red, larger nodes are those
...en revised more frequently than those
...yellow nodes. We gave more
...urrent and major revisions. The result
...ng articles which have been furiously

Most Actively Revised Articles

...is
2. Adolf Hitler
3. October 2003
4. Nintendo Revolution
5. Hurricane Katrina
6. India
7. RuneScape
8. Anarchism
9. Britney Spears
10. PlayStation 3
11. Saddam Hussein
12. Japan
13. Albert Einstein
14. 2004 Indian Ocean Earthquake
15. New York City
16. Germany
17. Muhammad
18. Pope Benedict XVI
19. Ronald Reagan
20. Hinduism

REFERENCES
[1] Denoyer, Ludovic & Gallinari, Patrick (2006). The Wikipedia XML Corpus. SIGIR Forum.
[2] Wikipedia network downloaded from http://www.zweipunktnull.at/Viszards07/. Accessed on November 2006.
[3] Wikipedia edit history data downloaded from http://download.wikimedia.org/enwiki/. Accessed on April 2007.
[4] Davidson, G. S., Wylie, B. N., & Boyack, K. W. (2001). Cluster stability and the use of noise in interpretation of clustering. Proc. IEEE Information Visualization 2001, 23-30.

ACKNOWLEDGEMENTS
We would like to thank the WikiMedia Foundation for freely making data dumps available for research, the many Wikipedians who have made Wikipedia the useful resource that it is, Vladimir Batagelj for organizing the Viszards session, Soma Sanyal and Shashikant Penumarthy for their input to this project, and the Cyberinfrastructure for Network Science Center at Indiana University for hosting our research. This research is supported by the National Science Foundation under IIS-0513650 and a CAREER grant under IIS-0238261. Any opinions, findings, and conclusions or recommendations expressed in this material are those of the author(s) and do not necessarily reflect the views of the NSF.

Online version available at http://scimaps.org

cyberinfrastructure for
NETWORK SCIENCE CENTER

NSF

Combining graphic design and data visualization, this 5-foot (1.5 m) image captures one moment of Wikipedia activity. Through visual representation, we are able to comprehend the colossal number of edits made to Wikipedia every minute.

Visualization:
Bruce W. Herr II

Data Mining:
Todd M. Holloway

Advisor:
Katy Borner, United States

*Getting lost while trying
to understand the mind is
a shared human experience.*

Rhonald Blommestijn,
The Netherlands

SECTION ONE

GETTING GRAPHICS

"The brain adds information to the raw visual impressions, which gives a richness of meaning far beyond the simple stimuli it receives."

ROBERT SOLSO, *Cognition and the Visual Arts*

The Meaning of Pictures

A picture is more than a two-dimensional marked surface. It reflects the creator's intent and signifies there is information to be communicated. It is the artifact of creative play and thoughtful decisions, produced to evoke a visual experience. Designers create graphics with the assumption that viewers will understand their message—that upon viewing that viewers will understand their communication will be transmitted. They assume the viewer will proceed through a graphic in an orderly sequence, controlled by the designer's expression of visual hierarchy.

But how can one know that a viewer will find meaning in a visual communication? How can a designer ensure that the audience will comprehend his or her intent? After all, picture perception can be a tricky affair. When looking at a picture, the viewer consciously or unconsciously experiences competing perceptions. A person perceives the two-dimensional picture surface while simultaneously viewing an illusory three-dimensional space. The viewer must reconcile these contradictory perceptions while at the same time attempting to understand and interpret a picture. A suspension of belief, however small, is often required.

Also, audience members differ in their perceptions and interpretations of a picture. We cannot know how an individual will perceive a graphic, nor what thoughts, emotions, knowledge, and expectations the viewer will bring to a visual encounter. When viewers look at a graphic, their perceptions are inevitably colored by their preconceived ideas, likes and dislikes, values, and beliefs. This can create a powerful bias toward seeing what one wishes to see, potentially missing the designer's intent. Age, gender, educational background, culture, and language are other potent influences on perception.

In a study that examined the gap between intended and perceived meaning, some audience groups misinterpreted the meaning of pictures more than half the time. The author's study concluded, "Despite what appears to be a cross-cultural ability to recognize objects depicted in pictures, the visual content of an illustration is frequently a vehicle to communicate a more complex meaning or intention. Unlike the subject content of the picture, this intended meaning may often be misunderstood or unrecognized by the viewer."[1]

The discrepancy between a designer's intention and a viewer's interpretation may also be due to the enhanced visual skills that artists possess compared to nonartists. When viewing art, the artist excels at synchronizing multiple regions of the brain, which creates a coherent and unified visual perception.[2] This advanced visual skill may be due to training in the arts, a well-developed visual imagination, and a natural inclination toward the visual. Specifically, when viewing a painting, art-trained viewers spend more time looking at background features and the relationships among elements, like shapes and color. Untrained viewers spend more time looking at central and foreground figures, focusing on objects and pictorial elements.[3] Due to this variance in perceptions between artist and nonartist, it is possible that during the act of creation, the designer cannot quite anticipate what the audience will perceive.

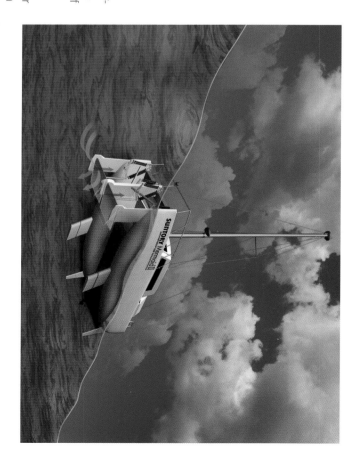

While viewing a graphic, we simultaneously perceive the flat two-dimensional picture plane and the three-dimensional picture space, exemplified in this catamaran information graphic for Popular Science *magazine.*

Kevin Hand, *United States*

Our perceptions are partially driven by concepts and emotions and influenced by age and cultural background. In this sex education spread for a magazine popular with Brazilian teenagers, Mundo Estranho, it is likely the teens will perceive and react to these graphics quite differently than their parents.

Reneta Steffen and Carlo Giovani, Carlo Giovani Studio, Brazil

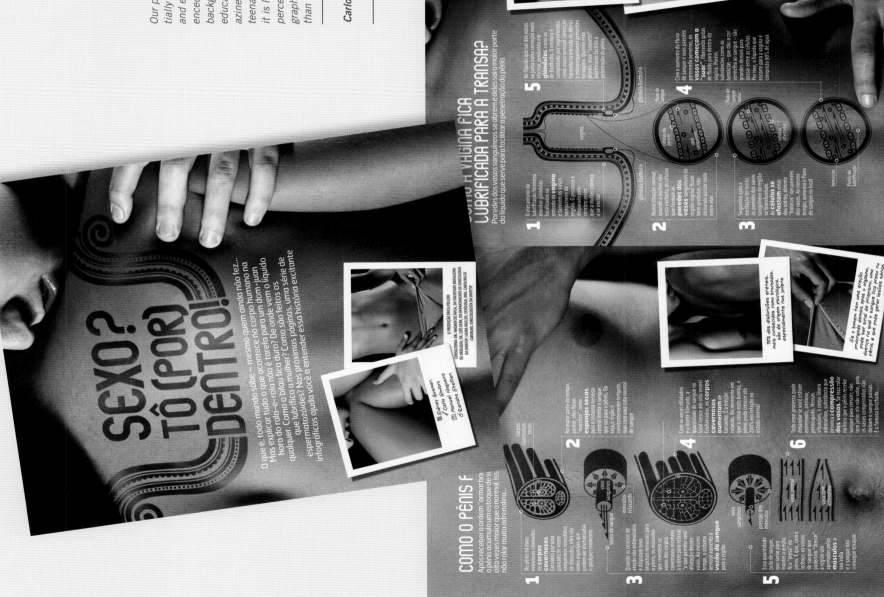

Despite these challenges, graphic designers seek to create clarity in their communications so viewers will accurately interpret the intended message. "This is the real measure of the performance of any and every piece of graphic design and the proof that graphic design cannot be understood in isolation but only within a communication context," writes Jorge Frascara in his essay "Graphic Design: Fine Art or Social Science?"[4] Understanding how people process visual information will increase the likelihood that a designer will produce graphics that audiences understand. This is because every aspect of a design and every design element is part of a visual language that conveys meaning to an audience. Fortunately, we can turn to cognitive science—the study of how we think and learn—for a plausible explanation of how people perceive and comprehend visuals.

Human Information Processing System

Cognitive science emerged from several fields, including cognitive psychology, computer science, neuroscience, philosophy, and linguistics, and makes use of the computer as a metaphor for how we process information. It relies on a model known as the *human information-processing system* to explain how raw data from the senses is transformed into meaningful information that we act upon or store away for later use. Not only does our nervous system continuously and instantaneously perform this remarkable feat, it cannot do otherwise.

Our information-processing system consists of three main memory structures—sensory memory, working memory, and long-term memory. The input to the system is raw sensory data that registers in sensory memory. A small portion of this data passes on to working memory—the equivalent of awareness—and is represented there. Some information is coded and stored in long-term memory as new knowledge; some information may simply result in performing an action. With the proper cues, we can retrieve information stored in long-term memory.

For example, when we look at *The Starry Night*, its colors, brushstrokes, and shapes register in sensory memory. The main features and elements of the scene are held in working memory. Simply seeing the painting is a cue to recall the painting's title and the painter's name from long-term memory. In addition, the experience of viewing *The Starry Night* will be stored in long-term memory. With this generic model of cognition, we can examine information processing in more detail, particularly in terms of how we extract visual information and interpret and understand pictures.

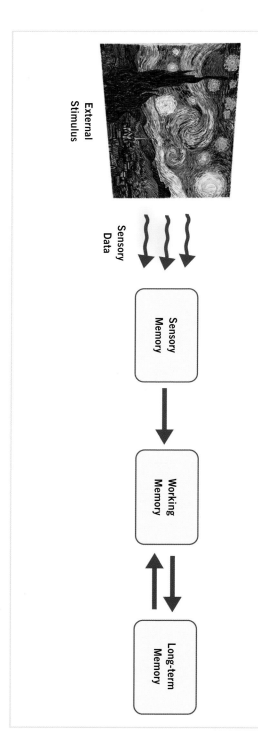

External Stimulus

Sensory Data

Sensory Memory

Working Memory

Long-term Memory

The human information-processing system is the model that cognitive scientists use to understand how people transform sensory data into meaningful information.

Visual Perception: Where Bottom-Up Meets Top-Down

We are able to see a picture because reflected or emitted light focuses on the retina, composed of more than 100 million light-absorbing receptors. The job of the retina is to convert this light energy into electrical impulses for the brain to interpret. One could say that the mechanics of visual perception center on the fovea, the region of the retina that gives us sharpness of vision. The fovea allows us to distinguish small objects, detail, and color. Because the fovea is small, just a limited part of our visual world is imaged on it at any moment in time. Most visual information falls on the peripheral areas of the retina, where the sharpness of vision and detail fall off rapidly from the fovea.

Our eyes must repeatedly move to keep the object of most interest imaged on the fovea. These rapid eye movements, called saccades, allow us to select what we attend to in the visual world. The eye performs several saccades each second. In between saccades there are brief fixations—around three per second—when the eyes are nearly at rest. This is when we extract visual data from a picture and process it. The visual system continuously combines image information from one fixation to the next.

Unlike data streaming into a passive computer, we perceive objects energetically, as active participants. Although our visual awareness is driven by the external stimulus, known as *bottom-up processing*, our perceptions are also driven by our memories, expectations, and intentions, known as *top-down processing*. Visual perception is the result of complex interactions between bottom-up and top-down processing.

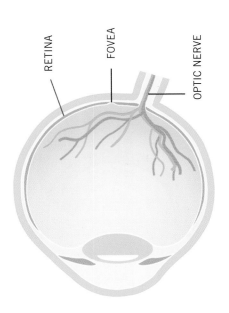

▲ The fovea is the part of the eye that gives us the greatest acuity of vision.

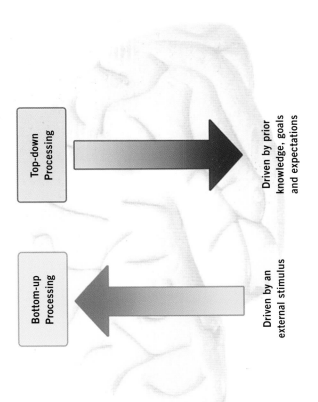

▼ Visual perception results from the complex interactions of bottom-up and top-down processes.

Top-down Processing

Driven by prior knowledge, goals and expectations

Bottom-up Processing

Driven by an external stimulus

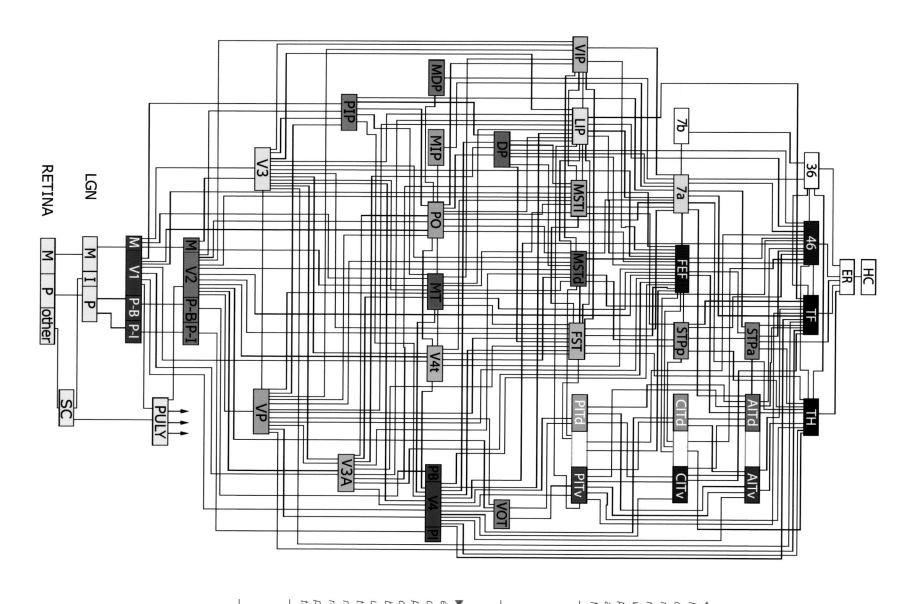

▲ Our visual system is highly attuned to visual composition. This diagram maps the many visual regions of a primate brain, which are specialized to process distinct visual attributes, such as motion, form, and color.

Published in Science magazine, for an article by David Van Essen, Charles Anderson, and Daniel Felleman

▼ In this visually rich explanation of Hindu cosmology, a viewer will preattentively see the colors and shapes through bottom-up processes. Then, using selective attention, the viewer will follow the numbered sequences and relate this information to prior knowledge through top-down processes.

Annie Bisset, Annie Bisset Illustration, United States

Bottom-up visual processing occurs early in the vision process without conscious attention or effort, propelled by the brain's persistent need to find meaningful patterns in the visual environment. When we happen to glance at a picture or a scene, we detect motion, edges of shapes, color, contours, and contrasts through bottom-up processes without conscious awareness.[5] As our brain processes these primitive features, it discriminates foreground from background, groups elements together, and organizes textures into basic forms. This occurs rapidly, helping us to recognize and identify objects. The output from bottom-up processing is quickly passed on to other areas of the brain and influences where we place our attention. This second phase of perception, top-down processing, is strongly influenced by what we know, what we expect, and the task at hand. We tend to disregard anything that is not meaningful or useful at the moment. Top-down processing so affects our visual perception that some say we see more with our mind than our eyes.

Events in our information-processing system occur rapidly and are measured in milliseconds or one thousandth of a second. As we interact with the world, we continually process sensory data in parallel. Different regions of the brain that are attuned to specific visual attributes of a picture, such as color or shape, are activated simultaneously. Accordingly, visual perception produces a network of activated neurons in the brain, rather than a single concentrated area of activated neurons. Massive parallel processing makes the act of perception fast and efficient. Perception and object recognition would be quite slow if data were passed from neuron to neuron in a serial fashion.

Sensory Memory: Fleeting Impressions

When we process sensory data, an impression or brief recording of the original stimulus registers in sensory memory. Sensory memory is thought to have at least two components: an iconic memory for visual informa-tion and an echoic memory for auditory information. Although the impression fades after a few hundred milliseconds, it is buffered long enough for some portion to persist for further processing.[6] In picture perception, the prominent features of the picture along with our conscious attention influence what will be retained.

Working Memory: Mental Workspace

Because we are compelled to understand what we see, we need a mental workspace to analyze, ma-nipulate, and synthesize information. This occurs in working memory, where conscious mental work is per-formed to support cognition. In working memory, we maintain and manipulate information that is the focus of attention, piece together sensory information, and integrate new information with prior knowledge. Like sensory memory, working memory processes informa-tion through two systems; visual working memory pro-cesses visual information and verbal working memory processes verbal information.

A profound aspect of working memory is how it helps us make sense of the world. To understand some-thing, we have to compare it with what we already know. Thus, as new information streams into working memory, we instantaneously search through related information in our permanent store of knowledge to find a match. If we find a match, we recognize the object or concept and identify it. If it is unfamiliar, we make inferences about it.

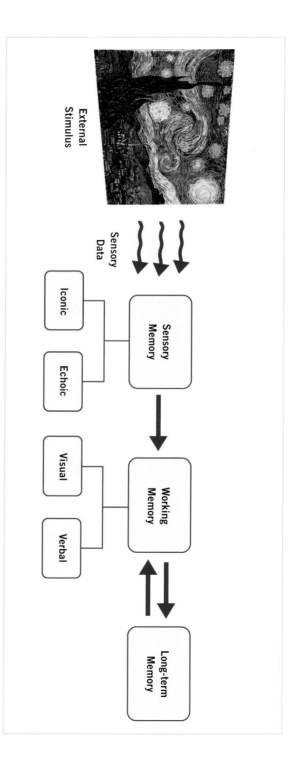

External Stimulus

Sensory Data

Iconic   Echoic

Sensory Memory

Visual   Verbal

Working Memory

Long-term Memory

Both sensory memory and working memory are thought to process informa-tion in separate channels: visual and verbal.

Analyze

Studying The Social Sciences at Holy Cross

Synthesize

Studying the Humanities at Holy Cross

The ability to analyze and synthesize are important aspects of cognition, as aptly expressed in these cover graphics for a college brochure.

David Horton, Philographica, *United States*

For example, upon viewing this map, we separate figure from ground and immediately try to identify the shapes as objects. We rapidly search through our knowledge base (long-term memory) to find a match for the shapes. This activates our associated knowledge of maps and geography. If the external depiction of the map matches our generalized internal representation, we are able to recognize the landmass as "the world" and to understand the symbols from reading the legend. If we cannot identify the landmass or have no knowledge of map reading, we will not understand the graphic. The comprehension of a particular graphic is dependent on a viewer's prior knowledge and ability to retrieve that knowledge.

Two well-known constraints of working memory are its limited capacity and short duration. Although the capacity of working memory is not fixed, it appears that on average, a person can manipulate around three to five chunks of information in awareness at one time.[7] Thus, working memory is considered a bottleneck in the information-processing system. One can easily sense the limits of working memory by performing a sequential mental operation, such as multiplying two large numbers. At some point, more partial results are needed to perform the multiplication problem than working memory can handle. That is when we typically reach for paper and pencil or a calculator.

This statistical map was created for a Newsweek Education Program for high school students to learn how to interpret and analyze information.

Eliot Bergman, *Japan*

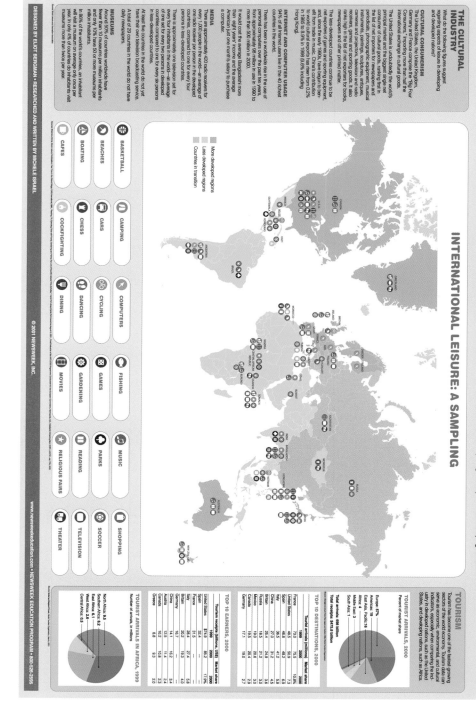

As portrayed in this graphic for Elegance magazine, information in working memory decays rapidly.

Rhonald Blommestijn, *The Netherlands*

In addition to its limited capacity, the short duration of working memory also affects our cognitive abilities. New information in working memory decays rapidly unless the information is manipulated or rehearsed. For example, we must mentally repeat directions until we can write them down or they will quickly fade away. Individual factors also affect the constraints of working memory. Age is a factor; working memory capabilities increase with maturation but decline in old age. Working memory is also affected by the speed with which an individual processes information. Speedier processing results in a greater capacity to handle information. Distractibility is another factor. People who are adept at resisting distractions, which are known to overload working memory, have a greater functional capacity. Finally, a person's level of expertise affects working memory. With a great deal of domain-specific knowledge, an expert is not as easily overwhelmed when performing associated tasks as is a novice.[8]

Conversely, the constraints of working memory can be considered advantageous. The transitory nature of information in working memory enables us to continually change cognitive direction, providing the flexibility to shift the focus of our attention and processing to whatever is most important in the environment. In terms of picture perception, this allows a viewer to instantly perceive and consider a newly discovered area of a picture that may be easier to comprehend or of greater importance. The limited capacity of working memory creates a highly focused and uncluttered workspace that may be the perfect environment for speedy and efficient processing of information.[9]

All About Stem Cells

**Stem cells are the origin of all cells in the body (every cell "stems" from this type).
Under the right conditions, stem cells can become any of the body's 200 different cell types.**

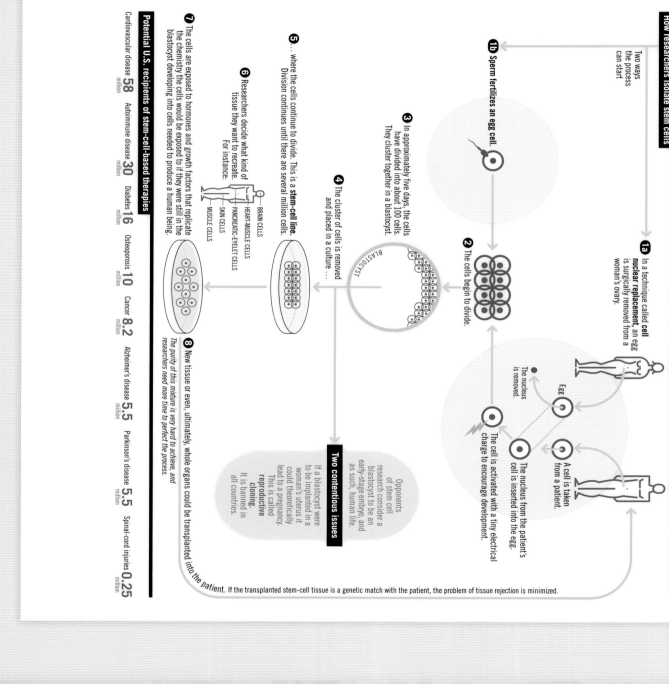

There are two types of stem cell

EMBRYONIC
also called **early** stem cells

"Pluripotent"
can give rise to all cell types
(except cells of the placenta)

	First isolated	**1998** at the University of Wisconsin	**1960s**
	Federal funding (1999 to 2004)	**$55 million**	**$2.24 billion**
	Results	**In animal trials** no human trials to date	**50+ human therapies**

ADULT
also called **mature** stem cells (much the rarer of the two types—
only one of every 10,000 cells in bone marrow, for instance)

"Multipotent"
can give rise to limited cell types

"Unipotent" stem cells are cells
that can self-replicate but not
become a different type of cell.

How researchers isolate stem cells

1b Sperm fertilizes an egg cell.

Two ways
the process
can start

1a In a technique called **cell nuclear replacement,** an egg is surgically removed from a woman's ovary.

2 The cells begin to divide.

3 In approximately five days, the cells have divided into about 100 cells. They cluster together in a blastocyst.

BLASTOCYST

4 The cluster of cells is removed and placed in a culture ...

5 ... where the cells continue to divide. This is a **stem-cell line.** Division continues until there are several million cells.

6 Researchers decide what kind of tissue they want to recreate. For instance:

BRAIN CELLS
HEART-MUSCLE CELLS
PANCREATIC-EYELET CELLS
SKIN CELLS
MUSCLE CELLS

7 The cells are exposed to hormones and growth factors that replicate the chemistry the cells would be exposed to if they were still in the blastocyst developing into cells needed to produce a human being.

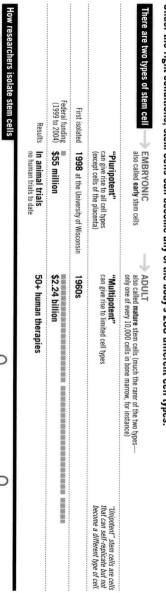

Egg

The nucleus
is removed.

A cell is taken
from a patient.

The cell is activated with a tiny electrical
charge to encourage development.

The nucleus from the patient's
cell is inserted into the egg.

Two contentious issues

Opponents
of stem cell
research consider a
blastocyst to be an
early-stage embryo, and
as such, human life.

If a blastocyst were
to be implanted in a
woman's uterus it
could theoretically
lead to a pregnancy.
This is called
**reproductive
cloning.**
It is banned in
all countries.

8 New tissue or even, ultimately, whole organs could be transplanted into the patient. The purity of this mixture is very hard to achieve, and researchers need more time to perfect the process.

... the patient. If the transplanted stem-cell tissue is a genetic match with the patient, the problem of tissue rejection is minimized.

Potential U.S. recipients of stem-cell-based therapies

Cardiovascular disease **58** million	Autoimmune disease **30** million	Diabetes **16** million	Osteoporosis **10** million	Cancer **8.2** million	Alzheimer's disease **5.5** million	Parkinson's disease **5.5** million	Spinal-cord injuries **0.25** million

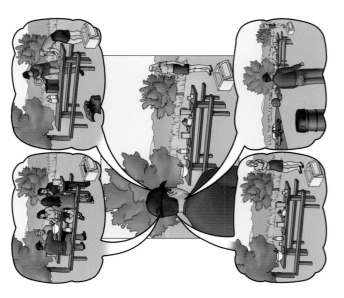

▲ *This illustration depicts the memories activated in one man as he observes a postpicnic scene. Long-term memory stores numerous types of memories.*

Joanne Haderer Müller,
Haderer & Müller
Biomedical Art,
United States

▼ *Challenging content increases the cognitive load on working memory. This graphic explaining stem cell research incorporates several effective techniques for reducing the load, such as iconic illustrations, sequencing, and arrows.*

Nigel Holmes,
United States

Cognitive Load: Demands on Working Memory

While many of the cognitive tasks we perform, such as counting, make little demand on working memory, other tasks are quite taxing. Demanding tasks include such things as acquiring new information, solving problems, dealing with novel situations, consciously recalling prior knowledge, and inhibiting irrelevant information.[10] The resources we use to satisfy the demands placed on working memory are known as *cognitive load*.

When a high cognitive load impinges on working memory, we no longer have the capacity to adequately process information. This overload effect often results in a failure to understand information, a misinterpretation of information, or overlooking of important information. Many challenging tasks associated with complex visual information make high demands on working memory. Designers of visual communication can reduce cognitive load through various graphical techniques and approaches that are discussed throughout this book.

Long-Term Memory: Permanent Storage

When we selectively pay attention to information in working memory, it is likely to get transformed and encoded into long-term memory. Long-term memory is a dynamic structure that retains everything we know. It is capable of storing an unlimited quantity of information, making it functionally infinite. Knowledge in long-term memory appears to be stored permanently—though we may have difficulty accessing it. Educational psychologist John Sweller describes its

significance: "Because we are not conscious of the contents of the long-term memory except when they are brought into working memory, the importance of this store and the extent to which it dominates our cognitive activity tends to be hidden from us."[11]

Long-term memory is not a unitary structure because not all types of memories are the same. We remember facts and concepts, such as basic color theory; we remember childhood events, such as playing our first instrument; and we remember how to perform a task, like riding a bicycle. Accordingly, long-term memory appears to have multiple structures to accommodate different types of memories. Semantic memory is associated with meaning; it stores the facts and concepts that compose our repository of general knowledge about the world. This includes the information we extract from pictures. Episodic memory is autobiographical. It stores events and associated emotions that relate to experiences. Procedural memory is the storehouse of how to do things. It holds the skills and procedures that enable us to accomplish a task.

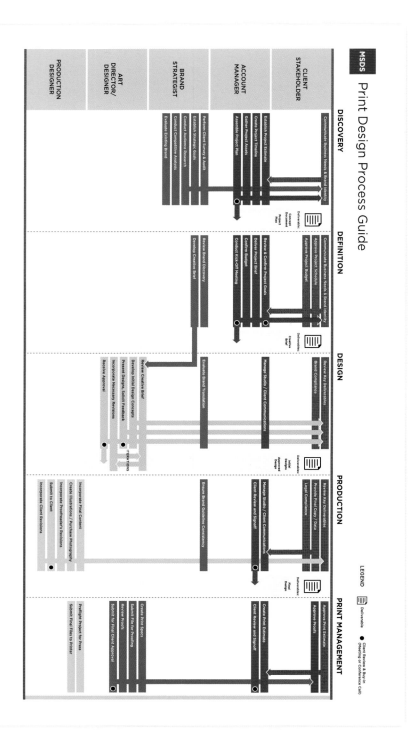

MSDS Print Design Process Guide

Encoding. Although some information is automatically processed from working memory into long-term memory without conscious effort, encoding into long-term memory generally involves some form of conscious rehearsal or meaningful association. Maintenance rehearsal is simply a matter of repeating new information until it is retained; elaborative rehearsal occurs when we analyze the meaning of new information and relate it to previously stored knowledge in long-term memory. Research suggests that the more ways we can connect new information with old information, the more likely it is to be recalled. In addition, connecting information from both the visual and verbal channels facilitates encoding to long-term memory.

Depth of processing. Cognitive researchers think that depth of processing significantly affects how likely it is that information will be recalled from long-term memory. When a viewer focuses only on the physical aspects of a word or graphic, the information is not stored as deeply as when the viewer focuses on the semantic aspects, which are those that have meaning. For example, if a viewer concentrates only on the shapes and colors of a graph, the information will not be processed as deeply as if the person studied the graph, followed the flow of explanations, and understood its meaning. Encoding at the semantic level is superior to encoding at the perceptual level. The important point that cannot be overemphasized is that we have a superior memory for anything that is processed at the level of meaning.

Depth of processing can be understood by observing this chart that depicts the processes of print design. Following the horizontal path of each process for a coherent understanding results in deeper encoding than focusing only on the layout, colors, and shapes of the elements.

Gordon Cieplak,
Schwartz Brand Group,
United States

SCHEMAS: MENTAL REPRESENTATIONS

To store a lifetime of knowledge in long-term memory, we need it in an accessible form. Not surprisingly, we achieve this by classifying and storing information in terms of what it means to us. "New information is stored in memory—not by recording some literal copy of that information but, rather, by interpreting that information in terms of what we already know. New items of information are 'fit in' to memory, so to speak, in terms of their meaning," write researchers Elizabeth and Robert Bjork.[12]

Cognitive scientists theorize that the knowledge in long-term memory is organized in mental structures called schemas. Schemas form an extensive and elaborate network of representations that embody our understanding of the world. They are the context for interpreting new information and the framework for integrating new knowledge. We rapidly activate schemas to conduct mental processes, such as problem solving and making inferences.

Unlike a perceptual experience that focuses on unique features, a schema is an abstract or generalized representation. There are schemas that represent objects and scenes and schemas that represent concepts and the relationships between concepts. When we see a house, we notice its architectural style, the materials from which it is built, its colors and textures, and the surrounding environment. Although each house is unique, each time we encounter one of these structures we are able to identify it as a house, whether it is a hut constructed of mud and straw, a farmhouse, or a townhouse. This is because we have a generalized schema of what constitutes a house. A general schema for house might include a place where people live; a structure with rooms, windows, doors and roof; and a place to sleep, eat, and bathe.

Our schemas are constantly changing, adapting, and accommodating new information, contributing to the dynamic nature of long-term memory. Every time we encounter new information and connect it to prior knowledge, we are adapting a schema to assimilate this new information. When schemas change or new schemas are constructed through analogy, we call this occurrence *learning*. And when a person becomes very skilled in a particular area, having constructed thousands of complex schemas in a particular domain, we consider the person an expert.

Retrieval. Our sole purpose in encoding information into long-term memory is to retrieve the information when we need it. Unfortunately, as we have all experienced, this is not always a straightforward process. According to the Bjorks, "The retrieval process is erratic, highly fallible, and heavily cue dependent."[13] Information recall is accomplished by a retrieval cue, which is the piece of information that activates associated knowledge stored in long-term memory. Retrieval cues can be of any form—an image, a fact, an idea, an emotion, a stimulus in the environment, or a question we ask ourselves.

When long-term memory is cued to retrieve stored memories, the cue activates associated schemas. Activation quickly spreads to other schemas in the network. A common experience occurs, for example, when a person hears an old song and tries to remember the band that recorded it. The song is the cue that retrieves associated schemas from long-term memory. If the right schemas are retrieved, the person will remember the band's name. A failure to remember something is often the result of a poor retrieval cue rather than a lack of stored knowledge.

Automaticity. Many schemas, such as word recognition, become automatic through practice. Over time and with repeated use, more complex mental operations also become automated with practice. When this happens, the procedure is processed with less conscious effort. Since working memory is the space where conscious work is performed, automaticity decreases the load on working memory.[14]

A good example of this occurs as someone learns to read. Upon one's first encounter with the word *cat*, three letters or three perceptual units are held in working memory while the word is deciphered. As a reader gains experience, the word *cat* is chunked into one perceptual unit until eventually, recognizing the word *cat* becomes an automatic process with little imposition on working memory. It is not uncommon for people with expertise in a field to perform a task without needing to pay deliberate attention to it. As the automaticity of the schema frees up cognitive resources, the expert can use working memory to competently deal with more complex tasks, such as solving problems or handling novel situations. This can be observed in experienced athletes, master teachers, and expert designers.[15]

Mental models. Whereas schemas form the underlying structure of memory, mental models are broader conceptualizations of how the world works. Mental models explain cause and effect and how changes in one object or phenomenon can cause changes in another. For example, users of graphic software have a mental model of how layers operate. The mental model contains knowledge of how a layer is affected

by moving it above or below another layer and the effect of increasing or decreasing its opacity. This mental model is easily transferred to any graphic software that uses the same paradigm. Thus, mental models help us know what results to expect.

With an understanding of schemas and mental models, graphic designers can begin to consider how an audience might understand a visual form of communication. When someone looks at a graphic, the objects, shapes, and the overall scene activate associated schemas and mental models that enable the viewer to make inferences about the visual and construct an interpretation of it.

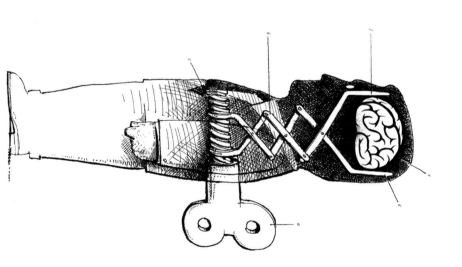

▲ Created for the NRC
Handelsblad, this graphic
suggests the automaticity of
many of our actions.

Rhonald Blommestijn,
The Netherlands

▼ This graphic portrays a
novel way of seeing the
interrelationships inherent
in cognitive processes.

Lane Hall, *United States*

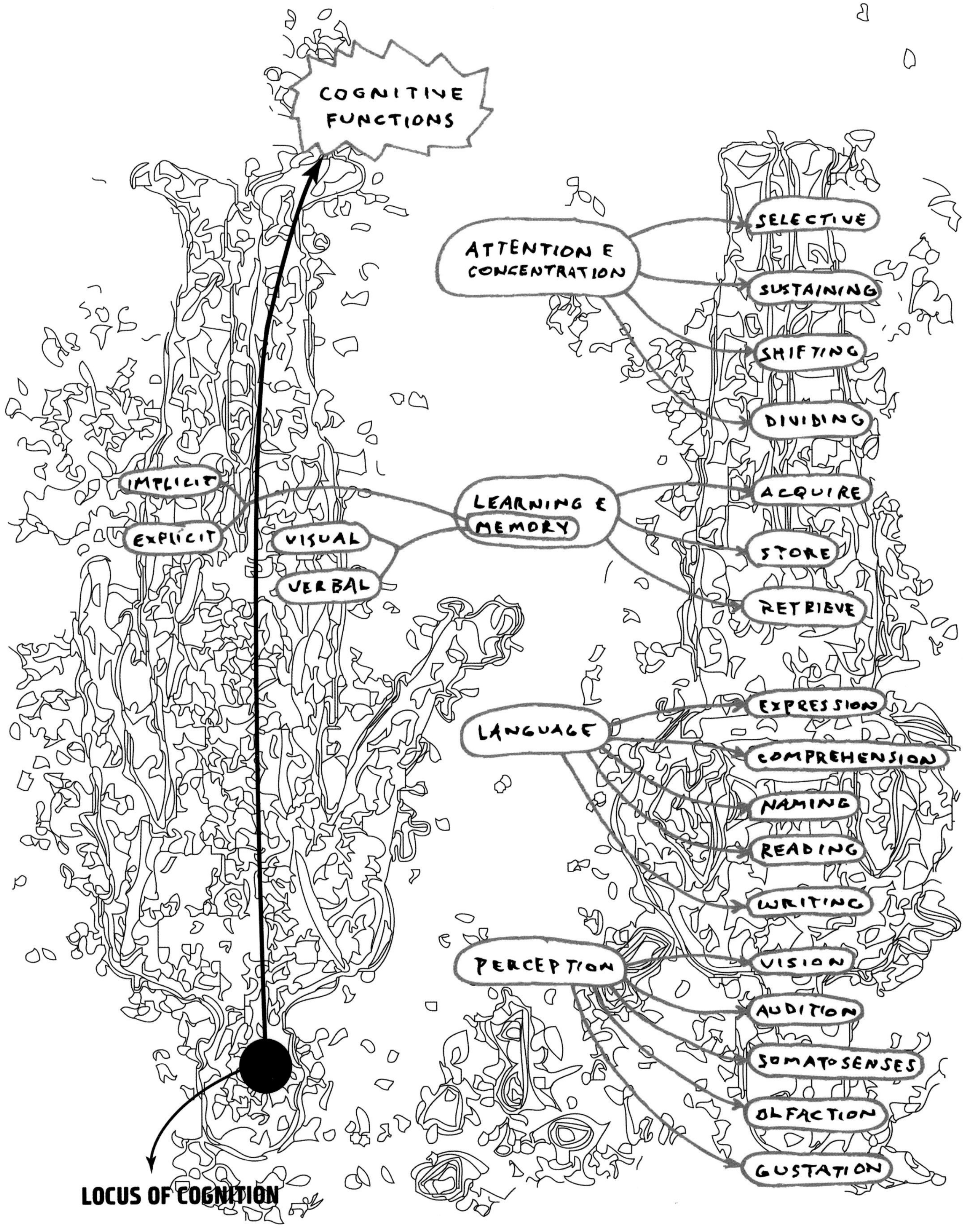

COGNITIVE FUNCTIONS

ATTENTION E CONCENTRATION
- SELECTIVE
- SUSTAINING
- SHIFTING
- DIVIDING

LEARNING E MEMORY
- ACQUIRE
- STORE
- RETRIEVE
- VISUAL
- VERBAL
- IMPLICIT
- EXPLICIT

LANGUAGE
- EXPRESSION
- COMPREHENSION
- NAMING
- READING
- WRITING

PERCEPTION
- VISION
- AUDITION
- SOMATOSENSES
- OLFACTION
- GUSTATION

LOCUS OF COGNITION

DUAL CODING: THE VISUAL AND THE VERBAL

Verbal and visual information appear to be processed through separate channels, referred to as dual coding. One channel processes visual information that retains the perceptual features of an object or picture and the information as words. Although the systems are independent, they communicate and interact, such as when both image and concept knowledge are retrieved from long-term memory. For example, upon hearing the name Salvador Dalí, a person might retrieve both image-based and verbal information from long-term memory. One might construct mental images of the artist's paintings and also recall biographical information about his life.

This dual system of processing and storage explains why memorized information is more likely to be retrieved when it is stored in both visual and verbal form. That is why associating graphics with text or using an audio track with an animation can improve information recall. Placing pictures together with words also allows these two modes of information to form connections, creating a larger network of schemas.

THE AUDIENCE'S COGNITIVE CHARACTERISTICS

It may not be possible to fully predict how an audience will perceive and interpret a picture because of the complex nature of human experience and the variable cognitive skills among individuals. Yet an awareness of an audience's cognitive characteristics can bring designers closer to this goal. In her book *Research into Illustration*, professor Evelyn Goldsmith categorizes the cognitive resources and abilities that could affect an individual's ability to comprehend a picture.

The first characteristic is developmental level. The implication is that development, rather than age, is a more accurate predictor of a person's cognitive abilities. A less skilled viewer may interpret a picture literally although the intended meaning is metaphorical. The ability to interpret more complex types of visual expression comes with mature development. Also, visual skills vary with developmental level. Visual skills such as depth perception, color differentiation, and acuity vary at different stages of development.

Distractibility is the ability to focus on what is important while inhibiting distraction from other events and information. In terms of graphic comprehension, an individual capable of inhibiting distractions will be better able to concentrate on relevant information in a visual. Not surprisingly, younger viewers find it more difficult to close their minds to extraneous information.

▼ *The cognitive characteristics of developmental level and distractibility come into play when designing for a young audience. These display graphics use bright colors and humorous illustrations for an aquarium exhibit.*

Greg Dietzenbach, McCullough Creative, *United States*

This information graphic visualizes the potential global usage of wind energy depicted in maps and graphs. Advanced developmental and visual literacy levels are required to comprehend complex graphics.

Kristin Clute, *University of Washington,* *United States*

Another characteristic at the top of the list is visual literacy. Although it may not take training to recognize the objects in an image, a comprehensive understanding of a picture involves the ability to fully decode the visual message. Knowledge of the symbols and graphical devices used in one's culture as well as an understanding of the context are required. Learning to accurately read a picture is a result of education and experience. For example, it takes an advanced level of visual literacy to analyze and interpret an information graphic using many types of graphs.

The audience's level of expertise should significantly affect design decisions. Experience with the content of a picture is an important predictor of a viewer's ability to comprehend a graphic. Experts are known to organize complex patterns in the visual environment into fewer perceptual units, which reduces cognitive load. Thus, viewers with domain-specific experience are less likely to get overloaded when perceiving a complex visual as compared to novices.

Motivation is an important factor in whether an audience member will have an interest in a picture. A viewer's motivation is typically based on his or her goals for viewing the graphic. Is the graphic being viewed for aesthetic appreciation or is it required for performing a task, such as fixing a bicycle? Does the graphic explain a complex concept that must be learned? Or is it a bland marketing mailer for which the viewer has no use? With enough motivation, a viewer will attend to and work at understanding a graphic.

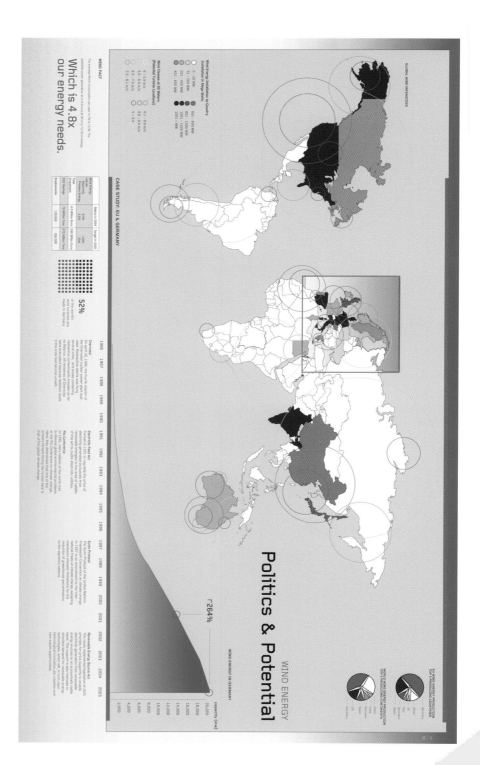

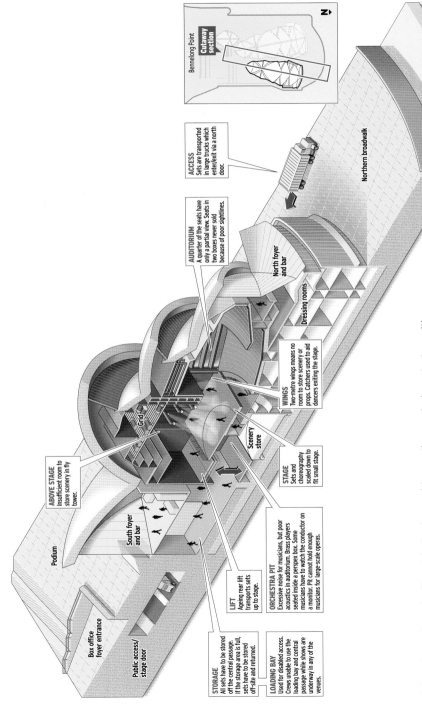

Bennelong Point

Cutaway section

N▶

North

ACCESS
Sets are transported in large trucks which enter/exit via a north door.

Northern broadwalk

AUDITORIUM
A quarter of the seats have only a partial view. Seats in two boxes never sold because of poor sightlines.

North foyer and bar

Dressing rooms

WINGS
Two-metre wings means no room to store scenery or props. Catchers used to aid dancers exiting the stage.

ABOVE STAGE
Insufficient room to store scenery in fly tower.

Grid

STAGE
Sets and choreography scaled down to fit small stage.

Scenery store

Podium

South foyer and bar

LIFT
Ageing rear lift transports sets up to stage.

ORCHESTRA PIT
Excessive noise for musicians, but poor acoustics in auditorium. Brass players seated inside a perspex box. Some musicians have to watch the conductor on a monitor. Pit cannot hold enough musicians for large-scale operas.

Box office foyer entrance

Public access/ stage door

STORAGE
All sets have to be stored off the central passage. If the storage area is full, sets have to be stored off-site and returned.

LOADING BAY
Used for disabled access. Crews unable to use the loading bay and central passage while shows are underway in any of the venues.

An important cognitive skill to consider in complex graphics is the reading level of the audience. In this information graphic for the Sydney Morning Herald, call-outs are extensively used to explain the cramped conditions at the Opera Theatre.

Ninian Carter, *Canada*

Culture is another significant factor in graphic creation. Many cognitive skills are culturally based—ways and patterns of thinking, symbol and color interpretation, and visual associations with verbal language, to name a few. Culture provides the context or lens through which people interpret a picture, and therefore culture affects cognitive processing. As the global exchange of people and ideas continues to increase, accommodating the cognitive conventions of a pluralistic culture is a fundamental requirement of effective design.

Reading skills often correspond to the user's understanding of a graphic. People with low reading levels may not be proficient at following a visual hierarchy or finding the most relevant information. They may not be experienced at allocating their visual attention to a picture in the most efficient manner and may miss important information.[16] Reading level also affects how well the viewer will read titles, captions, and call-outs and how he or she will integrate text and images.

INFORMATIVE VALUE

Another aspect of cognition relates to a graphic's informative purpose. In his book *Steps to an Ecology of the Mind*, Gregory Bateson writes that information "is a difference that makes a difference." This statement is profoundly true for visual communication. The visual language of a graphic and every compositional element it contains potentially convey a message to the viewer.

By determining a graphic's informative purpose, designers can strategically organize a graphic to invoke the most suitable mental processes. For instance, some graphics only request recognition from the viewer. They require the viewer to notice, to become aware—of an organization, an event, a product, or an announcement. These graphics must be magnetic to attract the viewer's attention and sustain it for as long as possible. The viewer's gaze must be directed to the most important information. And the graphic should be memorable, so that the viewer encodes the message into long-term memory.

Other graphics are created to extend the viewer's knowledge and reasoning abilities. The value of maps, diagrams, graphs, and information visualizations is to make things abundantly clear and move the viewer beyond what he or she could previously understand. Upon viewing one of these visuals, the viewer should be able to see new relationships. Here, the graphics must be clean and well organized and must accommodate ease of interpretation and reasoning. Then there are graphics designed to assist with a task or a procedure, such as assembling furniture. In order for the graphic to be effective when the viewer becomes a user, it must be accurate and unambiguous, leaving no room for misinterpretation.

By understanding the mental processes required to meet specific informative goals, designers can find the most suitable graphic approach for their purpose. The principles discussed in the next section of the book describe ways to achieve this.

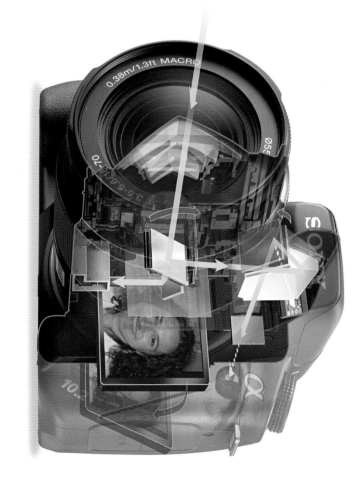

▼ The rich, striking textures in this promotional poster make it memorable.

Adrian Labos, X3 Studios, Romania

▼ An effective visual explanation, such as this depiction of how a digital camera operates, must be efficient and organized to promote ease of comprehension.

Kevin Hand, United States

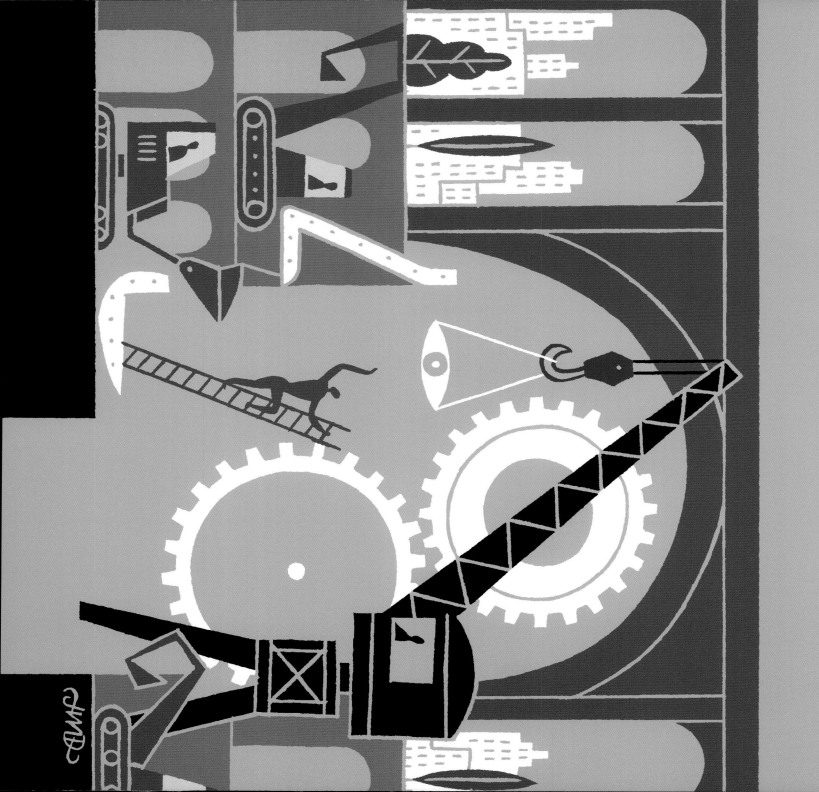

SECTION TWO
THE PRINCIPLES

"For design is about the making of things: things that are memorable and have presence in the world of mind. It makes demand upon our ability both to consolidate information as knowledge and to deploy it imaginatively to create purpose in the pursuit of fresh information."

KROME BARRATT, *Logic & Design in Art, Science & Mathematics*

Jean-Manuel Duvivier,
Jean-Manuel Duvivier
Illustration, Belgium

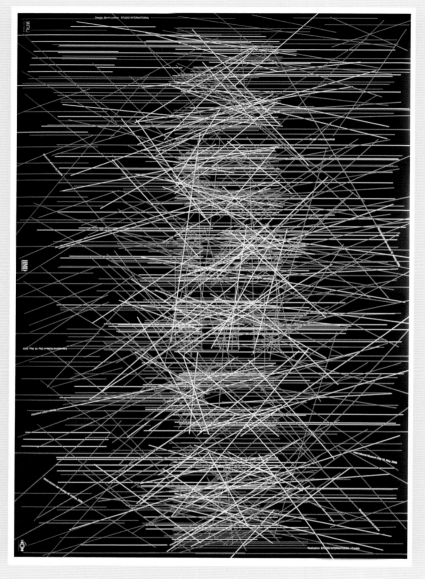

Our visual intelligence enables us to see the word museum in this poster, which is constructed using straight lines and three simple colors.

Boris Ljubicic, Studio International, *Croatia*

PRINCIPLE 1

ORGANIZE FOR PERCEPTION

"Vision is not a mechanical recording of elements, but rather the apprehension of significant structural patterns."

RUDOLF ARNHEIM, *Art and Visual Perception*

Our visual system is remarkably agile. It helps us perform tasks necessary for survival in our environment. Yet we are able to apply these same processes to perceiving and understanding pictures. For example, without conscious effort we scan our surroundings to extract information about what is "out there," noting if there is anything of importance in the environment. Similarly, without conscious effort we scan a picture to acquire information, noting if there is anything of importance in the visual display. All of this occurs effortlessly, before we have consciously focused our attention.

The processes associated with early vision, called preattentive processing, have generated a great deal of research that can be applied to graphic communication and design. By understanding how viewers initially analyze an image, designers can structure and organize a graphic so it complements human perception. The goal is to shift information acquisition to the perceptual system to speed up visual information processing. This is equivalent to giving a runner a head start before the race begins.

Early vision rapidly scans a wide visual field to detect features in the environment. This first phase of vision is driven by the attributes of an object (the visual stimulus), rather than a conscious selection of where to look. Upon detecting the presence of visual features, we extract raw perceptual data to get an overall impression. This data is most likely "mapped into different areas in the brain, each of which is specialized to analyze a different property."[1] From this rapid visual analysis, we create some form of rough mental sketch or representation.[2]

Later, vision makes use of this representation to know where to focus our attention. It is under the influence of our preexisting knowledge, expectations, and goals. For example, using the low-level visual system of early vision, we might register the shapes and color features we see in a graphic. Later, vision directs our attention to those same features and uses knowledge stored in long-term memory to recognize and identify the shapes and little understood interaction that provides us with a unique visual intelligence. These two stages of vision form a complex and little understood interaction that provides us with a unique visual intelligence.

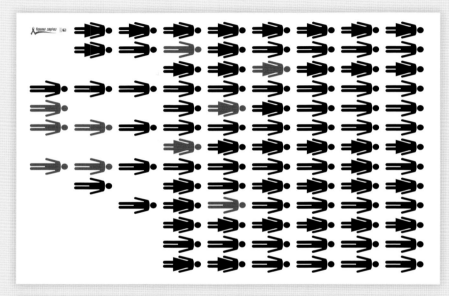

▶ Designed as a picto-
graph, this poster (left)
conveys the loss of life from
AIDS by taking advantage
of our ability to quickly
detect differences.

▶ In this poster (right), the
designer uses a pictograph
to depict the relationship
between the source of HIV
and humans.

Maziar Zand,
M. Zand Studio, Iran

Parallel Processing

The initial visual analysis of preattentive processing
is rapid because vast arrays of neurons are working
in parallel. We typically detect features with low-level
vision at a rate faster than ten milliseconds per item.[3]
To better understand the parallel nature of early visual
processing, search for the red symbols in this AIDS
awareness poster (above, left). Rather than perform a
serial search through every single figure in the graphic,
our low-level visual system immediately perceives
the red figures among the field of black ones. These
features tend to pop out and grab our attention.

Serial Processing

In contrast, later vision, which is guided by our selective attention, performs visual operations more slowly
through an item-by-item, or serial, search. Trying to
detect just the red female symbols in the more complex field of this second AIDS awareness poster is a
slower, more laborious process (above, right). Because
the female symbol shares a color property with two
other symbols, red is no longer a unique feature.

In these illustrations of an underwater landslide for Scientific American, *vivid textures enable us to distinguish between land and sea. The dynamic texture of the ocean projects a sense of the oncoming tsunami.*

**David Fierstein,
David Fierstien Illustration,
Animation, & Design,**
United States

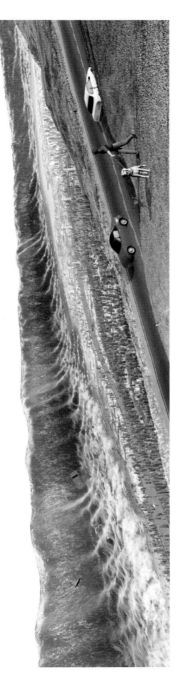

Perceptual Organization

The significance of early vision is that it organizes our perceptions and gives structure and coherence to sensory data. Without perceptual organization a picture might appear to be a chaotic set of disconnected dots and lines. During our preconscious visual analysis, we perform two primary types of perceptual organization—discriminating primitive features and grouping visual information into meaningful units.

Primitive features are the unique properties that allow a visual element to pop out of an image during a search, because they are the most salient or prominent. Examples of primitive features are color, motion, orientation, and size. We later merge these features into meaningful objects through the guidance of our focused attention. Primitive features also allow us to discriminate between textures, which we see as regions of similar features on a surface. When we see the discontinuation of a feature, we perceive it as a border or the edge of a surface. This process, known as texture segregation, helps us identify objects and forms and is a related preattentive process.

Whereas the detection and discrimination of primitive features tell us about the properties of an image, the preattentive process of grouping tells us which individual parts go together. Before consciously paying attention, we organize sensory information into groups or perceptual units. This provides information about the relationship of elements to each other and to the whole. A basic perceptual unit can be thought of as any group of marks among which our attention is not divided. A simple example of this concept occurs when we perceive a square. We tend to see the whole shape of the square rather than four straight lines intersecting at right angles. Application of the grouping concept can help a designer ensure that viewers perceive visual information in meaningful units.

Using visual language that speaks to a viewer's preattentive visual processes—discrimination of primitive features and grouping parts into wholes—enables a designer to quickly communicate, grab attention, and provide meaning. This principle can be applied to informational and instructional graphics, promotional materials, warning signs and wayfinding, information visualizations, and technical interfaces.

▼ This design demonstrates the principle of grouping, in which elements that are close together are seen as one perceptual unit. In an instant, our early perceptual system groups the circles into arrows.

Veronica Neira Torres,
Nicaragua

▼ In this identity design for a type foundry in Japan, the overall shape takes precedence over the smaller elements from which it is composed.

**Shinnoske Sugisaki,
Shinnoske Inc., Japan**

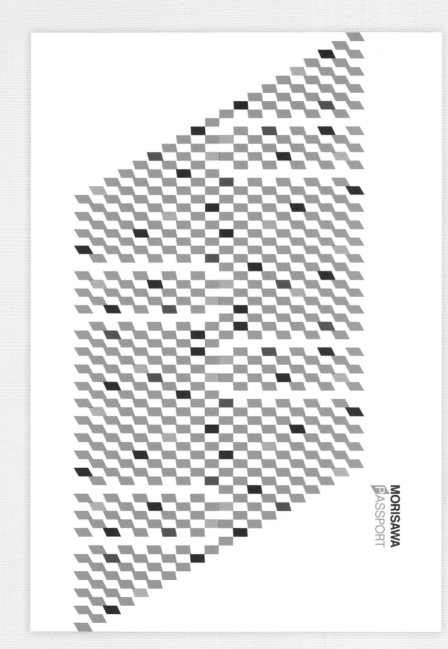

MORISAWA
PASSPORT

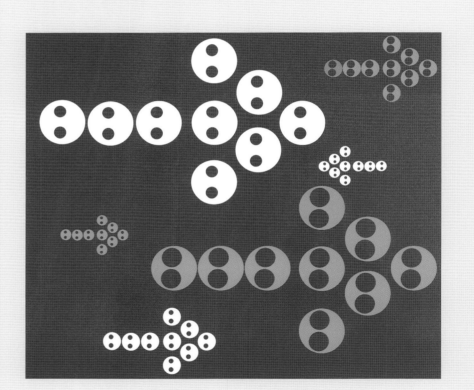

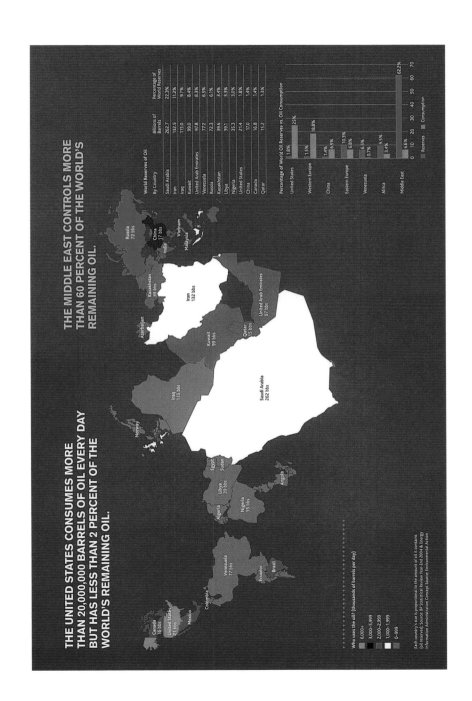

Boosting Cognition

Preattentive processes are initiated when something new appears in our visual field but is outside of our conscious attention. For example, a person may be walking along a city street and perceive the shape of a sculpture in front of a building without consciously paying attention to it. Preattentive processes screen this sensory data so that its meaning is subconsciously recognized. If the person has a particular interest in sculpture, the sensory data is passed on to higher processes so that the sculpture will come under the scrutiny of conscious attention. Sensory data that is not used for further processing simply decays.

Designing the visual structure of a graphic to take advantage of preattentive processes sets the stage for successful comprehension. A graphic's structure can influence how an audience perceives, recognizes, and interprets a picture. As educational psychologist William Winn notes, "Comprehension succeeds or fails to the extent that the information organized by preattentive processes can be assimilated to existing schemata (mental representations), or that schemata can be altered to accommodate that information."[4] This is because the bottom-up flow of information initiated by sensory input quickly influences and interacts with the top-down flow of information guided by our preexisting knowledge and expectations.

For example, emphasizing a primitive feature in a concert promotion poster, such as using bold colors, will quickly attract the audience to the essential message. Accentuating the size of important areas on a map will ensure the audience accurately understands the information. Grouping related information in a graph will help viewers know which data should be compared. Organizing a graphic's structure for early vision can have a domino effect on later vision, reducing the demands placed on working memory, facilitating interpretation, and ultimately enhancing comprehension. This approach to design should also speed information acquisition. When the audience is given a cognitive kick start, the intended message is more likely to be clear at the beginning of the process and there will be fewer opportunities for miscomprehension.

In this map showing oil-consuming nations, high-contrast colors and simplified flat regions enable the viewer to get a sense of the information early in the vision process.

Jennifer Lopardo,
Schwartz Brand Group,
United States

In this three-dimensional visualization of consumer electronics spending for Wired magazine, the individual bars with proximity and similar color form into their own perceptual group. The individual groups form into one whole graph because of proximity and preexisting knowledge of how to read bar graphs.

Arno Ghelfi, l'atelier starno,
United States

The primitive features of size and color in the title of this 2-mile-challenge poster create immediate emphasis and focus.

Mark Boediman,
Clif Bar & Company,
United States

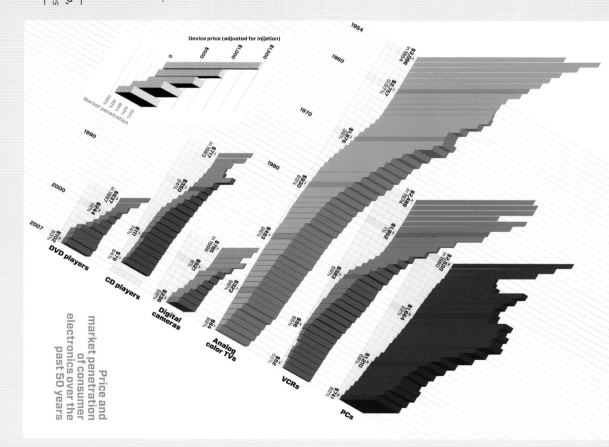

Price and market penetration of consumer electronics over the past 50 years

The way we preatten-tively organize textures into shapes can be clearly seen in this visualization of apoptosis (cell death).

Drew Berry, Walter and Eliza Hall Institute of Medical Research, *Australia*

Applying the Principle

Accommodating our preattentive visual processes through design requires thinking in terms of how the visual information will be detected, organized, and grouped. Fortunately, it is not difficult to predispose the viewer to a well-organized visual structure. The low-level visual system is continuously seeking a stimulus in the environment to provide focus and draw the eyes. When a design calls for quick recognition and response, graphics that emphasize one pronounced primitive feature, such as line orientation or shape, can be placed against a background with few distractors. This primitive feature will be detected during a preattentive rapid scan.

When a project requires an emphasis on aesthetic expression, the designer can take advantage of how early vision segregates features into textures. Using texture as a prominent feature can add visual depth and complexity to a graphic. And because we are adept at detecting texture differences, this can offload some of the processing normally placed on working memory to the perceptual system.

The low-level visual system also seeks to configure parts of a graphic into a whole unit when they are close together or have similar features. One example is how we perceive elements that have a common boundary as one unit. From a compositional perspective, grouping provides opportunities for emphasis, balance, and unity in a design.

By organizing the structure of a design through emphasis of primitive features or through grouping individual elements, viewers will quickly detect the organization of the graphic. Many designers intuitively use these organizing principles, but an awareness of the audience's preattentive capabilities is a way to intentionally improve the communication quality of any informative message.

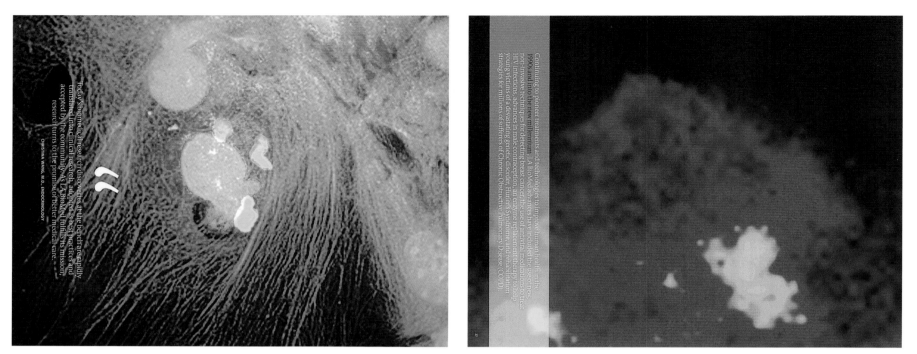

Today's biomedical research discoveries at the bench are rapidly translated into clinical research, and pioneer as best practices and accepted by the community as LA BioMed fulfills its mission: research turns to the promise of better medical care.

CHRISTINA WANG, M.D., ENDOCRINOLOGY

Continuing to pioneer treatments and technologies to improve human health in the 1990s and into the new millennium, LA BioMed advances have included the use of new non-invasive techniques for detecting breast cancer, the use of antiviral medications to treat HIV infections, advances in male contraception, an enzyme replacement therapy to help young victims of a devastating genetic disorder, Hurler's Syndrome, and rehabilitation strategies for millions of sufferers of Chronic Obstructive Pulmonary Disease (COPD).

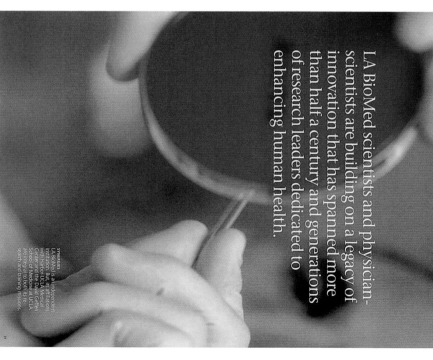

LA BioMed scientists and physician-scientists are building on a legacy of innovation that has spanned more than half a century and generations of research leaders dedicated to enhancing human health.

SYNERGIES
LA BioMed is an independent institution, but, in affiliation with Harbor-UCLA Medical Center and the David Geffen School of Medicine at UCLA, are integral to both its re- search and training missions.

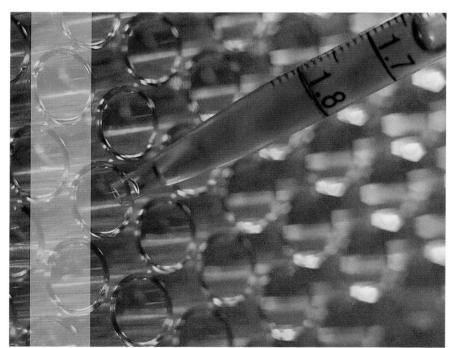

There is little question which object is intended as the focus in this rendering of New York City buildings for Bloomberg Markets magazine.

Bryan Christie,
Bryan Christie Design,
United States

▲ In this college campus map, outlined green areas accentuate regions within the campus. This helps us group the buildings within each region, facilitating the use of the map.

David Horton and
Amy Lebow,
Philographica,
United States

▼ The photographs and imagery in this annual report use an aesthetic approach to texture segregation, communicating a sense of medical competence for a biomedical research institute.

Jane Lee,
IE Design &
Communications,
United States

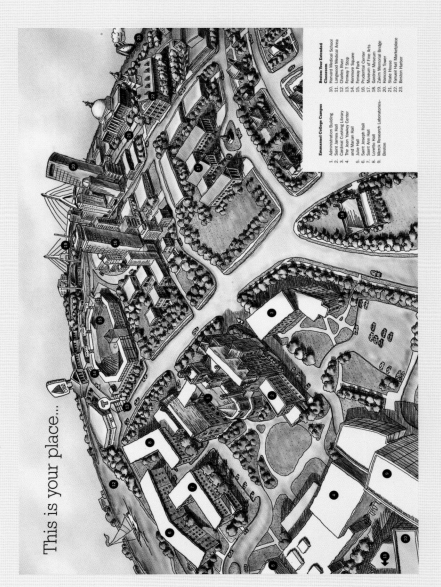

This is your place...

Emmanuel College Campus
1. Administration Building
2. Saint James Hall
3. Cardinal Cushing Library
4. The Jean Yawkey Center and Marian Hall
5. Julie Hall
6. Saint Joseph Hall
7. Saint Ann Hall
8. Loretto Hall
9. Merck Research Laboratories-Boston

Boston: Your Extended Classroom
10. Harvard Medical School
11. Longwood Medical Area
12. Charles River
13. Fenway T Stop
14. Kenmore Square
15. Fenway Park
16. Prudential Center
17. Museum of Fine Arts
18. Gardner Museum
19. Zakim Memorial Bridge
20. Hancock Tower
21. State House
22. Faneuil Hall Marketplace
23. Boston Harbor

FEATURES THAT POP OUT

The scientific term *pop out* aptly expresses how we perceive the most unique and conspicuous primitive features in a graphic during early vision. Before consciously paying attention, we rapidly analyze a graphic and register the features that pop out. The purpose is to get an accurate reading of whatever is important in our visual field. After a brief exposure, a feature with prominence or salience is more likely to attract our conscious attention in later vision than an inconspicuous feature.

Primitive features that both pop out and are most likely to control later attention include color, motion, orientation, size, depth, tilt, shape, line terminators (where a line ends), closure (an enclosed space), topological properties (such as a dot inside a circle), and line curvature.[5] Any of these features can be emphasized to establish visual prominence.

To perceive a feature as salient, we must be able to discriminate it from everything else. Through visual discrimination, we determine whether a property is the same as or different from other properties. "Two properties must differ by a large enough proportion or they will not be distinguished," writes professor and researcher Stephen Kosslyn in *Clear and to the Point*. Kosslyn explains that differences between two visual properties are not always detected because a difference is registered as a change in our brain cell activity. If the change in neuronal activity isn't strong, it might be confused with noise in the system, which is a natural occurrence in the brain. To effectively promote visual discrimination, therefore, the differences between two visual properties must be great enough to cause sufficient brain cell activity.

This is particularly relevant during preattentive processing, when discrimination occurs without our conscious awareness. Using two shapes with very different orientations or using two objects of very different sizes will result in effective discrimination. In general, make a primitive feature prominent; don't leave it up to the viewer to make fine or subtle visual discriminations.

REINVENTANDO UN LENGUAJE

DEMOCRACIA

ANTONIO MENA · 2005

▲ *In this poster commemorating the Democratic rebellion in Ecuador, the gestured hands pop out during preattentive processing because of color contrast.*

Antonio Mena,
Antonio Mena Design,
Ecuador

▼ *In these animation frames for the Croatian Architects Association, the letter A appears to pop out because of its contrasting color, shape, orientation, and novelty.*

Boris Ljubicic,
Studio International,
Croatia

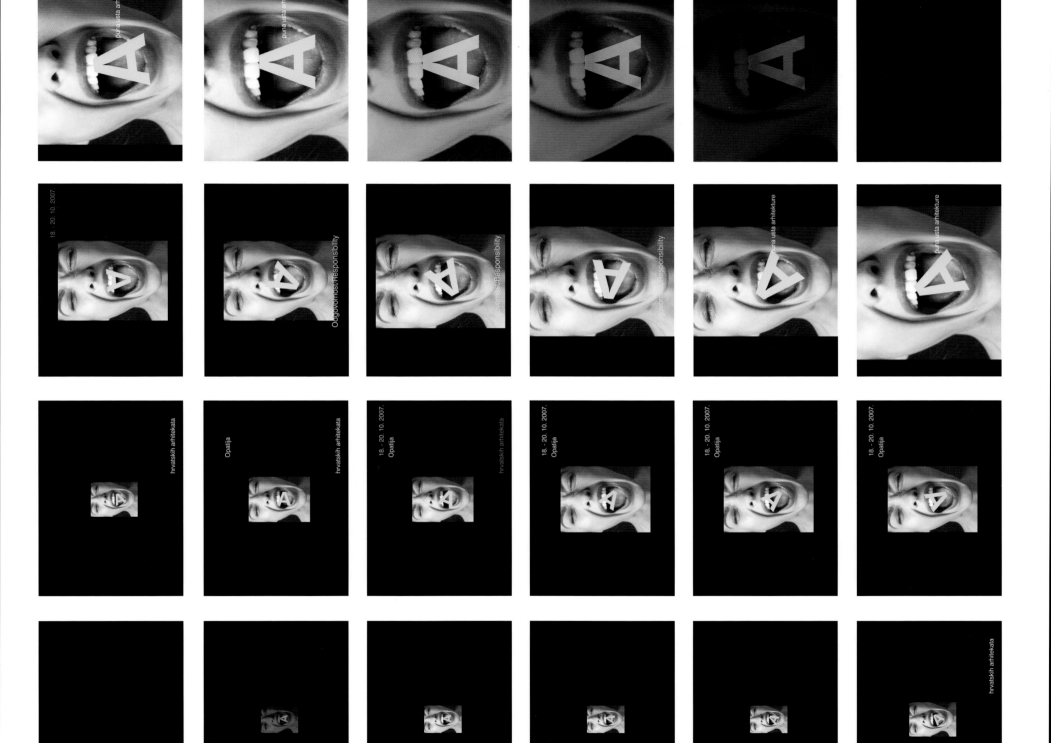

▲ In this elegant array of Iranian proverbs, the designer uses color contrast to ensure that the salient proverbs in white are the most prominent.

Majid Abassi,
Did Graphics, Iran

▼ This fifth-anniversary advertisement poster for a popular club exploits the primitive feature of depth to create an extreme pop-out effect.

Sorin Bechira,
X3 Studios, Romania

24-FUN
CEL MAI TARE GHID DIN ROMANIA
15 IUNIE
party
5 ani
ÎN CLUB ŞI ÎN CAFE
PARTY 24 DE ORE
PE TERASĂ: DEKO STAND-UP COMEDY

TEXTURE SEGREGATION

One of our first responses to the influx of sensory data is to organize primitive features into segmented regions of texture. In pictures, texture can be thought of as the optical grain of a surface. We unconsciously unify objects into regions that are bound by an abrupt change in texture. We perceive this change as defining where one object, or form, ends and where another begins. Once we segregate a region into textures, we then organize it into shapes or objects that we identify with conscious attention. Our knowledge of texture patterns helps us to identify objects.

Through texture segregation, we also separate foreground from background. When we perceive a difference between two textures, the textured area is typically seen as the figure or dominant shape and the area without texture is typically seen as the ground or neutral form. The relationship between figure and ground is a prerequisite for perceiving shapes and eventually identifying objects. Color and size, also contribute to the figure—ground perception.

Just as primitive features can induce the pop-out effect, so can regions of texture. For instance, when a surface texture is composed of uncomplicated primitive features, such as line orientation or shapes, it's

easy to distinguish the texture from its surroundings. When a form with a complex texture is placed on a busy background, the texture is harder to discriminate and loses its pop-out effect.[6]

Texture perception also presents spatial information by providing cues for depth perception.[7] The texture gradient on a surface contributes to our perception of how near or far an object appears. When the texture's pattern on a surface is perceived as denser and finer, an object appears to recede in the distance; when the pattern is perceived as less dense and coarser, the object appears closer.

Our ability to segregate textures during early vision is key to understanding the meaning of a graphic. An analysis of texture shows that it is constructed from contrast, orientation, and element repetition. Designers can manipulate these individual properties to convey meaning. Texture can be expressive, capturing the essence of an object or mood. Texture can also simulate surface qualities to help us identify and recognize objects. When given appropriate emphasis, texture can become more prominent than shape and line.

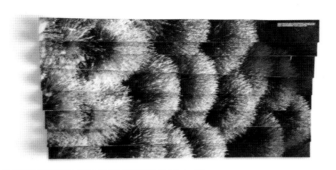

▲ *In these three-dimensional displays to promote tourism, the designer used organic textures to express the natural beauty of Croatia. Textures are easily perceived in the early vision process, which makes this example so compelling.*

Boris Ljubicic, Studio International, Croatia

▶ *One can almost feel the gooey, melting textures in this poster. The powerful type pops out even against the high-energy colors and shapes because of the contrasts in color and texture.*

Adrian Labos, X3 Studios, Romania

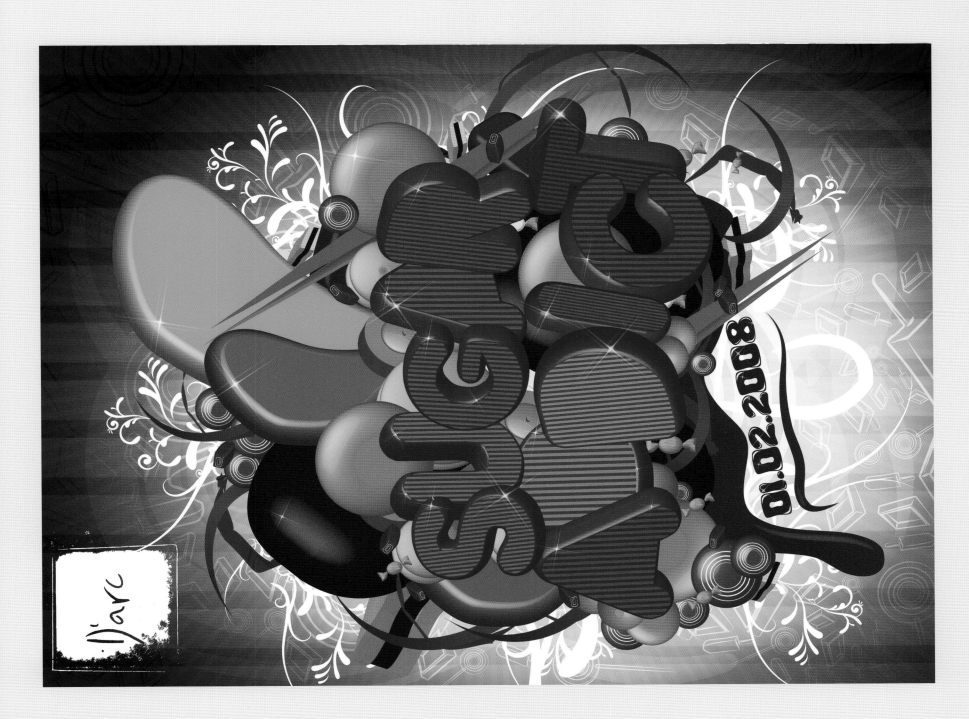

▲ This exploded view of a
processor setup is a good
example of how texture
segmentation helps us
perceive the figure—ground
relationship. The glossy,
smooth surfaces of objects
in the foreground contrast
with the duller receding
objects in the background
to create this effect.

Christopher Short,
United States

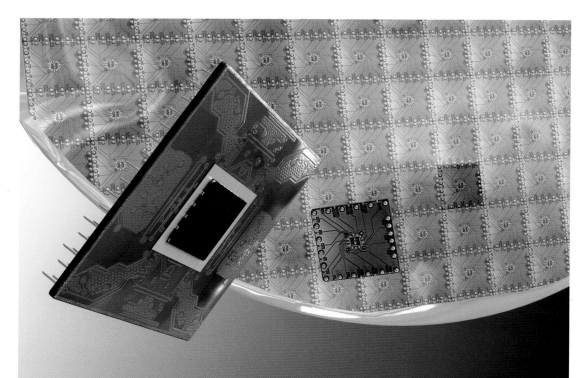

▼ In this rendering of
solder-based products, the
difference in texture density
between the chip in the
foreground and those in the
background provides cues
that help us perceive three-
dimensional depth. As an
object recedes in space, its
texture appears denser.

Christopher Short,
United States

The atmosphere of Tokyo is expressed through the busy textures and buzzing patterns in this poster advertising a café. Even in a dense design, the varied textures make it easy to perceive objects.

Ian Lynam, Ian Lynam Creative Direction & Design, Japan

Texture with Text

An appealing way to create texture is through the creative use of type, regardless of whether the type can be read. When type is repeated, varied, layered, or manipulated and altered, it creates an optical grain that conveys meaning. Often, the meaning is expressed on two levels: the words formed by the type communicate a literal message and the texture conveys meaning through design. Using type as texture is particularly appropriate in text-associated themes that relate to books, poetry, and language.

To create textures that are easy to discriminate, use a texture with a simple distinguishing homogenous feature separated from a contrasting region. There should be an easily perceptible difference where two objects or forms meet. Textures that are easy to discriminate might include those with different line orientations, contrasting rhythms of pattern, and regions composed of high-contrast patterns surrounded by regions of low contrast. The phenomenon of texture segregation provides many possibilities for communicating a message early in the perceptual process.

▲ Thick layers of overlapping type create poetic textures in this work for a collaboration exhibition by a poet and typographers.

Shinnoske Sugisaki,
Shinnoske Inc., Japan

▼ In this poster to commemorate the 200th year of the first reading room in Croatia, type is an appropriate design element for a textured background as it curves and bends through space. The glasses and their shadow emerge from the number 200.

Boris Ljubicic, Studio
International, Croatia

ZADAR, 1807. – 2007.
200 GODINA
Pokrovitelj:
Hrvatska akademija znanosti i umjetnosti
Organizatori svečanosti:
Nacionalna i sveučilišna knjižnica u Zagrebu
Gradska knjižnica Zadar
Suorganizatori:
Grad Zadar
Sveučilište u Zadru
Općina Novigrad
Program:
Petak, 29. lipnja 2007.
ZADAR
10.00 sati Gradska loža, Svečanost obilježavanja 200. obljetnice prve hrvatske čitaonice
Predstava Govorite li hrvatski? izvodi Joško Ševo
11.00 sati Narodni trg, Glazbeno-scenska svečanost
Scenu Prvvoj od slave iz Planina Petra Zoranića izvodi Kazalište lutaka Zadar
NOVIGRAD
12.30 sati Otvaranje Knjižnice i čitaonice Novigrad
13.00 sati prigodni program
Obrazloženje:
200
prva
hrvatska
čitaonica
družba
od štenja

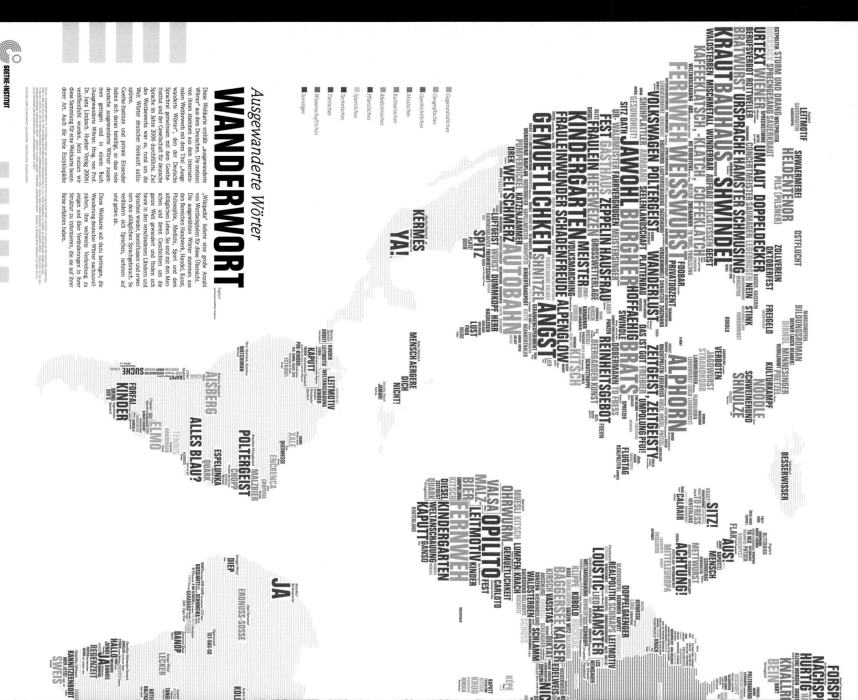

The repetition of type creates texture and geographical forms in this information graphic depicting German words used around the world.

Jan Schwochow,
Katharina Erfurth, and
Sebastian Piesker,
Golden Section Graphics,
Germany

GROUPING

Understanding where objects are located and how they are arranged in space is essential for moving through the environment. Perhaps that's why spatial organization is a fundamental operation of preattentive perception. The low-level visual system has a tendency to organize elements into coherent groups depending on how they are arranged and where they are located. This preattentive configuration of parts into wholes lets us know that a set of elements in a picture is associated and should be viewed as one unit. During later cognitive processing, the relationship among the perceptual units and their relationship to the whole becomes valuable information that conveys meaning in a graphic.

The perceptual organization of parts into wholes is based on theories promoted by the Gestalt psychologists in the early twentieth century. Their principles demonstrated that under the right conditions, combining parts into wholes takes precedence over seeing the parts themselves. A few of the Gestalt principles that determine whether a whole unit or its parts have visual precedence include proximity, similarity, and symmetry. Elements that exhibit proximity are close to each other in space or time. We perceive elements with proximity as belonging to the same group. We also perceive elements that have similar visual characteristics, such as shape and texture, as one unit. The symmetry principle states that we configure elements into a whole when they form a symmetrical figure rather than an asymmetrical one.

In the past few decades, research in the area of preattentive perception has added to our body of knowledge about the grouping phenomenon. These findings have extended the factors that are thought to influence our natural tendency to group parts into wholes. These newer principles include the concepts of boundary and uniform connectedness. The boundary principle states that if a set of elements is enclosed with a boundary, such as a circle, we group those elements together.[8] Thus, when a boundary encloses a set of items, we perceive this as a unit even though we would perceive the items as separate without the boundary. Connectedness describes our tendency to perceive elements as one unit when they are physically connected by a line or common edge.[9] This is generally how we perceive diagrams.

A design that arranges elements into meaningful units will influence how well the audience organizes, interprets, and comprehends a visual message. Grouping elements enhances the meaning of a graphic, because viewers know that clustered elements are associated. Visual search is speedier as a result of grouping because it is faster to find information that is placed in one location. Grouping elements together can also make new features emerge. For instance, a set of lines radiating from a center point might emerge as a Sun form. Designers can take advantage of the conditions that evoke grouping—proximity, similarity, symmetry, bounding, and connectedness—to facilitate visual communication.

Dining

EATING LOCATIONS

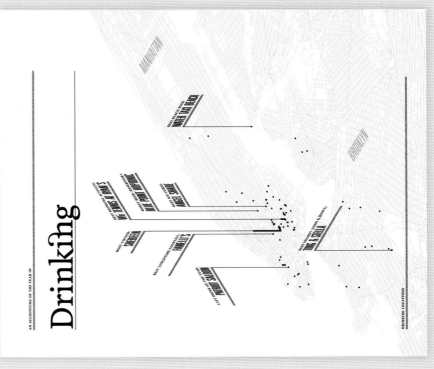

Drinking

DRINKING LOCATIONS

*In this visualization of din-
ing and drinking data from
the Feltron Personal Annual
Report, grouping occurs
by visual plane—the blue
line segments that form the
streets create a horizontal
group and the street signs
form a vertical group.*

Nicholas Feltron, Megafone,
United States

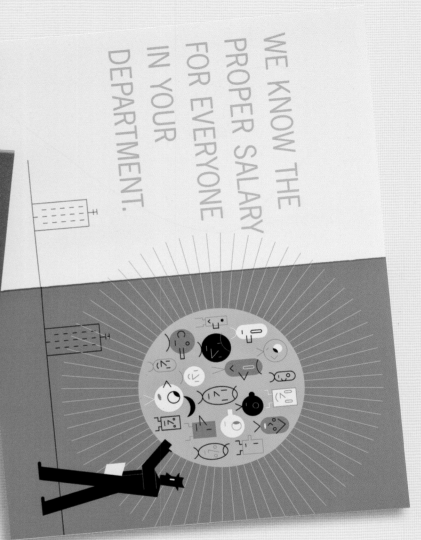

The boundary principle is exemplified in these schematic graphics for a compensation survey booklet. In each graphic, we perceive the collection of people as associated and belonging to one group because of proximity and enclosure.

David Horton and Amy Lebow, Philographica, United States

In this poster we perceive the circle that forms the clock face as more prominent than the individual lines. Soon after, we perceive the male and female symbols as the hands of the clock.

Maziar Zand,
M. Zand Studio, Iran

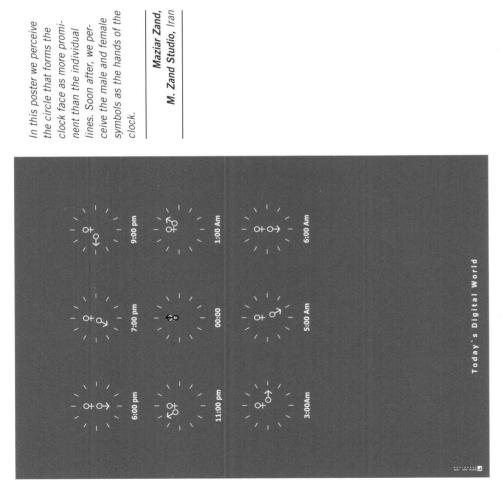

This graphic illustrates the concept of setting boundaries for children. Clearly, there is one element per group.

Angela Edwards,
United States

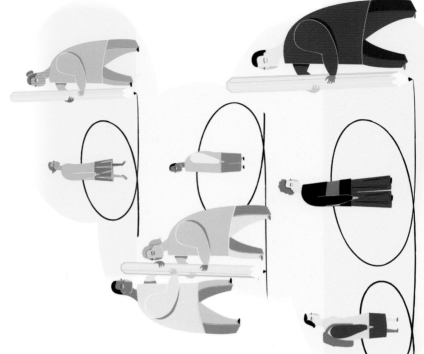

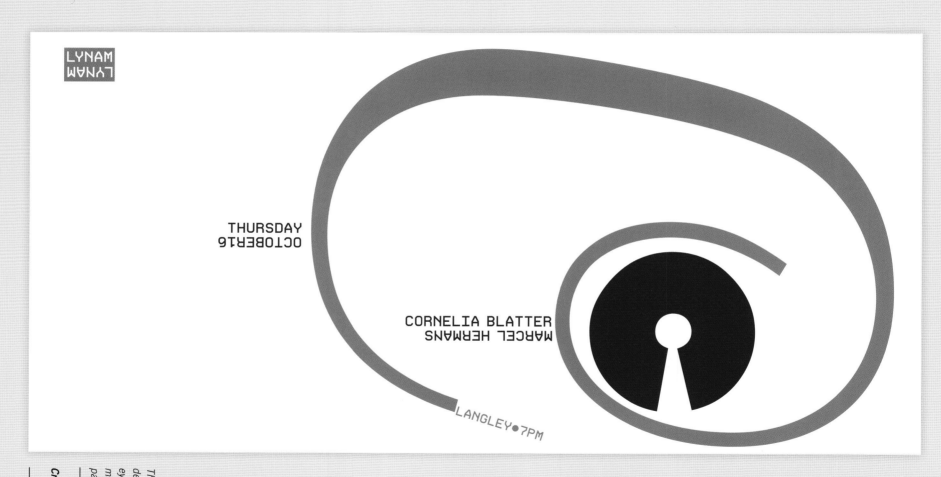

THURSDAY
OCTOBER16

CORNELIA BLATTER
MARCEL HERMANS

LANGLEY●7PM

This poster for a graphic
design lecture directs the
eyes to the important information along a spiraled
path.

Ian Lynam, Ian Lynam
Creative Direction & Design,
Japan

PRINCIPLE 2 | DIRECT THE EYES

"If the viewer's eyes are permitted to wander at will through a work, then the artist has lost control."

JACK FREDERICK MEYERS, *The Language of Visual Art*

Although we think of the brain as a system that can process massive amounts of data in parallel, the quantity of input coursing through the optic nerve every second is actually more than the brain can squeeze into conscious awareness. Thus, we shift our visual attention from one location to another in a serial manner to extract the information we want. An interesting feature in the environment may attract our eyes, or an internal goal may direct our attention. Likewise, when viewing a graphic we attend to what is most compelling. Prominent features in a graphic compete for our attention, so if we are not given visual direction we may dwell on the wrong information or become overwhelmed with too much information. To find meaning in what we see, we must selectively attend to what is important. A designer or illustrator can assist this process by purposefully guiding the viewer's eyes through the structure of a graphic. This is one of the more essential techniques visual communicators can employ to ensure that viewers comprehend their intended message.

Directing the eyes serves two principal purposes—to steer the viewer's attention along a path according to the intended ranking order and to draw the viewer's attention to specific elements of importance. When our eyes scan a picture, we do not glance randomly here and there. Rather, our eyes fixate on the areas that are most interesting and informative. We tend to fixate on objects, skipping over the monotonous, empty, and uninformative areas. This is not surprising, since we are continually seeking meaning in what we see. But it does mean that each individual may scan the same picture in his or her unique way depending on what the person considers informative.

Nevertheless, there are common tendencies and biases in how we move our eyes around a picture. The initial scanning process often starts in the upper left corner as the point of entry. We are biased toward left-to-right eye movements and top-to-bottom movements. Diagonal movements of the eye are less frequent. After the first several fixations, we most likely get the "gist" of a picture, and then our eye movements are influenced by the picture's content, its horizontal or vertical orientation, and our own internal influences. It is debatable whether the directional orientation of one's writing and reading system contributes to eye movement preferences.

The eye movements of the viewer are critical to graphic comprehension. Unlike other forms of communication, such as reading, listening to music, or watching a movie, the time spent looking at a graphic can be remarkably brief. Purposefully directing the eyes makes it likely that a viewer will pick up the most relevant information within a limited time frame. The designer can guide the viewer's eyes by using techniques implicit to the composition, such as altering the position of an element or enhancing the sense of movement. The designer can also guide the viewer to specific information by signaling the location with visual cues like arrows, color, and captions. Visual cues do not carry the primary message; their function is to orient, point out, or highlight crucial information.

BOLD YET
ACHIEVABLE

The Group's five year vision is to make Chiripal a leading Textile House with a place in the national top 10 and a significant global presence.

Lead the industry in commitment to world-class standards...further the Group's reputation for unparalleled reliability and growth. The ultimate goal is to make Chiripal a benchmark for quality.

In coming years, Chiripal aims to increase capacities by adding new product lines, expansion and diversification. A modern Plant to manufacture Synthetic Adhesives and Acrylic based emulsions for the Paint and Textile industry, is on the anvil.

Higher value added products for emerging markets, incorporation of new technology and materials will engineer the future of Textile and of Chiripal.

1 Show Room
2 Power Plant at Shanti Processors

SINGLE MINDED YET
MANY SIDED

Shanti Processors

The success of the Group's integration plans, Shanti Processors has passed many a milestone since 1985. Its state-of-the-art manufacturing facilities are capable of handling a wide range of fabrics irrespective of the count, construction or blend.

Various units such as Process Division, Knitting Division, Folar Plant Division, Pack Division, cater to the varied needs of customers from top readymade garment manufacturers to leading exporters and importers. That is multi-faceted.

Anything you can imagine, you can make real. That's the single-minded operating principle at Shanti Processors. With the setting up of its captive power plant, a collaboration with processing facility, expansion of production capacities and a manufacturing plant for flock binder and other raw materials, the Company now ensures a enviable name for value-addition and timely delivery.

1 Printing Machine, Polar Fleece Division
2 Finishing Machine, Polar Fleece Division
3 Stenter Machine, Polar Fleece Division
4 Packing, Pack Division

In these promotional graphics for a textile house, bold
fabrics attract attention and
guide the eyes to the copy
and photographs explaining
the company's operations.

**Sudarshan Dheer and
Ashoomi Dholakia, Graphic
Communication Concepts,**
India

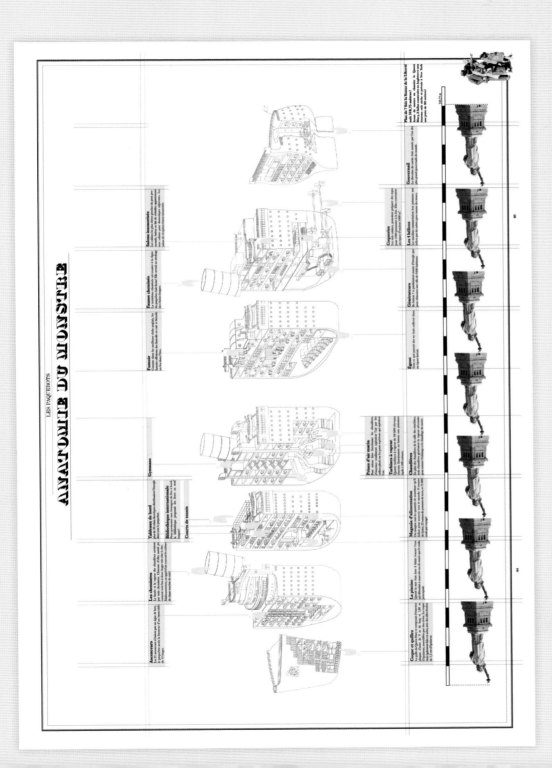

Both compositional and signaling techniques are effective at guiding the eyes because they make use of prominent features that are picked up early in the perceptual process. Even though eye movements are also controlled by the viewer's expectations and search goals, research shows that using compositional and signaling techniques to direct the eye can be quite effective. In one experiment that gauged eye movement based on compositional techniques, an experienced artist explained to the study authors precisely where he intended observers of his art to look. Observers were then allowed to view the art for thirty seconds while their eye movements were recorded. The scanning paths of the subjects proved to be in "considerable concordance" with what the artist intended.[1]

Signaling the viewer with arrows and color is known to be effective when used in explanatory and informational graphics. Studies show that when an area of a graphic is highlighted as it is being discussed, such as in a multimedia environment, viewers retain more information and are better able to transfer this information than those who did not view the highlighted visuals.[2] Other research has demonstrated that the use of arrows as pointing devices reduces the time it takes to search for specific information in a visual field.[3]

In this visual study of early transatlantic liners created for a student project, the pointing finger is a visual cue styled to fit the early era of transatlantic liners.

***Chronopoulou Ekaterini, La Cambre School of Visual Art,** Belgium*

Importance of Attention

The cognitive mechanism that underlies eye movement control is selective attention. When we extract sensory data from a picture, it is momentarily registered in our sensory memory in fleeting images. We must detect and then attend to these images through the process of selective attention to transfer visual information into working memory. Through selective attention, we send visual information onward through the visual information–processing system.

Cognitive researchers study eye movements because eye movements reflect mental processes. We typically move our eyes, and sometimes our head and body, to view an object with the fovea—the part of the eye with the sharpest vision. When doing this, our focus of attention usually coincides with what we are seeing. But the relationship between eye movement and attention is not absolute. We can move our eyes, as when we notice something in peripheral vision while looking straight ahead at someone speaking. In this circumstance, the movement of attention precedes the movement of the eyes.[4] Because attention and the eyes can be dissociated, intentionally directing the eye helps to ensure they are aligned.

As discussed in Principle 1 (Organize for Perception), attention can be captured preattentively through the bottom-up processing driven by a stimulus, or it can be captured during conscious attention through top-down processing. Designers can take advantage of either type of processing to direct the viewer's attention. Incorporating contrast or movement into a design will trigger attention through bottom-up processes. Indicating the steps of a sequence through numbers and captions will activate attention through top-down processes.

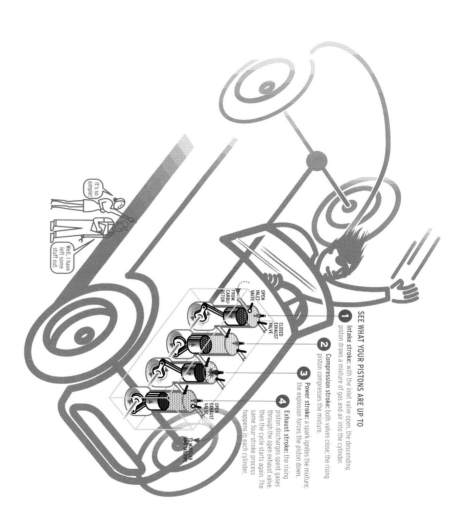

SEE WHAT YOUR PISTONS ARE UP TO

1 **Intake stroke:** with the inlet valve open, the descending piston draws a mixture of gas and air into the cylinder.

2 **Compression stroke:** both valves close; the rising piston compresses the mixture.

3 **Power stroke:** a spark ignites the mixture; the explosion forces the piston down.

4 **Exhaust stroke:** the rising piston discharges spent gases through the open exhaust valve, then the cycle starts again. The same four-stroke process happens in each cylinder.

This information graphic created for Attaché magazine explains how gasoline engines work, using a sequence of numbers to guide the viewer's attention.

Nigel Holmes,
United States

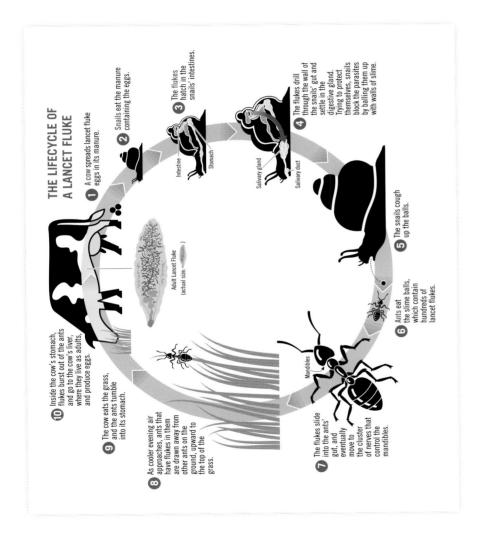

THE LIFECYCLE OF A LANCET FLUKE

1. A cow spreads lancet fluke eggs in its manure.

2. Snails eat the manure containing the eggs.

3. The flukes hatch in the snails' intestines.

Intestine
Stomach

4. The flukes drill through the wall of the snails' gut and settle in the digestive gland. Trying to protect themselves, snails block the parasites by balling them up with walls of slime.

Salivary gland
Salivary duct

5. The snails cough up the balls.

6. Ants eat the slime balls, which contain hundreds of lancet flukes.

7. The flukes slide into the ants' gut, and eventually move to the cluster of nerves that control the mandibles.

Mandibles

8. As cooler evening air approaches, ants that have flukes in them are drawn away from other ants on the ground, upward to the top of the grass.

9. The cow eats the grass, and the ants tumble into its stomach.

10. Inside the cow's stomach, flukes burst out of the ants and go to the cow's liver, where they live as adults, and produce eggs.

Adult Lancet Fluke (actual size:)

Enhancing Cognitive Processes

Promotes speedy perception. When an observer's visual attention shifts to a predetermined location or along a preconceived path, it enhances how the person understands a graphic in many ways. Directing the eyes promotes the efficiency and speed of visual perception, enhances visual information processing, and improves comprehension. Specifically, when a viewer scans a complex graphic, it takes time to get oriented, to determine what is most important, and to extract essential information. Viewers are known to overlook important details in complex illustrations unless they are shown where to attend. When a viewer is directed to a precise location, however, search time is reduced and efficiency is increased.

Improves processing. During preattentive processing, attention is unconsciously directed to features that are most salient. Studies have demonstrated that viewers can be distracted by powerful but irrelevant visual information that captures their attention even against their intentions.[5] Directing the eyes can help ensure that irrelevant information is neither dwelled upon nor

processed. Moreover, when a viewer is quickly guided to the essential information, it diminishes the demands placed on working memory that would have been applied to finding important information. More resources are then available for organizing and processing information as well as assimilating new information.[6] This results in better understanding and retention.

Increases comprehension. Directing the eyes can also assist in the comprehension of a picture. The types of visual cues used in informational and instructional graphics, such as arrows and highlights, are more likely to be understood than if instructions were presented in a written form. Comprehension is also aided by visual cues that provide structure, such as adding numeric captions to emphasize the order of a process. Organization is known to improve comprehension because it provides a cognitive framework. Well-organized information helps viewers construct coherent representations in working memory, making it easier to assimilate new information into existing schemas.

This circular format portraying the life cycle of a parasite directs the eyes with a continuous arrow and a number sequence, providing a structure that facilitates comprehension.

Nigel Holmes,
United States

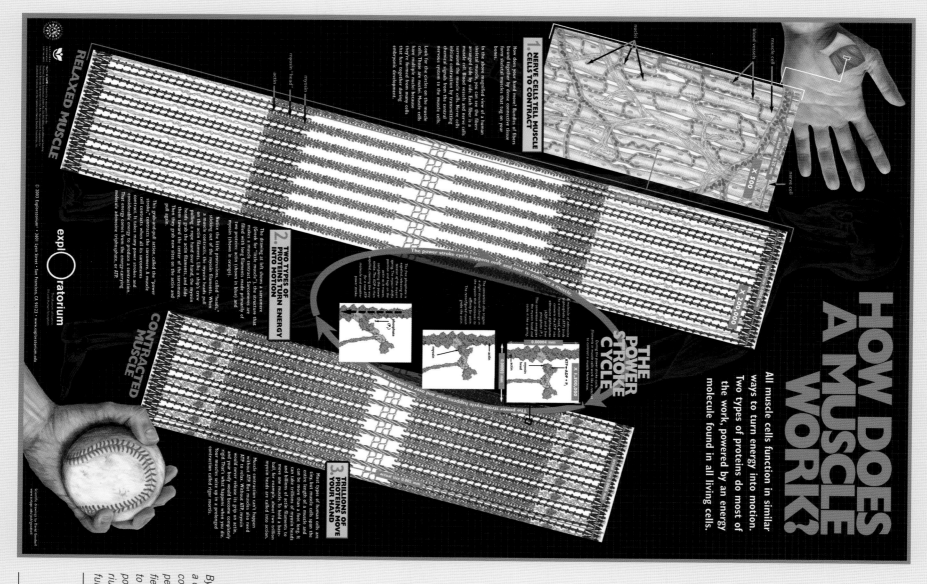

HOW DOES A MUSCLE WORK?

All muscle cells function in similar ways to turn energy into motion. Two types of proteins do most of the work, powered by an energy molecule found in all living cells.

1. NERVE CELLS TELL MUSCLE CELLS TO CONTRACT

How does your hand move? Bundles of fibers bound together by dense connective tissue form skeletal muscles that tug on your bones.

In the above magnified view of a human skeletal muscle, you can see the fibers arranged side by side. Each fiber is a muscle cell. Blood vessels and nerve cells surround the muscle cells. Nerve cells initiate contraction by transmitting chemical signals from the central nervous system to the muscle cells.

Look for the circles on the muscle cells. Those are nuclei. Muscle cells have multiple nuclei because they're formed from many cells that fuse together during embryonic development.

2. TWO TYPES OF PROTEINS TURN ENERGY INTO MOTION

The drawing at left shows a sarcomere (Greek for "little muscle"), the structure that makes a muscle contract. Sarcomeres are filled with long filaments made primarily of two proteins: actin (shown in blue) and myosin (shown in orange).

Notice the little protrusions, called "heads," sticking out of the myosin filaments. When a muscle contracts, the myosin heads pull on the actin filaments. Like a ship's crew pulling a rope hand over hand, the myosin heads grab the actin filaments, and slide them toward the center of the sarcomere. Then they grab new sites on the actin and pull again.

This grab-and-pull action called the "power stroke," contracts the sarcomere. A muscle cell contracts when all its sarcomeres contract. It takes many power strokes and considerable energy to produce a contraction. That energy comes from the energy-carrying molecule adenosine triphosphate, or ATP.

3. TRILLIONS OF PROTEINS MOVE YOUR HAND

Most types of human cells are tiny, but muscle cells span the entire length of a muscle and can be more than a foot long. It can take trillions of myosin heads to move one muscle, to hold a baseball, for example, about two trillion myosin heads are called into action.

Muscle contraction can't happen without ATP. But muscles also need ATP to relax. Without ATP, myosin would never release its grip on actin, and your body would become completely rigid. That's what happens when you die. Your muscles seize up in a prolonged contraction called rigor mortis.

THE POWER STROKE CYCLE

The power stroke cycle happens over and over to contract a muscle.

RELAXED MUSCLE

CONTRACTED MUSCLE

Mark McGowan,
David Goodsell,
Exploratorium,
United States

By leading the viewer along a diagonal path from the context graphic in the upper left through magnified views of muscle fibers to the bottom right, this poster for the Exploratorium reveals how muscles function.

© 2003 Exploratorium ® 3601 Lyon Street · San Francisco, CA 94123 · www.exploratorium.edu

Scientific drawings by David Goodsell
www.nirogov.edu/pdb/goodsell

explOratorium
The Museum of Science
Art & Human Perception

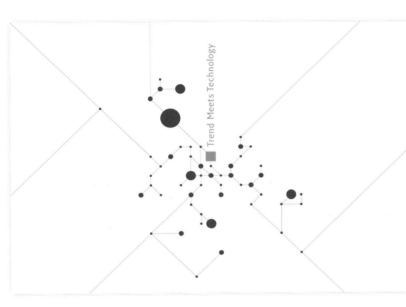

Trend Meets Technology

Applying The Principle

In the visual arts, the focal point, the magnetic area to which the eyes are drawn, is a principal aspect of a composition. "If a design has no focal point, drawing attention inward, it may seem to fall apart, making it difficult for the viewer to organize what is going on," write Paul Zelanski and Mary Pat Fisher in *Design Principles and Problems*. All of the elements within the frame of a composition have a relationship to one another and to the whole. The focal point can be the largest shape in a graphic or the one with the brightest color; it can be isolated from other elements or placed in a compelling position. We perceive it because our brains are wired to seek and detect differences. To our visual processing system, these differences are informative, causing the eye to pause and extract information. Creating several focal points with varying degrees of weight gives rise to a relative order of importance that guides the viewer's attention and eyes through the flow of information.

Several compositional techniques can be used to direct the eyes. Positioning and emphasis are two powerful ways to achieve this. Positioning refers to the importance associated with an element's location. Emphasis refers to the stress given to an element. In addition to structure, movement also guides the eyes. A picture tends to move and flow according to the directionality and energy of line, shape, and texture. For example, the downward flow of wine pouring from a bottle directs the viewer's eyes along the vertical axis into the wine glass. When the patterns of a texture move in a specific direction, this also guides the eyes. Position, emphasis, and movement provide a visual language for orienting and directing the viewer's vision along an intended path.

In addition, explicit techniques that are overlaid onto a graphic call attention to critical attributes and provide directional information. Explicit cues facilitate attention when used alone or in combination, as long as they are placed correctly and used judiciously. The designer should ensure that the chosen cues are appropriate to the cognitive characteristics of the audience. For example, a younger audience may not know that a dashed line implies directionality. Also, children are not as adept as adults at shifting their attention to important information.

Whether guiding the eyes through a graphic or directing the eyes to a specific location, designers should consider the informative purpose of the graphic, its degree of visual complexity, and the characteristics of the audience when deciding on an approach. Implicit, compositional techniques have an aesthetic dimension that will enhance promotional graphics. For instance, powerful lines that guide the eye are also appealing to the senses. Explicit cueing techniques that indicate location are appropriate in information and instructional graphics and diagrams.

The diagonal lines of this graphic draw the viewer into its kinetic center, as the eyes jump to several focal points derived from contrasts in color, shape, and size.

Shinnoske Sugisaki, *Japan*

K & L WINE MERCHANTS

▲ These explanatory line drawings illustrate how ancient Aztec writing is formed. Visual cues include numbers, arrows, and dashed lines, all of which direct the eye.

Lorenzo De Tomasi, Italy

▲ The cover image of this wine merchant's brochure uses a compositional technique to guide the viewer's eyes through the flowing motion of pouring wine.

Christine Kenney,
IE Design +
Communications,
United States

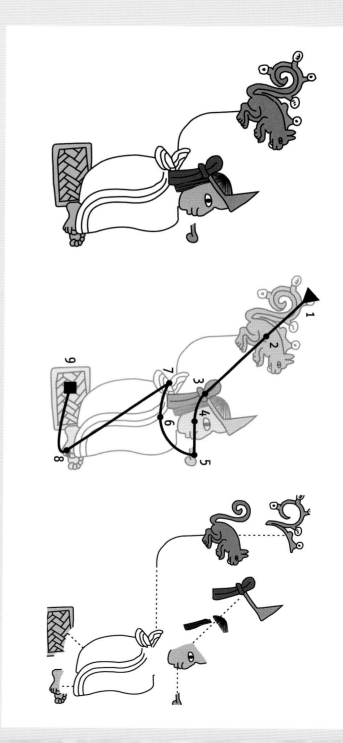

POSITION

The boundaries that define the edges of a graphic, referred to as the frame, have a powerful effect on a composition. Regardless of whether it encloses a post-card, a page, a poster, or a screen, the frame creates meaning for the elements it bounds. Among aesthetic theorists, it is generally accepted that the position of an object within a frame creates a perceptual force or tension that affects the perceived importance of an object and hence where we place our attention.[7]

Through the thoughtful placement of elements, a designer can establish a visual hierarchy to direct the viewer's eyes. The position of each component conveys a progression of relative importance, starting with the element of the highest rank and continuing to those with lesser rank. For example, in a magazine spread, the information graphic might be the most dominant element, followed by a headline and then explanatory text. A standard visual hierarchy consists of three levels—primary, secondary, and equivalent.

Our understanding of positioning in a frame is a metaphor for how we view hierarchies in the world. We speak of people who have important positions as being at the top. Likewise, we have an expectation of this convention in pictures. We anticipate that elements at the top of a page will be the most important.

In fact, research shows that objects in the top half of a picture are considered to be more active, dynamic, and potent. In other words, they have more visual weight.[8] Another study found that viewers spend more time viewing areas appearing on the left and upper half of the field than on areas located on the right and lower half. This appeared to be true in both sym-metrical designs and in a double-page spread.[9] Of one thing we can be certain: Varying the position of an object in a frame changes its impact on the observer.

▶ This information graphic for Condé Nast Portfolio establishes an effective visual hierarchy to explain the auction of mobile band-widths.

John Grimwade and Liana Zamora, Condé Nast Publications, United States

▼ In this poster for a London museum, the designer used a classic approach to positioning by placing the name of the historical exhibition above the fold in an old-timey newspaper design.

Cog Design, United Kingdom

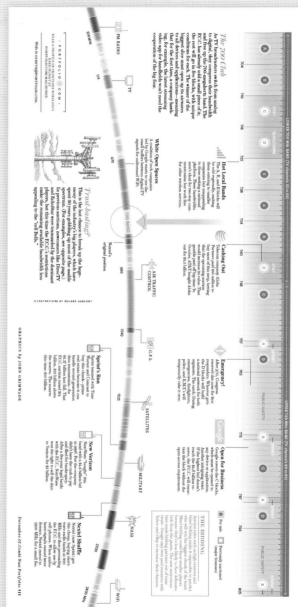

Battle of the Cell Bands

The F.C.C. is selling the last bit of bandwidth suitable for mobile phones in an auction that could raise $30 billion and determine the future of wireless technology ... BY GENEVIEVE SMITH

The Auction
On January 24, the Federal Communications Commission will open bidding on 1,099 licenses for the last slice of airwaves suit-able for mobile phones. The F.C.C. has conceded that the industry's big four—Verizon, AT&T, Sprint, and T-Mobile—which came to dominate this country, to change that, which has already attracted a gaggle of prospec-tive new players, including Google. For America's 240 million cell-phone subscribers, the outcome of this auction could be the difference between the same old cell-phone service and a bold new wireless horizon.

The 700 Club
As TV broadcasters switch from analog to digital, they compress their bandwidth and free up the 700-megahertz band. The F.C.C. has already sold a small piece of it; the rest will go in five blocks, with unique conditions for each. The winner of the biggest slice must open up its airwaves to all devices and applications—meaning that for the first time, a company hawk-ing, for example, the latest streaming video app for handhelds won't need the cooperation of the big four.

Hot Local Bands
Telecom company Aloha has been paying $6 million to buy most of this strip, betting that the upcoming auction would increase its value. That gamble paid off. Page One: In October, AT&T bought Aloha out for $2.5 billion.

White Open Spaces
A coalition of tech companies led by Google wants to use the small buffers between digital-TV signals for unlicensed WiFi.

Cashing Out
After 9/11, Congress set aside this band for first responders. Wherever goes the 700-megahertz band, they will build a national network for each of the 3 blocks will build out the 24 MHz band. The outfit During emergencies, firefighters, police, and EMTs will tune into this block without inter-ference and they can lease the open-access requirements.

Trust-busting? This is the last chance to break up the logo-many of the industry's big players, which have spent 90 years gobbling up most of the usable spectrum. (For example, see opposite page.) In previous auctions, newcomers like DirecTV and EchoStar were trumped by the dominant players, but this time the F.C.C.'s restrictions make the remaining available bandwidth less appealing to the "cell Bells."

Emergency!
After 9/11, Congress set aside this band for first responders. Wherever goes the 700-megahertz band, which must be opened to any device or application. Another intriguing twist: If the highest bid doesn't reach the $4.6 billion re-serve, the F.C.C. will reauc-tion that block without the open-access requirements.

Open for Business
Google covets the C-block, part of which is reserved for a open network.

THE BIDDING
Auction rules set a high reserve and limit individual bids. In a stroke, who will stop bidding? should the block sell, whoever wins that block could lose money—but filibid holding could force smaller players to sell out cheap—then big companies could snap them up. Yahoo and eBay to increase their licenses.

Sprint's Run
Sprint teamed up with Time Warner and Comcast to buy this chunk—prime real estate because it can handle second-generation data transmission—for $2.7 billion last fall. That didn't sit well with the F.C.C., and it forced a do-over: After a three-way legal battle with the F.C.C., Sprint won the rights to which then won the right to Verizon for $5 billion.

New Verizon
NextWave "bought" this band with a $4.8 billion bid in 1996. But the company didn't have the cash to pay its bid, and it defaulted. After a decade-long battle with the F.C.C., Verizon won the right to this band by buying old phones. When mobile signals caused inter-ference, Nextel moved to 800 MHz for a small fee.

Nextel Shuffle
Nextel runs Sprint; got this cheap, buying short-wave radio bands at 800 MHz and then promising the F.C.C. to allow use by old phones. When mobile signals caused interference, Nextel moved to 800 MHz for a small fee.

ILLUSTRATIONS BY ROLAND SARKARY

GRAPHICS by JOHN GRIMWADE

December.07 Condé Nast Portfolio 111

EMPHASIS

A design needs varying degrees of emphasis to capture and guide the viewer's attention. Without emphasis, a graphic feels flat and lifeless, offering a limited sensory experience and diminished possibilities for directing the eye. On the other hand, a design with emphasis is energetic. It attracts the eyes with prominent areas of focus, creating a dominant-subordinate hierarchy by endowing important elements with relative weight and stress. As the observer instinctively moves from the most prominent component to the least, emphasis directs the eyes around a graphic.

Emphasis can be accomplished through techniques that create contrast, which is characterized by a dramatic change in visual information. When we glance at a picture, contrast attracts our attention. We sense that areas of sameness are not as informative as areas of difference. It is through contrast that we discriminate foreground from background and differentiate shapes, textures, and patterns. Through contrast, prominent elements of a graphic emerge and become more visible than their surroundings.

A successful design uses contrast at varying levels so that every element has a place in the hierarchy, avoiding a competition for dominance. An element is most likely to be perceived as a primary focal point when the change is abrupt and the polarity between the element and its surroundings is vivid. The primary focal point must create impact. Secondary and tertiary elements should be progressively toned down.

The options for creating contrast are achieved by juxtaposing elements that differ along one or more dimensions of size, tone, color, texture, and shape. In his book *Art and Visual Perception*, Rudolf Arnheim notes that when all other factors are equal, the visual weight of an element is most dependent on its size. Others suggest that contrast in tonal values has the greatest impact. Regardless of the attribute selected, any contrast between elements should enhance the message, as the audience will interpret a difference as meaningful.

Incongruence can also be used to create emphasis because it provides a focal point. Incongruence refers to the placement of an unexpected object in a familiar context, such as a bathtub in the middle of the desert. It can also be achieved by using an attribute in an unexpected way, such as reversing the size of people so that babies are larger than their parents. Incongruence attracts our attention because we construct schemas of how the world looks, sounds, and works. Incongruence challenges our schemas because what we see is unfamiliar and fails to match our prior knowledge. Our interest is heightened as we attempt to mentally accommodate an unusual juxtaposition or an unconventional attribute.

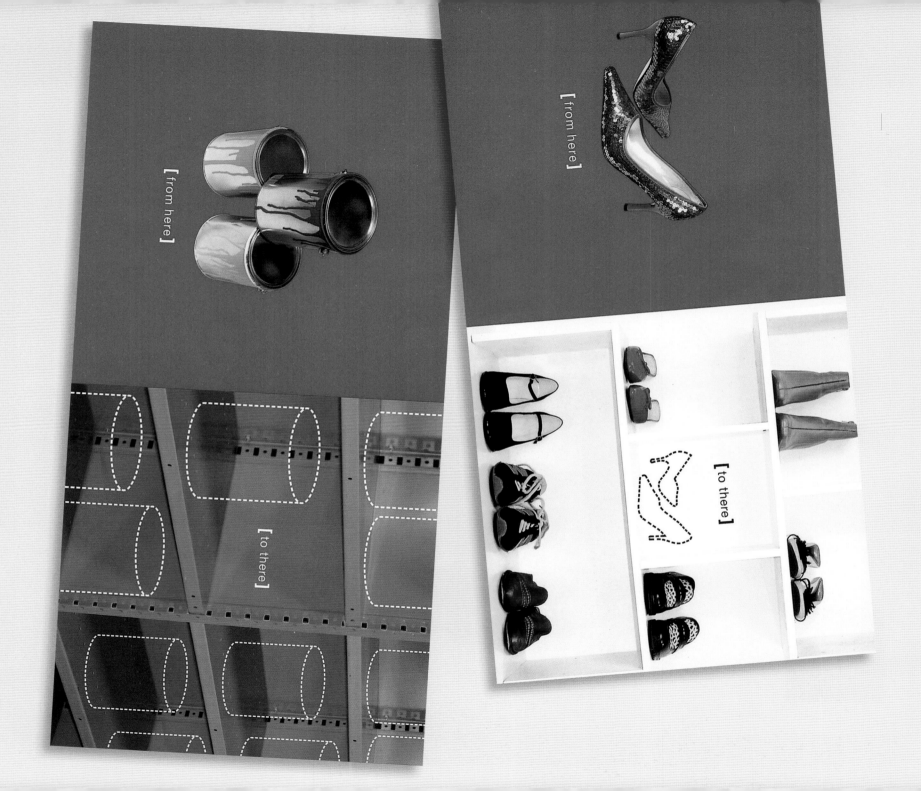

▼ Isolation is one way to
establish prominence, as
shown in these postcards
for retail merchandising
software.

Luis Jones,
Fusion Advertising,
United States

▲ The unexpected shape
of a foot creates emphasis
through contrast and sur-
prise in this graphic for
the Guardian newspaper.

Jean-Manuel Duvivier,
Jean-Manuel Duvivier
Illustration, Belgium

MOVEMENT

When a graphic conveys a dynamic sense of movement, our eyes seem to glide across its surface. Movement can be explained as an energetic force or tension embodied in and between the lines, textures, shapes, and forms of a graphic. Movement is more than the repetition of patterns; rather, it sweeps the viewer's attention through a picture. It is a powerful way for graphic designers to direct the viewer's eye to the important elements in a graphic.

When we perceive movement in a static picture, we perceive its directionality, sensing whether it moves in fits and starts, rounds back onto itself, or takes us off the page. Rudolf Arnheim suggests that the direction of visual forces in a picture is determined by three factors: the attraction exerted from the visual weight of surrounding elements, the shape of objects along their axes, and the visual direction and action of the subject.[10]

That we can perceive directionality and movement in a static two-dimensional picture is a remarkable feat of the eyes and brain. We perceive kinetic information in a still picture because we know the experience of our own physical movement and we understand the motion of objects. In fact, our ability to perceive movement in a static graphic is associated with regions of the brain that we use for observing physical motion. In one study, researchers found that action photographs activated areas of the brain that are sensitive to real motion, whereas photos depicting people in still positions did not activate these areas. According to the study's authors, motion cues in a graphic appear to create the perception that an object is leaping out from its static surroundings.[11] Although this study was based on photographs of people in action, it is likely that our perception of compositional movement is also due to motion-detecting neurons.

In this field hockey equipment catalog, motion shots create the perception of movement and capture the intensity of the sport.

Greg Bennett, Siquis,
United States

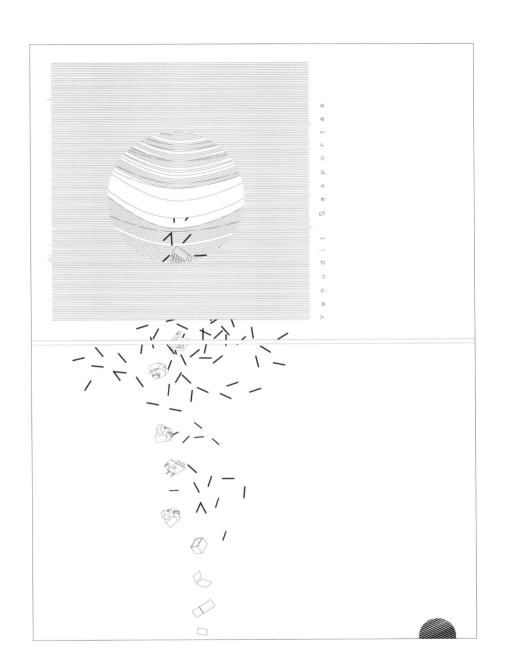

Yehudit Sasportas

Graphic designers can exploit the expressive quality of lines and shapes to create movement based on the rhythm of elements. For example, curved lines and undulating shapes create smooth and flowing movement. Jagged lines create tension and make the eyes dart and pause. It is interesting to note that movement that extends in a left-to-right direction is considered easier to perceive. In a survey of art from many cultures, including Chinese, Japanese, Indian, Persian, and Western, this left-to-right asymmetry of emphasis was found to be a common phenomenon.[12] The survey found that across cultures, important elements tended to be located to the left of those that were less important, causing the eyes to flow in a rightward movement. Thus, the left-to-right preference may be neurological rather than cultural.

Designers can also create movement by creating the illusion of three-dimensional perspective, which draws the viewer's eyes into the depth of field. Viewers deduce depth perception in a picture because of their knowledge of how things appear in the physical world. Objects that are larger in size are assumed to be in the foreground. Viewers also perceive the illusion of depth because converging lines create a sense of depth and cooler colors create a sense of distance. Depth perception also creates a visual hierarchy. Most viewers consider objects in the foreground more important than objects in the distance.

This promotional poster for an artist's lecture exemplifies how the visual direction of shapes can create dynamic movement.

Ian Lynam,
Ian Lynam Creative
Direction & Design, *Japan*

Three-dimensional perspective effectively directs a viewer's attention further into the depth plane, as illustrated in this cover for SMT magazine.

Christopher Short,
United States

The movement of fire carries the viewer across the page in this typography poster, based on a Persian traditional tale.

Maziar Zand,
M. Zand Studio, Iran

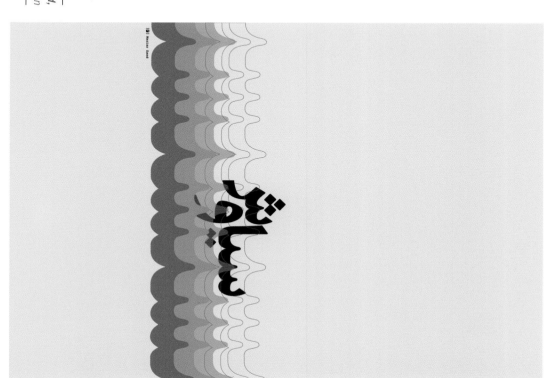

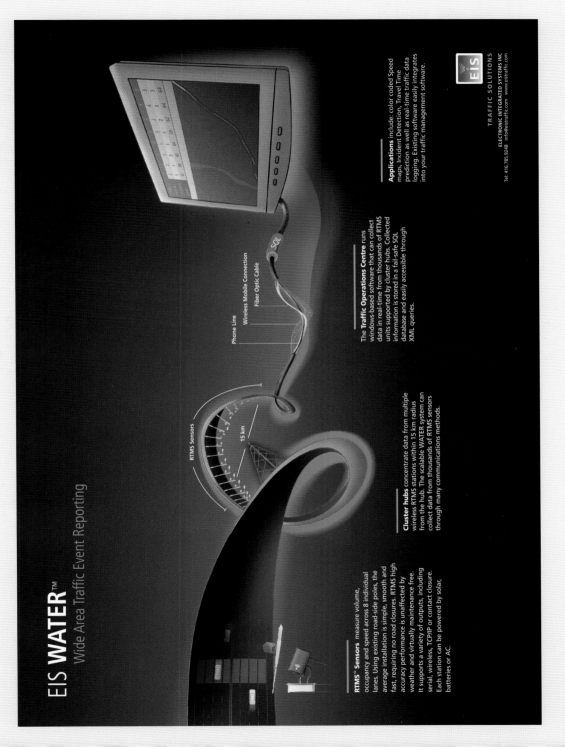

EIS **WATER**™
Wide Area Traffic Event Reporting

RTMS™ Sensors measure volume, occupancy and speed across 8 individual lanes. Using existing road-side poles, the average installation is simple, smooth and fast, requiring no road closures. RTMS high accuracy performance is unaffected by weather and virtually maintenance free. It supports a variety of outputs, including serial, wireless, TCP/IP or contact closure. Each station can be powered by solar, batteries or AC.

RTMS Sensors

15 km

Phone Line
Wireless Mobile Connection
Fiber Optic Cable
SQL

Cluster hubs concentrate data from multiple wireless RTMS stations within 15 km radius from the hub. The scalable WATER system can collect data from thousands of RTMS sensors through many communications methods.

The **Traffic Operations Centre** runs windows-based software that can collect data in real-time from thousands of RTMS units supported by cluster hubs. Collected information is stored in a fail-safe SQL database and easily accessible through XML queries.

Applications include: color coded Speed maps, Incident Detection, Travel Time prediction as well as real-time traffic data logging. Existing software easily integrates into your traffic management software.

TRAFFIC SOLUTIONS

ELECTRONIC INTEGRATED SYSTEMS INC
Tel: 416.785.9248   info@eistraffic.com   www.eistraffic.com

The undulating visualization of this traffic event-reporting system guides the viewer through the information flow—from an explanation of the hardware to the software and finally to the end-user advantages.

Patrick Keenan and Alan Smith, *The Movement, Canada*

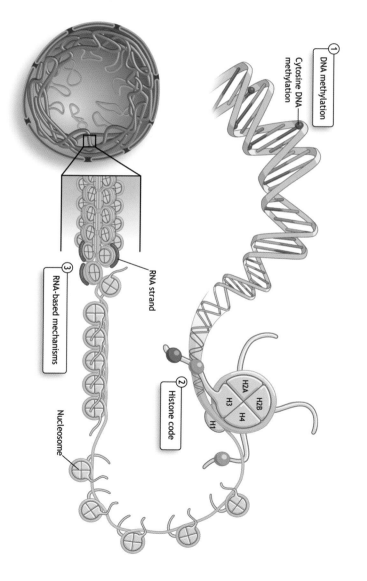

▼ The curvature of this biological graphic moves the viewer through the mechanisms and processes of gene expression.

Daniel Müller, Haderer & Müller, Biomedical Art, United States

① DNA methylation

Cytosine DNA methylation

RNA strand

③ RNA-based mechanisms

Nucleosome

② Histone code

H2A
H2B
H3
H4
H1

▲ Shapes and lines create rhythmic movement in this AIGA poster reflecting a 1930s artistic style.

Dale Sprague and Joslynn Anderson, Canyon Creative, United States

▼ In this information graphic for the Cleveland Plain Dealer, the curves in the highway take the viewer along a path to the most important information.

Stephen J. Beard, Plain Dealer, United States

TRAFFIC MYSTERY: THE 'SHOCKWAVE'

Making sense of red lights, construction zones and other roadway phenomena

Why do freeways come to a stop?

It happens to most drivers at least a few times a year. You're sailing along on the freeway when you're forced to come to a stop, or at least a crawl. You can't see why things are slowing around the bend — and when you get there, traffic is moving better.

Traffic planners call this a "shockwave."

1 Traffic is rolling along at 60 mph when someone slows to 50 mph. In this example, the driver of Car B does so to avoid hitting Car A, whose driver swerves at the last second to exit.

2 The next driver slows to 45 mph to maintain a safe distance from cars A and B.

3 Drivers farther back see the brake lights and begin slowing down.

4 The pattern continues, and more drivers apply their brakes until traffic comes to a crawl. By the time the rear of the jam catches up to where the shockwave began, the offending parties are long gone and there is no sign of what caused the problem.

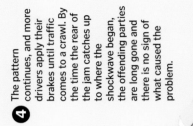
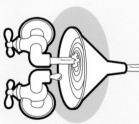

The funnel effect

Cuyahoga County transportation engineer Jamal Husani compares rush-hour traffic to a funnel.

Just the right amount of water can go through as fast as it's put in the funnel.

But add extra water to the funnel, and the whole thing backs up.

"The first few drivers could have a big impact," Husani said. "Their behavior in the peak time has a huge ripple effect, even if it doesn't look that bad to them."

STEPHEN J. BEARD AND RICH EXNER | THE PLAIN DEALER

FIRST IN A SERIES

"Traffic Mystery" will appear occasionally in The Plain Dealer's Metro section. To reach this reporter: rexner@plaind.com, 216-999-3505.

EXIT
THIS LANE ONLY

Cleveland

EYE GAZE

It isn't surprising that we are drawn to pictures of people—our brains appear to have specialized mechanisms for detecting and recognizing human faces. Regardless of whether the face appears as a photograph, a painting, a sketch, or a simple schematic figure, specific neural networks are activated in the brain upon perceiving anything configured as a face.[13] In addition, specialized regions of the brain respond to the recognition of at least one facial feature in isolation—the eyes.[14] We are attuned to detecting faces and eyes because we are communicative beings, and facial expressions convey important emotional and interpersonal information.

A secondary and intriguing characteristic of facial awareness is that we automatically shift our eyes in the direction where someone else is looking. In a long list of studies, eye gaze has been found to orient a viewer's attention.[15] According to researchers Stephen Langton and Vicki Bruce, "Neuropsychological, neurophysiological, and behavioral evidence is emerging in support of the position that there is a functionally specific mechanism devoted to the task of detecting eyes and computing where in the environment eye gaze is directed."[16] Support for this specialized mechanism is found in the fact that infants as young as three months of age can detect the direction of an adult's gaze and will shift their own attention in that direction.[17]

Although it is unclear whether this is innate or learned, gaze perception triggers what is known as joint attention, or shifting our eyes in the direction of someone else's gaze. As a survival mechanism, it is clear that shifting attention to where someone else is looking could prove quite helpful in times of danger. As a social mechanism, joint attention could provide significant information about another person's momentary interest and perhaps their psychological state.

This seemingly automatic ability transfers to pictures. When an observer views a static image of a face, it triggers the viewer's attention to look in the direction of the subject's gaze. Graphic designers can take advantage of this eye gaze reflex to focus attention on a particular graphic by using photographs or illustrations that depict a person gazing in the desired direction.

▶ Eye gaze is a magnetic attraction for pulling in the viewer.

Ola Levitsky,
B.I.G. Design, Israel

▼ This poster for an art exhibition features the artist and his wife gazing downward, absorbed in their tasks. Following the direction of their gaze takes the viewer deeper into the graphic.

Ida Wessel,
BankerWessel, Sweden

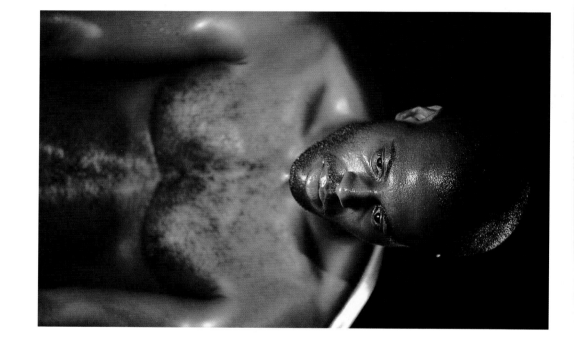

The performer's hypnotic stare in this theater program guide makes it difficult to look away.

Francheska Guerrero,
Unfolding Terrain,
United States

▼ In this CD cover for typographer Kurt Weidemann, the designer's eye gaze leads the viewer to the contents of the CD.

A. Osterwalder,
P. Bardesono, S. Wagner,
A. Bromer and
M. Drozdowski,
i_d buero, Germany

Illustrated depictions of eye gaze also direct the eyes to crucial areas of a picture.

Jean-Manuel Duvivier,
Jean-Manuel Duvivier
Illustration, *Belgium*

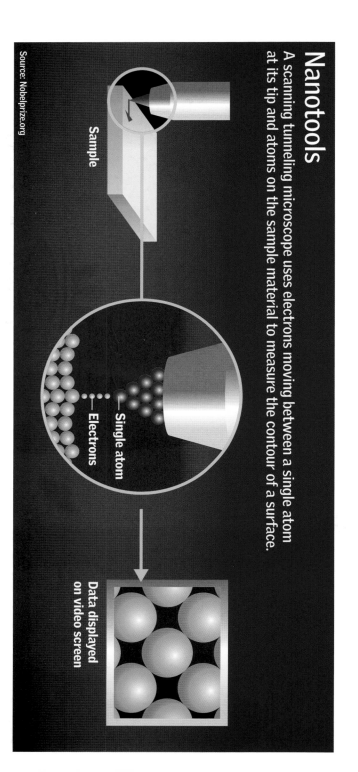

Source: Nobelprize.org

Nanotools

A scanning tunneling microscope uses electrons moving between a single atom at its tip and atoms on the sample material to measure the contour of a surface.

Sample

Single atom
Electrons

Data displayed
on video screen

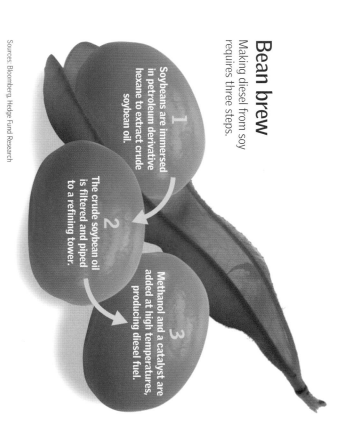

Bean brew

Making diesel from soy requires three steps.

1 Soybeans are immersed in petroleum derivative hexane to extract crude soybean oil.

2 The crude soybean oil is filtered and piped to a refining tower.

3 Methanol and a catalyst are added at high temperatures, producing diesel fuel.

Sources: Bloomberg, Hedge Fund Research

VISUAL CUES

Some of the first tasks a viewer performs when scanning a picture are to search for informative areas, prioritize the information, and select what is most important. The time it takes to locate important information depends on the number of eye fixations that a viewer makes, because the eyes fix on static points much of the time during the search process. Visual complexity makes it more difficult to find important information and increases the number of fixations needed to perform a search.

Designers can facilitate the early tasks of searching, prioritizing, and selecting by signaling the viewer's attention to the location of the most essential information. This involves adding visual cues such as arrows, color, and captions to a graphic. Visual cues optimize the viewing experience by providing a shortcut to relevant information, rendering the need for a visual search unnecessary. Furthermore, visual cues have been shown to improve a person's recall of information.[18] They also enable a viewer to attend to a single area of visual information rather than dividing attention among competing stimuli. There is evidence that when a viewer's attention is divided, the size of the perceived visual field is actually reduced, whereas a visual cue pointing to a target increases the perceived visual area. This speeds up the search for important information.[19]

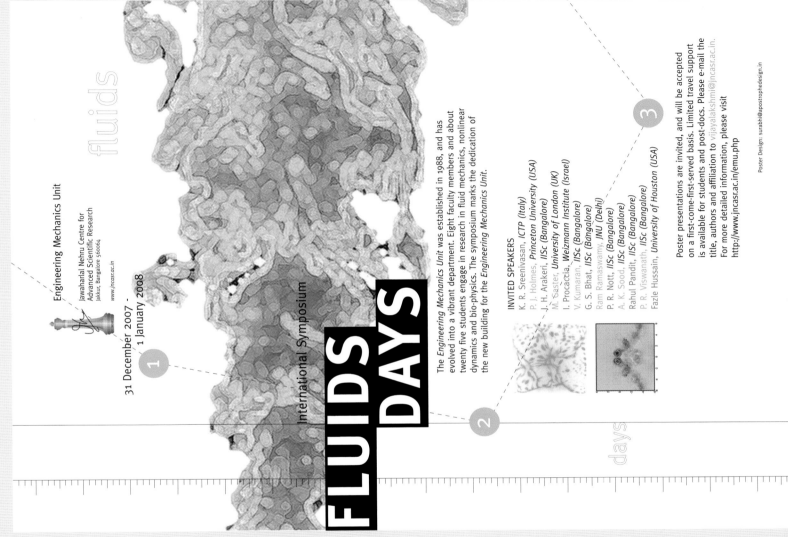

Engineering Mechanics Unit

Jawaharlal Nehru Centre for
Advanced Scientific Research
Jakkur, Bangalore 560064
www.jncasr.ac.in

31 December 2007 -
1 January 2008

International Symposium

FLUIDS DAYS

fluids

days

The *Engineering Mechanics Unit* was established in 1988, and has evolved into a vibrant department. Eight faculty members and about twenty five students engage in research in fluid mechanics, nonlinear dynamics and bio-physics. The symposium marks the dedication of the new building for the *Engineering Mechanics Unit*.

INVITED SPEAKERS
K. R. Sreenivasan, *ICTP (Italy)*
P. J. Holmes, *Princeton University (USA)*
J. H. Arakeri, *IISc (Bangalore)*
M. Gaster, *University of London (UK)*
I. Procaccia, *Weizmann Institute (Israel)*
V. Kumaran, *IISc (Bangalore)*
G. S. Bhat, *IISc (Bangalore)*
Ram Ramaswamy, *JNU (Delhi)*
P. R. Nott, *IISc (Bangalore)*
A. K. Sood, *IISc (Bangalore)*
Rahul Pandit, *IISc (Bangalore)*
P. R. Viswanath, *IISc (Bangalore)*
Fazle Hussain, *University of Houston (USA)*

Poster presentations are invited, and will be accepted on a first-come-first-served basis. Limited travel support is available for students and post-docs. Please e-mail the title, authors and affiliation to vijayalakshmi@jncasr.ac.in. For more detailed information, please visit
http://www.jncasr.ac.in/emu.php

Poster Design: surabhi@apostrophedesign.in

▼ These information graphics for Bloomberg Markets magazine show the value of signaling even for brief visual explanations.

Eliot Bergman, Japan

▲ In this scientific symposium poster, numbers and dashed lines are visual cues that lead the viewer to the essential information.

Surabhi Gurukar, Apostrophe Design, India

Arrows and the Like

The arrow is an ever-present pictorial device frequently found in explanatory graphics, diagrams, and wayfinding. It is used so often because it is exceedingly effective; the arrow not only directs our attention and our eyes, it guides cognition. Because the arrow is derived from an asymmetric shape—a triangle—it brings a sense of dynamism to a graphic.

The arrow is a symbol, and as such it stands for something else and must be decoded by the viewer. The viewer must recognize the triangular shape of the arrow's head, shaft, and tail as one perceptual unit and associate this shape with one or more "arrow schemas" stored in long-term memory. For those familiar with the arrow symbol, its recognition and meaning are easy and automatic. Upon perceiving a visual cue like an arrow, the viewer rapidly evaluates its directional meaning. Context plays an important part in arrow comprehension. We do not interpret any triangle lying on its side as an arrow, but in the appropriate context, such as in a diagram or when representing a "continue" or "play" button, we interpret a sideways triangle as an arrow.

When the arrow points to a specific location, it helps the viewer filter out extraneous information and focus on the essentials. Cueing the observer's selective attention to important information is the first step in comprehension. When designing the pointer arrow, it must be sufficiently dominant to capture the viewer's attention, but it should not overpower the holistic perception of the graphic.

Bold arrows in this information graphic for Condé Nast Traveler represent the time it takes to travel from London to Paris by various modes of transport. The arrows are the dominant element that leads the viewer from one piece of essential information to the next.

John Grimwade,
Condé Nast Publications,
United States

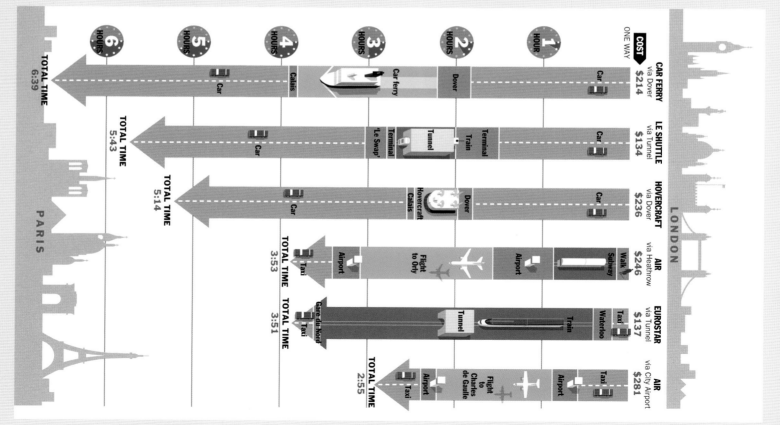

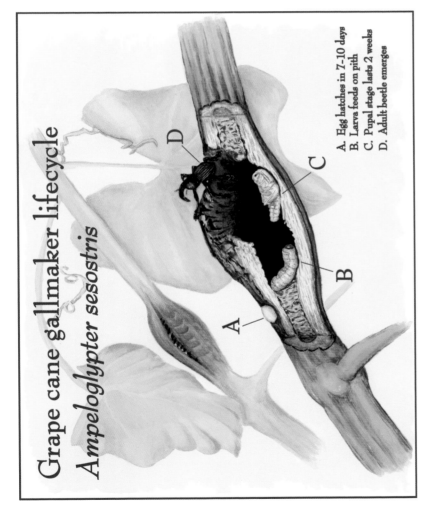

Grape cane gallmaker lifecycle
Ampeloglypter sesostris

A. Egg hatches in 7-10 days
B. Larva feeds on pith
C. Pupal stage lasts 2 weeks
D. Adult beetle emerges

▼ Unobtrusive lines both point to crucial information and effectively blend with the graphic in this illustration of a beetle's life cycle.

**Melisa Beveridge,
Natural History Illustration,**
United States

About pollutants

Sediment

...can keep sunlight from reaching the plants that need it to choke animals that need to breath in the water. Other pollutants, like bacteria, are often carried by sediment.

Bacteria and viruses

...commonly come from animal and human waste, and can make animals and humans who use the water sick. Cleaning up after your dog and putting trash in a trash can helps reduce bacteria and viruses in urban runoff.

Nutrients

...often come from fertilizer because they help plants grow. But they also can cause some plants in the water, like algae, to grow so much that other plants and animals cannot survive and the water isn't good for swimming or boating.

Metals

...can build up to toxic levels in fish and other animals, which can kill them or contaminate human food supplies, especially in the case of fish.

Oil and grease

...often come from activities related to cars. Oil and grease can be toxic to aquatic animals.

Wrongville or Rightville
WHICH TOWN DO YOU LIVE IN?

What makes a healthy watershed?

▲ These graphics are part of a comprehensive signage program explaining environmental content in a wetlands park. In both signs, arrows are well integrated into each graphic as pointers to associated information.

**Claudine Jaenichen and
Richard Turner,
Jaenichen Studio,**
United States

Color Cues

In a rich array of visual information, viewers need a way to filter out what is extraneous in order to attend to the information that is relevant to their task. Time and again, color has proven to be a compelling way to attract attention and prompt the viewer to attend to the most relevant details. As an explicit cueing device, contrast in color—in the form of a circle, a line, or other shape—acts as a signal to direct the eyes. Color is one of the primitive features we detect in preattentive vision, and it can play a dominant role in guiding attention and reinforcing a message.

Color facilitates the interpretation and comprehension of visual information in several ways. In complex visuals, it helps viewers rapidly search through a large quantity of visual information to locate what is most important. Also, viewers have an easier time noticing and distinguishing between objects in a colored graphic as compared to a monochrome one because color often emphasizes figure—ground contrasts. In addition, when a color cue becomes a visual attribute of an object, it helps to make the information memorable.

Color cues are effective in most types of visual communications. During animation sequences, color cues are needed because important information can fly by quickly. In maps and diagrams, color cues are often used to indicate key information. In learning materials, the explicit use of color cues is known to help students comprehend and retain information. There is evidence that color helps us organize and categorize visual information. [20] For information to get noticed quickly, a color cue must vary sufficiently from the background and surrounding objects. Designers should avoid using too many colors.

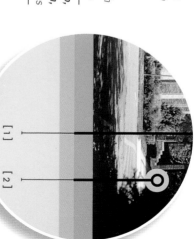

In this visitor's guide for a house and garden tour, the designer uses color cues to signal the location of the most important aspects of the house. Explanatory information associated with each cue is detailed below.

Francheska Guerrero,
Unfolding Terrain,
United States

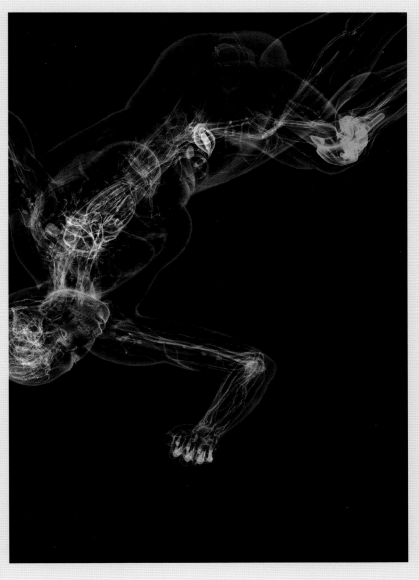

▶ Color cues highlight medical device implants in this futuristic super-woman rendered for Wired magazine.

Bryan Christie,
Bryan Christie Design,
United States

▶ This informational bro-chure promotes pine forest conservation. The maps use bright colors as visual cues to show the few regions of undeveloped, protected forest where Monterey pines still stand.

Karen Parry
and Louis Jaffe,
Black Graphics,
United States

What's the Threat?
Our Native Forest is Being Destroyed

Sadly, the native forests in the Monterey region lack a unified conservation plan. Since European colonization began, our forests have become fragmented, diseased and compromised by development, invasive plants and genetic contamination. Half of our native forest has already been removed. Much of the remaining forest is in private hands and subject to development. The long term survival of the remaining forested lands on the Monterey Peninsula is in jeopardy.

Safeguards are Needed Now

Though not a new idea, the conservation of the remaining native Monterey Pine Forest is now of critical importance. The proposed Jacks Peak Conservation Area is the largest tract of unfragmented native Monterey Pine Forest in the world. Conserved lands in the Jacks Peak Conservation Area could span over 3000 contiguous acres to safeguard both the heart of remaining undeveloped native forest, as well as the forest margins that grade into woodland, grassland and scrub. Benefits of conserving land around Jacks Peak include:

- Maintaining open space and establishing the largest protected area of native Monterey Pine Forest in the world.

- Retaining crucial wildlife corridors and connections between the northern Santa Lucia Range, the Carmel River, Fort Ord backcountry and Carmel Valley ridgelands.

- Enhancing property values that strengthen the regional economy and surrounding communities.

- Increasing recreation opportunities near urban centers.

- Lowering fire risk by reducing development in forested lands.

- Enriching the local quality of life by protecting viewsheds and watersheds that help sustain our healthy and inspiring environment now and into the future.

The Monterey Pine Forest:
Vanishing Treasure or Living Forest Legacy?

What's Our Plan?
Create Monterey Pine Forest Conservation Areas

Establishing Monterey Pine Forest Conservation Areas will help conserve outstanding scenic, recreational, economic and biological values in a region rich with distinctive landscapes. The proposed Conservation Areas – Del Monte Forest, Jacks Peak and Point Lobos – contain exceptional examples of native Monterey Pine Forest habitat and unusual Maritime Chaparral, Oak Woodland and Coastal Prairie, that support special status plants and animals. Portions of the Conservation Areas are threatened with incompatible land uses that will degrade the integrity of these unique and irreplaceable areas that help keep our water pure, our air clean, and our natural world healthy and beautiful. Programs could be developed in the Conservation Areas to facilitate long term protection of the native Monterey Pine Forest, including acquisition, restoration, conservation easements, stewardship incentives for private land owners, public lands management plans, and incorporation of conservation policies into County and City planning processes.

Historic Extent of Monterey Pine Forest

Present Extent of Undeveloped Monterey Pine Forest

Protected Monterey Pine Forest Habitat

Jacks Peak County Park

Potential Park Expansion

Non-Monterey Pine Forest Habitat

This illustration provides a clear explanation of how a crew team functions. A team member's location in the boat is most significant, so the individuality of each person is de-emphasized so the audience stays focused on the essential information.

Jonathan Avery,
University of North Carolina,
United States

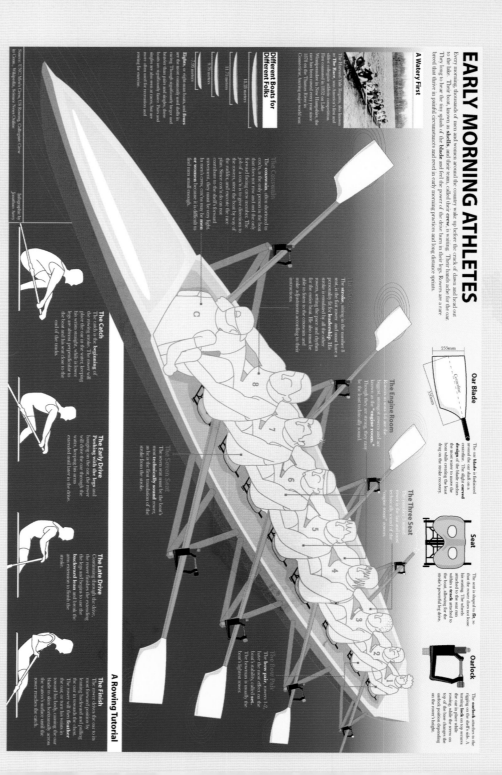

EARLY MORNING ATHLETES

Every morning, thousands of men and women around the country wake up before the crack of dawn and head out to the lake. Their boat, known as **shells**, and their team, called their **crew**, is waiting. Their hands ache for the oar. They long to hear the tiny splash of the **blade** and feel the power of the drive burn in their legs. Rowers are a rare breed that thrive in painful circumstances and revel in each morning practices and long-distance sprints.

A Watery First

The Harvard-Yale Regatta, also known as The Race, was America's first and oldest collegiate athletic competition. First raced on New Hampshire's Lake Winnipesaukee in 1852, the two-mile race has been rowed every year since 1878 on the Thames River in Connecticut, leaving many a world war.

Different Boats for Different Folks

— 19.9 meters

— 11.75 meters

— 18.28 meters

The Coxswain
The **coxswain**, often shortened to cox, is the only person in the boat that does not row and is the only forward-facing crew member. The job of a cox is to give directions to the rowers, steer the boat by way of the rudder, and execute the race plan. Since cox is do not add to the shell's forward momentum, they must be very light, maximum, they can be very light. In rowing's crew, cox must be **men** or **women** because it is difficult to find ones small enough.

Eights, or eight-man boats, and **fours** are the most commonly used shells in racing. Though significantly large and heavier than pairs and singles, these boats are slightly faster. Pairs and singles are also seen as faster, but are more often used for recreation and rowing for exercise.

Oar Blade
The oar **blade** is fashioned around the oar shaft on a centerline. The slight curved **design** of the blade catches the most water to move the boat while creating the least drag on the make recovery.

255mm

The Stroke
The **stroke**, sitting in the number 8 seat, at the first rower and must have a personality fit for **leadership**. His job is to set the pace and rhythm for the entire boat. He also must be able to listen to the coxswain and make adjustments according to their instructions.

The Engine Room

The rowers in the center of a boat are referred to as the "engine room" or the "water room." Though they are not always easy to spot, they provide the bulk of the power.

The Three Seat
The three seat rower is the middle of the boat and most technically sound rower.

Seat
The seat is shaped to **fit**, so that the rower does not lose his seating. The wheels attached to the seat can move within a **track** attached to the boat, allowing for the stroke's powerful leg drive.

Oarlock
The **oarlock** attaches to the rigging outrigger on the shell's side. A turning **lock** on top secures the oar and holds it in place while rowing, while the screw on top of the base changes the oarlock position depending on the rower's height.

The Seven Seat
The seven seat must be the boat's most **technically sound** rower, as he is the first translation of the stroke from the stroke.

The Bow Pair
The **bow pair**, rowers 1-2, have the most effect on the boat's stability, called **set**. The bowman is usually the boat's lightest rower.

A Rowing Tutorial

The Catch
The catch is the **beginning of** the rowing stroke. The rower will place the oar in the water, keeping his oar in the water, keeping his wrists straight, while is lower legs are almost perpendicular to the boat and his seat close to the end of the tracks.

The Early Drive
Pushing with the legs and hanging on the oar, the rower will drive the oar through the water, keeping his arms extended until later in the drive.

The Late Drive
Continuing through the drive, the rower finishes the extending his legs and begins to use the **backward lean** and break the arm extension to finish the stroke.

The Finish
The rower drives the oar to its most forward position as by leaning backward and pulling the oar in towards the chest. The rower will then **feather** the oar, or turn his wrists to toward the body, causing the oar blade to skim horizontally across the water's surface until the rower reaches the catch.

Infographic by Jonathan Avery

Source: UNC Men's Crew, USA Rowing, Collegiate Crew in Conn., Wikipedia, Science News Online

PRINCIPLE 3 | REDUCE REALISM

"The simplest way to achieve simplicity
is through thoughtful reduction."

JOHN MAEDA, *The Laws of Simplicity*

There are times when the ideal expression of a message can be achieved through visual shorthand. An effective way to do this is to reduce the realistic qualities embedded in a graphic.

One way to think about realism is in terms of fidelity, or how much an image resembles something recognizable. On a continuum, visuals with the highest fidelity are photographs in full and natural color, and photorealistic 3-D renderings. The high-fidelity visual contains detail, depth, shadow, texture, and nuance of color as close as possible to interpreting what we see in our environment. On the other end of the continuum are visuals with low fidelity, such as line drawings, silhouettes, and iconic images. The low-fidelity image uses fewer visual elements and qualities that resemble a recognizable object. Reducing realism reduces the fidelity of the image.

Low-fidelity graphics are effective when the goal is to focus on essential details, induce a quick response, strengthen the impact of a message, or provide an explanation, particularly to those with nominal knowledge of the content. For example, the designer may consider reducing the realism of graphics in a beginner's cookbook to help a novice understand how to follow the recipes. In contrast, high-fidelity images might work best in a cookbook for experienced chefs.

The communicative intent of the message, the characteristics of the audience, and the appropriateness of the content should influence the degree of image realism used in a design. Images with reduced realism are best suited for general audiences who need to quickly comprehend the message being conveyed, such as wayfinding signage, educational materials, explanatory graphics, and promotional materials.

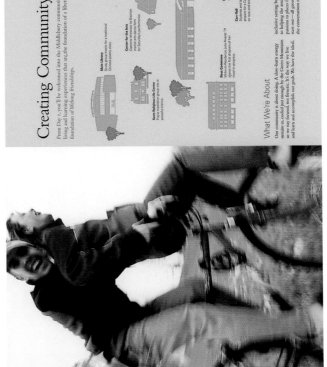

*The spread in this college
viewbook smoothly incorporates both high-fidelity
(on the left) and low-fidelity
imagery (on the right) to
suit different purposes.*

**Amy Lebow
and Purnima Rao,
Philographica,**
United States

Efficient Visual Information Processing

Designing with a minimalist approach has many advantages when it comes to graphic comprehension. Minimalism makes every phase of the human information-processing system more efficient as we perceive a graphic, hold information in working memory, internally represent information, and interpret it.

When we read an image, we scan it to extract significant information. As our neurons work in parallel, we perceive the primitive features of an image, such as color, shape, and depth. After this initial perception, we extract more complex information that we synthesize into a coherent form. A graphic composed of primitive features, such as a line drawing, will take less time to scan and assimilate compared to one that is more complicated, such as a natural scene in a photograph.

Working memory has a limited capacity and is easily overloaded. When viewing a high-fidelity graphic composed of superfluous elements, the additional information can overload working memory, acting as a barrier to comprehension. Distilling a graphic down to its essential visual elements minimizes the information processing required to understand it.

Low-fidelity graphics require fewer transformations to get them ready for encoding into long-term memory. As the brain processes visual information gleaned from an image, it removes the nonessential sensory input and retains the crucial information, converting it into a bare-bones representation. Some cognitive theorists think we may encode images as "sketchy, cartoon-like representations ... that exaggerate or highlight critical distinctions."[1] Because graphics with reduced realism inherently match how we most likely represent information internally, it takes less effort to recognize them and to prepare them for long-term storage.

The presence of unnecessary elements can distract the viewer from focusing on the key message and potentially cause misunderstandings. Francis Dwyer, professor and researcher of instructional systems, notes that images with highly realistic details are not always successful at communication. "Probably my most surprising finding is the ineffectiveness of realistic images. The very polished, most highly sophisticated visuals don't always work."[2]

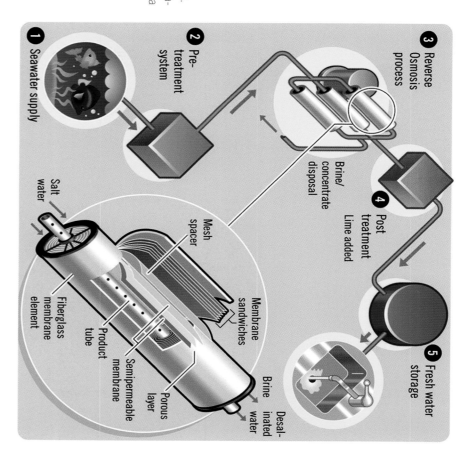

1 Seawater supply

2 Pre-treatment system

3 Reverse Osmosis process

Brine/concentrate disposal

4 Post treatment
Lime added

5 Fresh water storage

Salt water

Mesh spacer

Membrane sandwiches

Fiberglass membrane element

Product tube

Semipermeable membrane

Porous layer

Desal-inated water

Brine

▶ *Reduced realism is ideal for explaining a process such as desalination, shown here. The geometric forms, smooth surfaces, and flat areas of color make the components easy to perceive and comprehend.*

Colin Hayes,
Colin Hayes Illustrator,
United States

▼ *Flat areas of color without texture create low-fidelity maps—all the information that is needed for showing the location of this organization's projects.*

Benjamin Thomas,
Bento Graphics, Japan

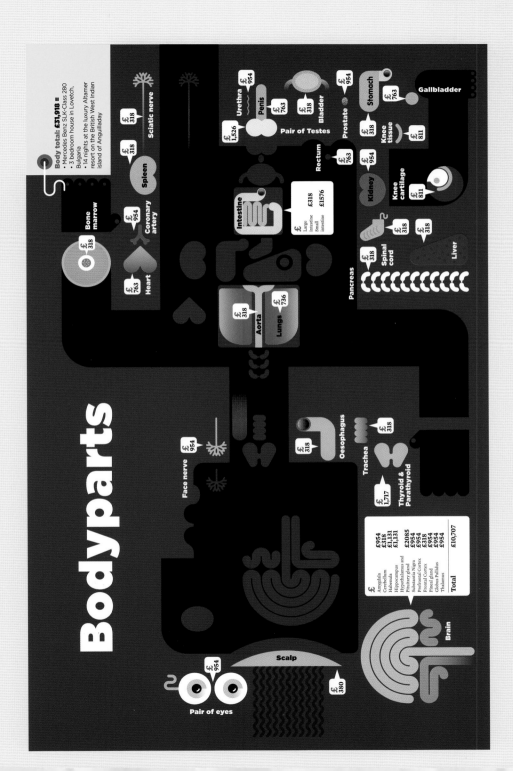

Bodyparts

Body total: £31,918 =
- Mercedes Benz SLK-Class 280
- 3 bedroom house in Lovetch, Bulgaria
- 14 nights at the luxury Altamer resort on the British West Indian island of Anguilladay

Bone marrow £318

Spleen £318

Sciatic nerve £318

Coronary artery £954

Heart £763

Aorta £318

Lungs £736

Urethra £954

Penis £763

Bladder £318

Prostate £954

Stomach £763

Gallbladder £318

Knee tissue £318 / £811

Pair of Testes £1,526

Rectum £763

Kidney £763

Knee cartilage £954 / £811

Intestine
£318
£1576
Large intestine £318
Small intestine £1576

Pancreas £318

Spinal cord £318

Liver £318

Oesophagus £318

Trachea £318

Thyroid & Parathyroid £1,717

Face nerve £954

Brain	
Amygdala	£954
Cerebellum	£318
Habenula	£1,131
Hypothalamus and Pituitary gland	£2085
Substantia Nigra	£954
Prefrontal Cortex	£954
Frontal gland	£318
Pineal gland	£954
Globus Pallidus	£954
Thalamus	£954
Total	**£10,707**

Scalp £380

Pair of eyes £954

▲ In this graphic for Esquire magazine, every object is reduced to its essential but recognizable characteristics.

Peter Grundy, Grundini,
United Kingdom

Reduce Realism 105

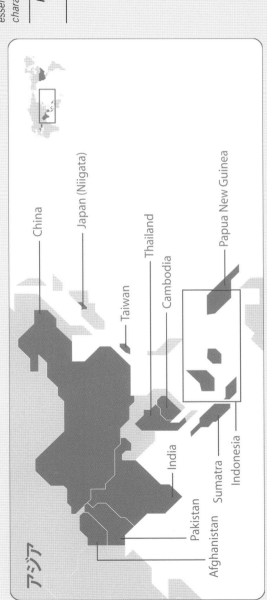

アジア

China

Japan (Niigata)

Taiwan

Thailand

Cambodia

Papua New Guinea

India

Pakistan

Afghanistan

Sumatra

Indonesia

Applying the Principle

We tend to define a picture as realistic if it appears to be a successful copy of its referent. By definition, however, all pictorial representations deviate to some degree from the objects in our physical environment. Manfredo Massironi explains this in *The Psychology of Graphic Images*, "Any graphic representation is always an interpretation, no matter how faithful to reality it is in proportion and attention to detail. Thus, graphics are always attempts to explain reality." Reduced realism is an attempt to interpret reality through visual abstraction and simplification.

To achieve greater abstraction, the designer needs to reduce the degree of detail and limit the expression of one or more visual dimensions, such as color, depth, or texture. The pictorial dimension that is reduced and the details that are included will affect the meaning of the message and the response of the audience. It takes careful consideration to choose which features to convey, which to ignore, and the degree to which a feature will be emphasized. Most important is to convey the information that is consistent across different views of an object.[3]

According to perception research, several qualities affect how a viewer perceives image realism. A hard shadow is perceived as less realistic than a soft shadow, and a smooth surface is perceived as less realistic than a rough surface.[4] Sharp color and sharp contours are perceived as less realistic, while the appropriate blurring of objects in the distance is more realistic. Designers can implement those qualities that make a graphic seem less realistic.

Another approach to reducing realism is to severely limit the number of elements in a graphic, in contrast to our physical environment, which is overloaded with visual information. This allows the viewer to quickly focus on the crucial element of importance. For example, in a brochure advertising ceramic art, the designer could choose to display an array of photographs showing potters at work or a simple photograph of one ceramic vase. The simplified approach has greater impact.

In their book *Reading Images: The Grammar of Visual Design*, Gunther Kress and Theo van Leeuwen note, "The naturalistic image, whatever it may be about, is always about detail." Conversely, the image with reduced realism is always about less detail. As a general guideline, designing to reduce realism is a process of selective abstraction with a focus on the essential intent of a message. While a sufficient amount of visual information must remain for the viewer to form an appropriate mental impression, irrelevant information must be eliminated so the viewer perceives the correct information. The end result should be an idealized and processed version of the real thing.

The designer should not be overly concerned that the audience will miss the point when using graphics with reduced realism—viewers can easily fill in missing details based on prior knowledge of familiar objects.[5] Through experience with pictures, viewers have a common knowledge of the way that objects are often depicted. Upon seeing an abstracted version of a familiar object, they easily recognize it as a conventional portrayal. Reducing visual noise, designing with silhouettes or line drawings, using abstracted imagery, and limiting the number of elements are approaches that can reduce the time it takes for a viewer to perceive and comprehend a graphic.

An image with simple shapes and uniform regions of color stands out in a cluttered environment—an essential quality for concert promotion posters.

Jonas Banker,
BankerWessel, *Sweden*

folk Implosion+
support: Alaskal & Mia Doi Todd

07/5 Copenhagen - Loppen
08/5 Stockholm - Södra
Teatern/Kgb
09/5 Oslo - SoWhat
10/5 Malmö - KB

Nytt album "The New Folk Implosion" ute nu!

Inger: OBC & DKBMúur presenterar

DR HIGGINS

BUZZCOCKS (UK)
DJ PER SINDING LARSEN

LIVE
Stockholm
21 MAJ KL 20.00 OCH 23.00

Christine Walker,
stressdesign, United States

The rich visual qualities
of one clay vase capture
the essence of pottery with
— an economy of design in
this brochure for a pottery
distributor.

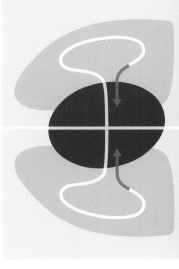

Minimalism is put to effective use in these frames from an animated exhibit on the circulatory system. When each frame is reduced to its essential details, cognitive operations are more efficient.

Stephanie Meier, D. B. Dowd, Taylor Marks, Sarah Phares, Sarah Sisterson, Enrique Von Rohr, and Amanda Wolff, Visual Communications Research Studio- Washington University, United States

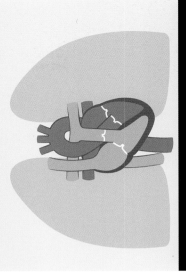

Here's a more detailed look.

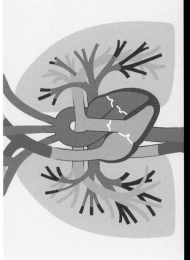

Oxygenated blood, shown as red, goes back to your heart to be pumped out to your body.

Your body is powered by oxygen and nutrients carried in your blood.

Your heart is really a muscle—a very powerful one.

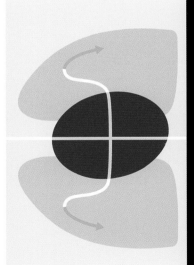

Oxygenated blood (red) enters from the lungs.

This blood passes through your heart to your lungs, where it picks up oxygen.

VISUAL NOISE

In the context of 3-D graphics, visual noise enhances the perception of realism in imagery. It simulates the rich quality of our physical environment, usually through texture and shading. According to researchers in the field, "A real environment is unlikely to be pristine but will have accumulated dirt, dust, and scratches from everyday use. Although human observers do not perhaps consciously take note of these phenomena, the absence of such features ... may indeed affect the viewer's perceived realism of the virtual environment."[6]

Although visual noise adds realism to an image, it can also distract the audience from the real message. The greater the quantity of meaningless information in a communication, the harder it is to decode. For example, because our brains are wired to detect patterns, the viewer may notice and then focus on unintentional patterns found in excessive texture or detail. Minimizing the visual noise in an image is an effective approach to reducing its perceived realism. To do this, the designer can create an environment

that approaches an artificial or pristine world. The graphics shown here demonstrate the hyperreal environment of reduced realism. Figures are extradefined, colored regions are crisp and flat, and surface textures are simplified.

Graphics that are used to support comprehension and learning or as aids to performing a procedure should contain little or no visual noise. The visual information in these types of graphics must be accurately understood. The visual content is often stored in long-term memory and transferred to real-world situations. Visual noise might congest the processing and reduce assimilation of new information.

In both 3-D and 2-D graphics, visual noise can be attributed to high-contrast surface textures, gradated regions of color, the illusion of depth, and detailed or patterned backgrounds. To minimize visual noise, reduce extreme variations in texture, experiment with flat and uniform areas of color, diminish shadows and shading, and lessen background interference.

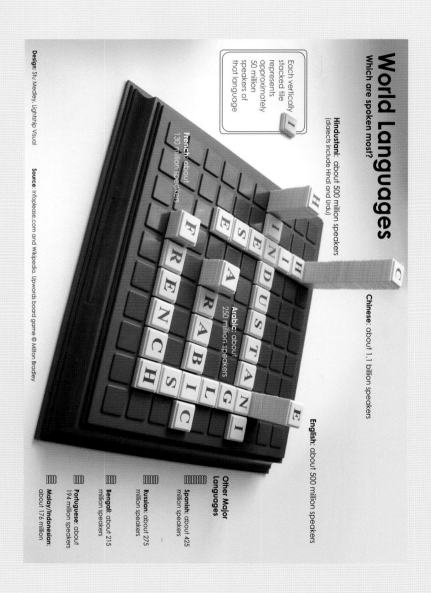

World Languages
Which are spoken most?
(dialects include Hindi and Urdu)

Hindustani: about 500 million speakers

Chinese: about 1.1 billion speakers

English: about 500 million speakers

Each vertically stacked tile represents approximately 50 million speakers of that language

French: about 130 million speakers

Arabic: about 250 million speakers

Other Major Languages

Spanish: about 425 million speakers

Russian: about 275 million speakers

Bengali: about 215 million speakers

Portuguese: about 194 million speakers

Malay/Indonesian: about 176 million

Design: Stu Medley, Lightship Visual

Source: infoplease.com and Wikipedia. Upwords board game © Milton Bradley

This comparison of world languages created for Figures magazine creates an environment with little visual noise. The designer uses sufficient detail to depict the board game metaphor and statistical data, but not enough to overwhelm or distract the viewer.

**Stu Medley,
Lightship Visual,** Australia

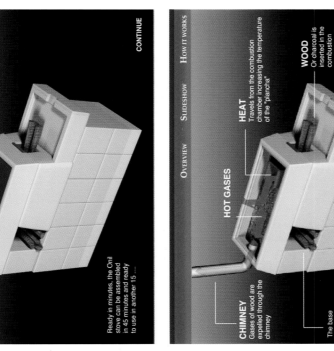

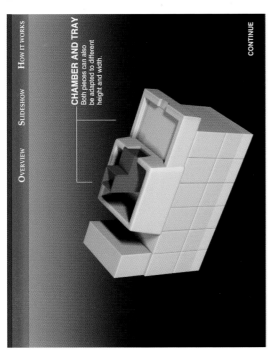

These frames from an interactive exhibit for the Houston Chronicle create a noiseless 3-D world to explain the workings of a high-impact, low-tech stove design. Low-contrast textures and hard shadows add enough realism to replicate the stove and burning wood but do not interfere with accurate perception and interpretation of the animation.

Alberto Cuadra,
Houston Chronicle,
United States

▲ Viewers have difficulty perceiving small differences between similar objects. By minimizing the detail on the jets, viewers can focus on the measurements in red.

Eliot Bergman, Japan

▲ The illustrations on this medical card show a health care audience how to evaluate the condition of an endoscope (used for looking inside the body). The problems with the three faulty tubes on the right are clearly portrayed through an emphasis on the important features and a lack of extraneous detail.

Aviad Stark, Graphic Advance, United States

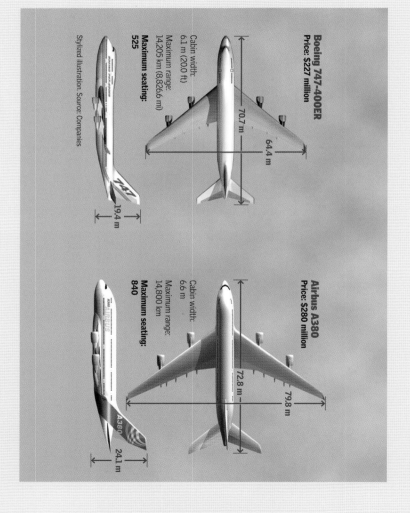

Boeing 747-400ER
Price: $227 million
Cabin width:
6.1 m (20.0 ft)
Maximum range:
14,205 km (8826.6 mi)
Maximum seating:
525
70.7 m
64.4 m
19.4 m

Airbus A380
Price: $280 million
Cabin width:
6.6 m
Maximum range:
14,800 km
Maximum seating:
840
72.8 m
79.8 m
24.1 m

Stylized illustration. Source: Companies

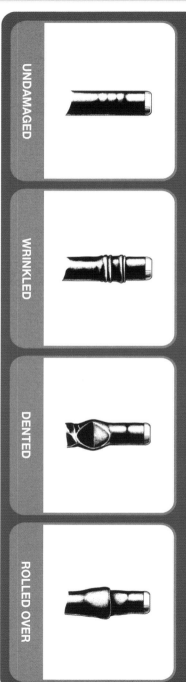

VISION SCIENCES

FLEXIBLE ENT SCOPE
INSERTION TUBE EVALUATION TEMPLATE

Vision Sciences ENT-1000
Karl Storz 11101SK1
Machida ENT-2L
Olympus ENF-XP
Pentax FNL-7RP3

Vision Sciences ENT-3000
Vision Sciences ENT-2000
Vision Sciences E-F100
Karl Storz 11101IP
Karl Storz 11101RP-1
Smith & Nephew / Gyrus Duraview OL-1
Welch Allyn RL-150
Xion EF-NS

Machida ENT-3L
Machida ENT-30PIII

Machida ENT-4L
Olympus ENF-V
Pentax FNL-13S
Pentax VNL-1330
Pentax VNL-1130
Pentax VNL-1170K

Olympus ENF-P4
Olympus ENF-P3
Olympus ENF-GP

Pentax FNL-10P2
Pentax FNL-10S
Pentax FNL-10RBS
Pentax FNL-10RP3

UNDAMAGED

WRINKLED

DENTED

ROLLED OVER

Use this card to evaluate your flexible endoscope prior to using the Slide-On™ ENT Sheath. If your ENT scope shows signs of damage (see below) or will not pass through the size gauge provided, contact the scope manufacturer for repair.

For more information about the Slide-On™ EndoSheath® System, please contact Vision-Sciences, Inc.
Vision-Sciences, Inc. • 9 Strathmore Road • Natick, MA 01760 • T: 800.874.9975 • T: 508.650.9971 • F: 508.650.9976 • www.visionsciences.com

C05164 Rev D

SILHOUETTES

The reduction of an object or scene to its essential profile, as in a silhouette, is an effective technique for minimizing realism. A silhouette typically depicts a form through the outline of its shape, an interior without detail or texture, and a fill of uniform color often within a flat pictorial space. A silhouette evokes recognition by retaining the most important shape information derived from its edge, whether it is a portrait, human form, or object.

A silhouette promotes quick perception and speedy comprehension when it maintains a faithful resemblance to the contours of a real-world form. Although it provides information on the shape dimension alone—without the illusion of depth—human visual perception is remarkably adept at recognizing what it represents.

The silhouette offers many possibilities for expression, depending on its shape, gesture, and context. In its most neutral state, a silhouette is often the visual equivalent of a generalization, conveying the sense that it speaks for all objects in the class it represents. Thus, a silhouette of a man symbolizes Everyman; a silhouette of a mountain symbolizes all mountains.

In a design that evokes emotion, a silhouette can imply anonymity or isolation, as in someone lacking identity. It can quickly convey a sense of mystery, representing a shadowy world devoid of detail. In cartoons, the frame with a silhouette provides a pregnant pause, allowing the audience to step back before the punch line. When a silhouette is given a quantitative value, it becomes a symbol, as in a pictogram. However it is used, a well-designed silhouette is a compact expression of compressed information that can be understood with a minimum of cognitive effort.

Because the silhouette is a closed and featureless form, it can potentially be difficult to perceive. This happens when the shape is ambiguous or cannot be distinguished from its background, causing figure–ground reversal. To avoid perceptual concerns, ensure that the silhouette shape is easy to detect and recognize. Use a formless region for the background and differentiate the figure with a well-defined boundary or color contrast. Do not allow negative space to intrude on the figure. Consider decreasing the size of the foreground objects, as smaller shapes tend to be perceived as the figure rather than the ground.

Expressive silhouettes convey a celebratory theme in this accordion poster for an in-house project. With little effort, we are able to recognize the representations of family and healthy living.

Janet Giampietro, Langton Cherubino Group,
United States

Antonio Mena,
Antonio Mena Design,
Ecuador

The repetition of silhouette shapes provides visual impact in this poster for the Icograda Exhibition in Cuba. Silhouettes provide the base for adding the single distinguishing detail on each form.

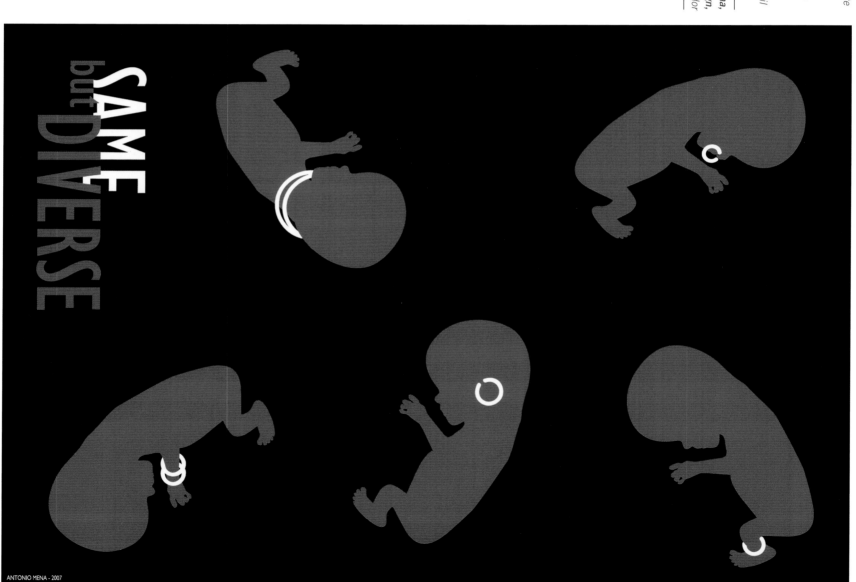

Symbols of music exploding
from the hair of this silhouette capture the energy of
the festival it advertises.
Creative layering makes
the silhouette work as both
foreground and background.

Cog Design,
United Kingdom

Appealing silhouettes grace
the lesson introductions of
these science education
materials, suggesting the
mysteries the books will
unravel for young students.

Heather Corcoran,
Colleen Conrado,
Jennifer Saltzman,
and Anna Donovan,
Plum Studio and Visual
Communications Research
Studio, United States

Lesson 2

What is the
life cycle of a
vertebrate?

Vertebrate life cycle discussion

Students will discuss vertebrate life cycles.

**How does
pollination
occur?**

Lesson 3

Global Crisis

40,000,000 people are currently infected with HIV

25,000,000 people have died as a result of AIDS

6,000 children lose a parent to AIDS every day

2 children die as a result of AIDS every minute

Your $20 each month will

**CARE FOR ORPHANS AND
OTHER CHILDREN**

Your ongoing monthly gift can help provide health
care and nourishing food, supply seeds, tools, and
agricultural training; equip medical clinics; provide
school materials and fees to help children stay in
school; and provide vocational training.

Jan. Mar. May Jun.
Feb. Apr.

USE YOUR VOICE

In this brochure to raise
awareness for children
orphaned from AIDS, the
silhouette depicts a universal figure, expressing that
everyone should take action
and get involved.

*Jay Smith, Juicebox
Designs, United States*

Photographic silhouettes reduce individuals to essential shape and posture.

Jane Lee,
IE Design & Communications, *United States*

ICONIC FORMS

The word *icon* has many meanings in art and graphic design. In this book, an iconic form refers to a highly distilled or stylized depiction that captures the essential characteristics of an object or concept. In contrast to the silhouette that communicates through shape alone, the iconic form communicates through an efficient use of shape, line, and color. When an iconic form is a symbol, its meaning is often culturally dependent and must be learned or deduced. Icons embody a quality that cognitive theorists call computational efficiency, meaning they minimize the processing required for an accurate interpretation. Thus, iconic forms are quickly recognized and processed, and their meanings are memorable.

When we think of iconic images, we may picture an abstracted representation of a familiar object, such as the simplified image that indicates a bus stop. Although these types of icons are prolific, iconic forms can also be rendered as simple schematic representations, such as a human face composed of geometric shapes. Though many iconic forms resemble an object in the environment and have a corresponding meaning, others have an associative value and are considered symbols. Context is a strong contributor to the meaning of an iconic form. For example, in one context, an iconic form of concentric curved lines can represent a rainbow, and in another context it can represent wireless service.

Graphic designers may benefit from an icon classification system proposed by professor Yvonne Rogers for user interface design. In her system, icons are categorized by how they depict the concept they represent.[7] This structure provides a way to think about the potential uses of iconic forms. Resemblance icons directly portray the object to which they refer, such as the icon for the ticket counter at the airport. Exemplar icons depict a common example of the class of objects to which they refer, such as a knife and fork to signify restaurant. Symbolic icons convey a concept that is at a higher level of abstraction than the object depicted, as when a cracked wine glass is used to indicate that the contents of a package is fragile. Arbitrary icons have no relationship to an object or concept, and their association must be learned, such as the symbol indicating no entrance.

Resemblance Icon   **Exemplar Icon**

Symbolic Icon   **Arbitrary Icon**

An iconic classification system adapted from icons by Russell Tate

**Russell Tate,
Russell Tate Illustration,**
Australia

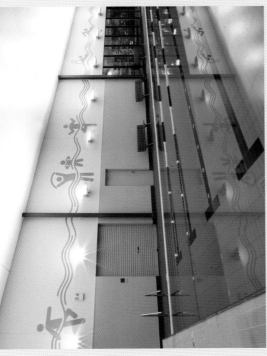

Playful iconic forms representing exercise and activity decorate the walls of this leisure center in Australia.

Simon Hancock, THERE, *Australia*

Iconic forms are appropriate for many uses because they facilitate quick communication. They are effective in signage, maps, technical displays, catalogs, diagrams, and graphs. The iconic form is effective as a memory device or mnemonic, often helpful in training aids and reference materials. Icons can help in the categorization and classification of content, providing meaning to seemingly random information. Icons also succeed as symbols for representing numerical data, as when an icon of a person equals a specific value in a pictograph.

If the goal is to express a message that is direct and immediately understood, the iconic form must be precise and use a simple, effective orientation. Designers may find that the most recognizable version of an object is its side view. When creating an iconic symbol, a corresponding association is more effective than an arbitrary one that must be learned or inferred. Nigel Holmes provides this insight regarding icon design in his book, *Designing Pictorial Symbols*: "It is visually precise; it attempts to get at the essence of an idea—either by being a literal, miniature drawing, or by being a non-literal, visual metaphor. A symbol can give an identity to a subject and, by repeated use, can come to equal it."

These stylized iconic forms for Europe's Thalys train are distilled to their minimum attributes for quick comprehension.

**Jean-Manuel Duvivier,
Jean-Manuel Duvivier
Illustration, Belgium**

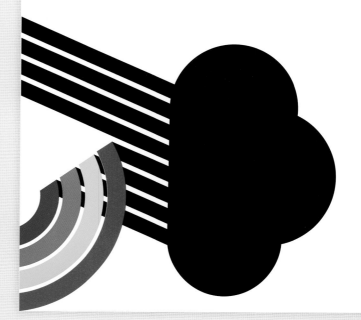

In this poster, the iconic symbol of rain transforming into a rainbow represents the freeing of Nelson Mandela from prison when South Africa was referred to as the Rainbow Nation.

**Emmi Salonen, Emmi,
United Kingdom**

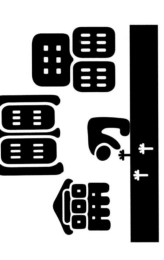

▼ Iconic forms can be expressive, as in these illustrations for a book of urban stories. The figures represent the concepts of monotony, play, inspiration, and urban planting.

Tamara Ivanova, Germany

▶ This reference card instructs office employees on how to be a good neighbor. The icons work as a mnemonic device to help people remember the rules of office etiquette.

Wing Chan, Wing Chan Design, United States

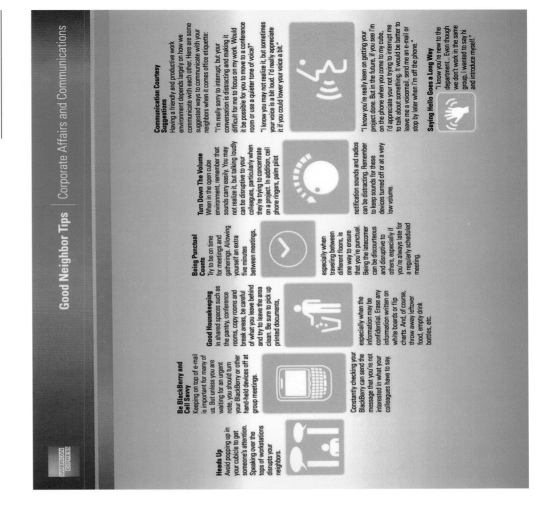

Reduce Realism **121**

LINE ART

The simple line drawing that focuses on the outline of an object is a graceful way to achieve reduced realism. Often with minimal tonal value or depth, the line drawing describes the shape of an object and its essential details with a few strokes. It is thought that early in the vision process, the brain quickly extracts linear features from a picture or scene. This includes line curvature, line orientation, and the ending point of a line. When we scan an image or an object, most of the visual activity occurs on the edges. Thus, depicting an outline alone is sufficient to convey meaning. Similar to understanding silhouettes, the dimension of shape helps us recognize objects. This may be due to our familiarity with picture conventions. Even though lines do not bind objects in the physical world, we perceive outline drawings "as depicting shapes rather than arrangements of wires."[8]

Our perceptual tendency to organize units into wholes comes into play in line perception. Known as the Gestalt principle of closure, it states that we organize sensory input by closing simple figures to make them whole. In addition, during later stages of vision we transform an image into something that fits with our experience and expectations. For example, we add a third dimension to an image from small depth cues. Although line art appears to be simple, it projects a great deal of information.

In addition to effectively conveying the human figure, line drawings are excellent for technical and explanatory graphics that describe the inner workings of the body or a machine. These drawings typically provide all the necessary detail and omit anything superfluous. Explanatory line drawings are effective as illustrations in documentation and textbooks, as infographics, and for assembly instructions. Surprisingly, people identify the objects in line drawings as easily as the objects in photographs, and line drawings are superior to photographs in terms of making the information conveyed in the picture memorable.[9]

As in other approaches to reducing realism, the line drawing does not need extensive detail, but must capture the contours and prominent features of an object while filtering out irrelevant information. The designer or illustrator must analytically and intuitively seek the few elements that will convey the idea, emotion, or object. Although the drawing and the object will not be equivalent, the visual impression it creates will suffice—the audience will add their knowledge of the world to the interpretation of those few lines.

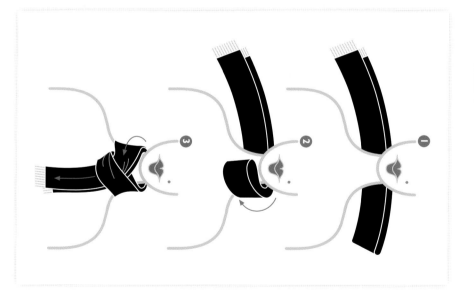

Evolution of the Thermometer

The Galileo Thermoscope 1592

A Galileo thermometer or thermoscope, which is named after the Italian physicist Galileo Galilei, is a thermometer made of a sealed glass cylinder containing a clear liquid and a series of objects whose densities are designed to sink in sequence as liquid is warmed and decreases in density

The Galileo thermometer works due to the principle of buoyancy. Buoyancy determines whether objects float or sink in a liquid. The only factor that determines whether a large object will float or sink in a particular liquid relates the object's density to the density of the liquid in which it is placed. Small objects can float through the surface tension. Only if the object's mass is greater than the mass of liquid displaced, the object will sink. If the object's mass is less than the mass of liquid displaced, the object will float.

Galileo discovered that the density of a liquid is a function of its temperature. This is the key to how the Galileo thermometer works. As the temperature of water increases or decreases from 4oC, its density decreases.

In the Galileo thermometer, the glass bulbs are partly filled with a different coloured liquid. This liquid may contain alcohol, or it might be water with food coloring added in.

The bubbles are all hand-blown glass, they are not exactly the same size or the same shape.

Once the handblown bulbs have been sealed, their effective densities are adjusted by means of the metal tags hanging from beneath them.

Even though these bulbs expand and contract with changing temperatures, the effect on their density is negligible. The heating and cooling of the coloured liquid and air gap inside the bulbs won't greatly affect the bulbs' density in any way at all.

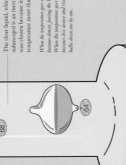

The clear liquid, which the bulbs are then submerged in, is an inert hydrocarbon, which was chosen because its density varies with temperature more than water.

When the temperature goes down, the fluid becomes denser, forcing the bulbs upward. When the temperature goes up, the fluid becomes less dense and rises, forcing the bulbs down one by one.

Fluid Temperature: 55   Fluid Temperature: 67

Reading the Thermoscope

If there are some bulbs at the top and some at the bottom, but one floating in the gap, then the one floating in the gap tells the temperature. If there is no bulb in the gap then you take the temperature of the bulbs at the bottom of the gap, add it to the temperature at the top of the gap, and divide the result by two. This will then give you an approximate measurement.

1000s — Abu Ali ibn Sina (Avicenna) develops an early air thermometer which can measure the level of water controlled by expansion and contraction of air.

1592 — Galileo Galilei builds a thermoscope, known as the thermoscope using the contraction of air to draw water up varying sized tubes.

1643 — Evangelista Torricelli invents the first mercury barometer.

1714 — Daniel Gabriel Fahrenheit invents the mercury-in-glass thermometer

1821 — Thomas Johann Seebeck invents the thermocouple

1864 — Henri-Louis Le Châtelier builds the first optical pyrometer

1900s — The electronic digital thermometer was developed to measure body temperature and was found to be safer than mercury filled since it is based on heat – sensitive liquid crystals rather than mercury.

Line art is used to instruct students on permitted and prohibited school dancing in this humorous illustration for the Seattle Weekly. Although the illustrations portray the top portion of each figure, our minds complete the missing information as a result of expectations and prior knowledge.

Eric Larsen, Eric Larsen Artwork, United States

NOTICE: Freak-dancing is not permitted at school-sponsored activities

Fig.1 Excellent

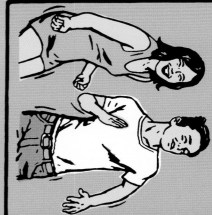

Fig.2 Acceptable

Fig.3 Prohibited

NOV 11, 2006

GALLERY WALK

DESIGN DISTRICT

Using the low-fidelity imagery of line art, this poster expresses the fun and lightness of Miami's Gallery Walk. Line art may closely match how we store visual information in long-term memory.

Sarah Cazee, Cazee Design, United States

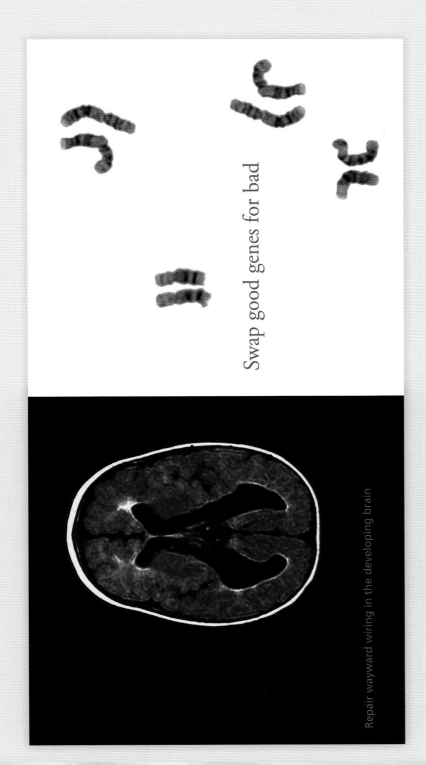

Repair wayward wiring in the developing brain

Swap good genes for bad

To promote the expertise of a children's hospital, this booklet reduces the number of design components on each page as a way of reflecting a childlike artistic simplicity.

Erica Gregg Howe and Amy Lebow, Philographica, United States

QUANTITY

Our natural environment is visually dense and complex. One way to reduce realism is to reverse what we typically see in the environment by strictly limiting the quantity of elements in a design. This allows the viewer to focus on the few essential components needed to understand the intended message. Restricting quantity means limiting the number of images, shapes, lines, and type.

In a quick glance, we can accurately and rapidly perceive a limited number of elements in a visual scene. This capability for quickly judging the number of items without counting is known as *subitizing*. We can automatically subitize up to around four objects.[10] This is similar to the number of elements we can typically hold in visual working memory at one time. By reducing the number of elements, working memory can operate at normal capacity without overload; visual processing is not overwhelmed; and the amount of information to store away is minimal.

Limiting the quantity of elements creates visuals with impact. With this approach, every element has an intentional function, so its message is clear. This approach also makes it easier for designers to rank elements in terms of dominance and subordination. One effective method for reducing the quantity of elements is the subtractive approach, or determining what can be eliminated from a design. Some ways to achieve this are to remove extraneous imagery, shorten text, clean up the background, and cluster items within a border so they are perceived as one unit. The design must continue to work after any element is removed.

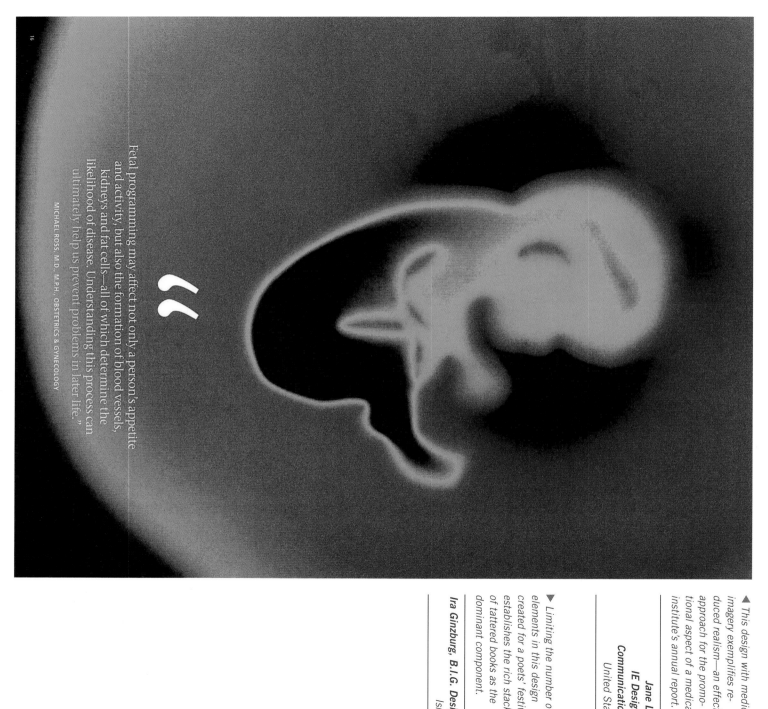

"
Fetal programming may affect not only a person's appetite and activity, but also the formation of blood vessels, kidneys and fat cells—all of which determine the likelihood of disease. Understanding this process can ultimately help us prevent problems in later life."

MICHAEL ROSS, M.D., M.P.H., OBSTETRICS & GYNECOLOGY

▲ This design with medical imagery exemplifies reduced realism—an effective approach for the promotional aspect of a medical institute's annual report.

**Jane Lee,
IE Design &
Communications,**
United States

▼ Limiting the number of elements in this design created for a poets' festival establishes the rich stack of tattered books as the dominant component.

Ira Ginzburg, B.I.G. Design,
Israel

BIG design studio

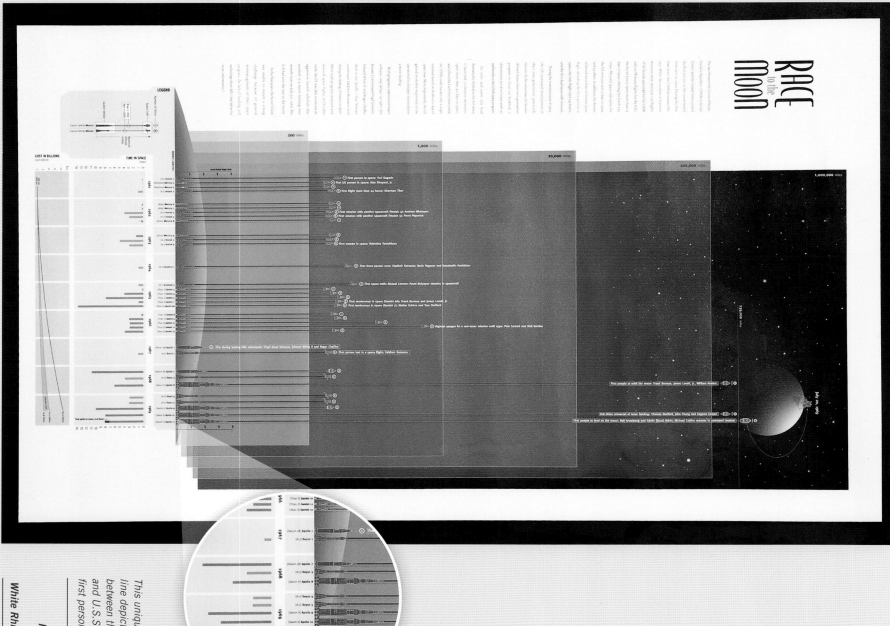

RACE to the moon

**Larry Gormley,
History Shots, and
Dan Greenwald,
White Rhino,** United States

This unique historical timeline depicts the competition
between the United States
and U.S.S.R. to land the
first person on the moon.

PRINCIPLE 4

MAKE THE ABSTRACT CONCRETE

"The progress of civilization can be read in the invention
of visual artifacts, from writing to mathematics, to maps,
to printing, to diagrams, to visual computing."

STUART CARD ET AL., *Readings in Information Visualization*

Visuals help us think. We sketch a map to give directions, draw a diagram to express a complex idea, and read graphs to understand financial data. Visual thinking is an integral aspect of cognition, and the visualizing of abstract concepts helps us understand the world and communicate about it. The contribution that visuals make to our analytical, reasoning, and problem-solving abilities is far reaching. In his book *Things That Make Us Smart*, Donald Norman writes, "The power of the unaided mind is highly overrated. Without external aids, memory, thought, and reasoning are all constrained."

We gain enormous insights from representing information in a visual form. From ancient maps to interactive visualizations, the graphical depiction of data and concepts has created new ways of seeing things and new approaches to solving problems. Two significant examples from the early history of graphs exemplify this point. In 1854, Dr. John Snow visually plotted where deaths were occurring from a cholera epidemic in London. By analyzing his statistical graph, Dr. Snow was able to locate and eliminate the contaminated source of water, which stopped the further spread of cholera. Not too many years later, during the Crimean War, Florence Nightingale invented a new type of statistical chart proving that British soldiers were dying at a much higher rate from preventable diseases than from the wounds of battle. Because Nightingale was able to visually represent the magnitude of preventable disease among soldiers, her petition to improve sanitation conditions was more compelling. Visual portrayals create new forms of knowledge.

Diagrams, charts, graphs, visualizations, maps, and timelines are referred to by many names—abstract, nonrepresentational, logical, and arbitrary graphics. Regardless of their name and form, their purpose is the same—to concretize abstract ideas and concepts. Although abstract graphics were once the domain of statisticians and cartographers, graphic designers and illustrators are frequently called upon to produce them for editorial publications; scientific, technical, and business journals; annual reports; educational and training aids; and promotional materials.

How Abstract Graphics Work

Not only do abstract graphics enhance communication, they also enhance the credibility of a message. There is a sense of objectivity to the nonrepresentational graphic, similar to the way photographs appear to be objective renderings of reality. After all, abstract graphics represent facts and data, concepts, and systems. People expect them to reflect accuracy and precision, believing they are the final word. In truth, however, every abstract graphic is inherently the result of numerous subjective design decisions. The designer must determine such things as what information can fit and what must be excluded; whether the elements should be represented as symbols, icons, or illustrations; which colors and patterns will enhance communicability; and which conventions should be followed and which ignored.

Abstract graphics are unique in that each element has a one-to-one correspondence with what it represents. Each element has only one unambiguous and exclusive meaning.[1] In a map, for example, the icon of a picnic area has a unique meaning—it symbolizes "picnic area." Anyone familiar with maps knows that this symbol has no other interpretations. In a line graph, each point represents a single value, and in a diagram, each component represents one object or concept. This is quite different from pictorial representations like paintings and photographs, where the elements and symbols can have many meanings based on a viewer's subjective interpretation.

Another distinguishing characteristic of abstract graphics is that they depict relationships. Diagrams and charts represent systems and the relationships between the systems' components; graphs represent quantitative relationships; visualizations create patterns that represent complex data relationships; maps represent spatial relationships among geographical locations; and timelines represent the relationships between temporal events. Hybrid graphics that combine two or more forms, such as the combined timeline and graph shown in the NASA infographic (on page 132), represent several levels of relationships.

Abstract graphics are prevalent in technical, scientific, and business publications because they provide a concrete reference for understanding difficult content and facilitate analysis and problem solving. They succeed at depicting intangible concepts that are difficult to express in words. Abstract graphics are also pragmatic, as in the maps we use for navigation and weather information. Many abstract graphics have a powerful aesthetic dimension associated with the rich beauty of information display. They can also serve as vehicles for artistic expression and for making political and social statements.

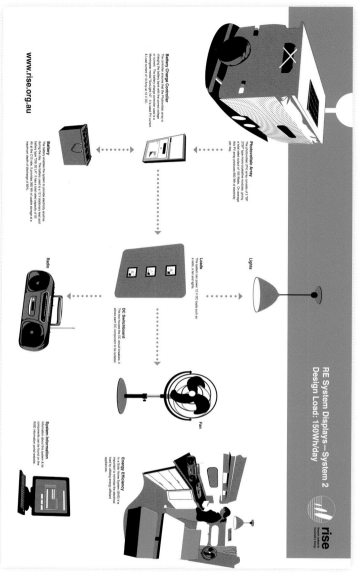

www.rise.org.au

RE System Displays—System 2
Design Load: 150Wh/day

Photovoltaic Array

Battery Charge Controller

Battery

Loads

Lights

Radio

DC Switchboard

Fan

System Information

Energy Efficiency

▲ This diagram created for a research institute uses minimalist art and text to explain the practical uses of solar-powered systems. Note how every element in the diagram represents one object or concept.

Stuart Medley, Lightship Visual, Australia

▼ In this provocative statement against breast augmentation, statistics blend with creative imagery to make a powerful social statement. A breast formation was arranged with 32,000 Barbie dolls, which equals the number of elective breast augmentation surgeries performed monthly in the United States in 2006, according to the artist.

Chris Jordan, United States

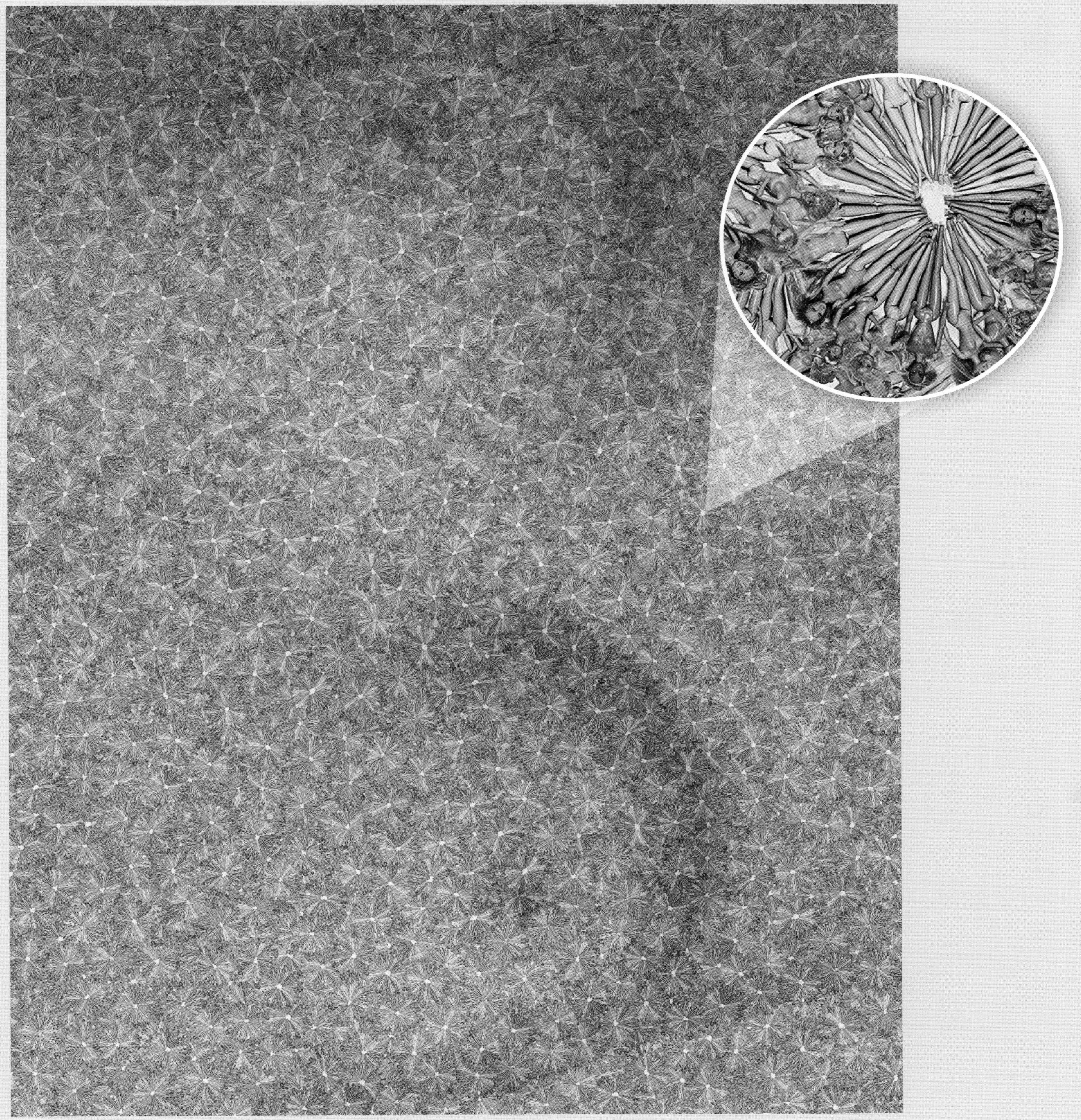

These graphics explain the toxic effects of mining and burning coal through many types of abstract graphics. Adding imagery to an abstract graphic, such as this photograph of visible pollution, is a helpful way to quickly communicate a message.

Sean Douglass, University of Washington, United States

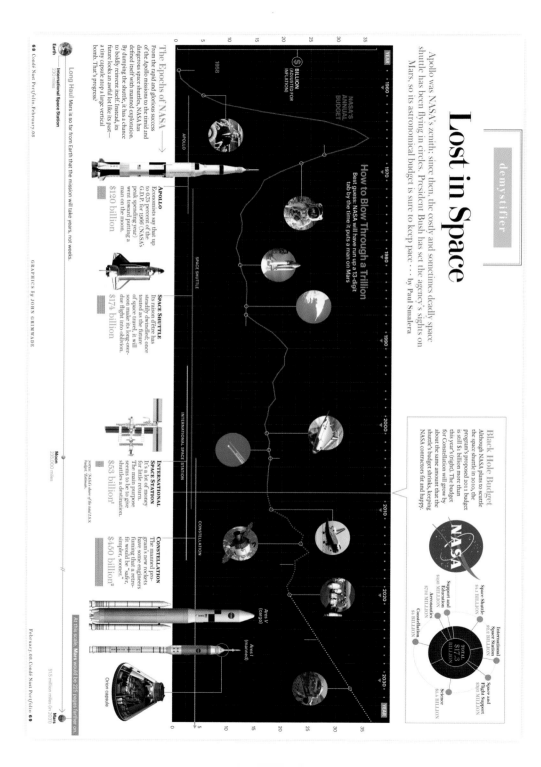

demystifier

Lost in Space

Apollo was NASA's zenith: since then, the costly and sometimes deadly space shuttle has been flying in circles. President Bush has set the agency's sights on Mars, so its astronomical budget is sure to keep pace . . . by Paul Sinatra

How to Blow Through a Trillion
Best guess: NASA will have run up a 13-digit tab by the time it puts a man on Mars

The Epochs of NASA
From the rapid and glorious success of the Apollo missions to the timid and dangerous space shuttles, NASA has defined itself with manned exploration. By dumping the shuttle, it has a chance to boldly reinvent itself. Instead, its future looks an awful lot like its past—a tiny capsule atop a large vertical bomb. That's progress?

APOLLO
Economists say that up to 0.75 percent of the G.D.P. for 1966 (NASA's peak spending year) went toward putting a man on the moon.
$120 billion

SPACE SHUTTLE
Its raison d'être has steadily dwindled; once touted as the future of space travel, it will soon make its long-over-due flight into oblivion.
$174 billion

INTERNATIONAL SPACE STATION
It's a lot of money for little return. The main purpose seems to be to give shuttles a destination.
$53 billion[1]

CONSTELLATION
The manned program's new rockets have some engineers fuming that a retro-fit would be "safer, simpler, sooner."
$450 billion[2]

Black Hole Budget
Although NASA plans to scuttle the space shuttle in 2010, the program's proposed 2011 budget is still $1 billion more than this year's (right). The budget for Constellation will grow by about the same amount that the shuttle's budget shrinks, keeping NASA contractors fit and happy.

Space Shuttle $6.4 BILLION
Support and Education $5.6 BILLION
Aeronautics $500 MILLION
International Space Station $2.8 BILLION
Space and Flight Support $820 MILLION
Science $4.4 BILLION
Constellation $8 BILLION
TOTAL $17.3 BILLION

Ares V (cargo)
Ares I (manned)
Orion capsule

NASA'S ANNUAL BUDGET
$ BILLION (ADJUSTED FOR INFLATION)

APOLLO — SPACE SHUTTLE — INTERNATIONAL SPACE STATION — CONSTELLATION

Earth
International Space Station 230 miles
Moon 235,000 miles
Mars

Long Haul Mars is so far from Earth that the mission will take years, not weeks.
At this scale, **Mars** would be 225 leagues farther on.

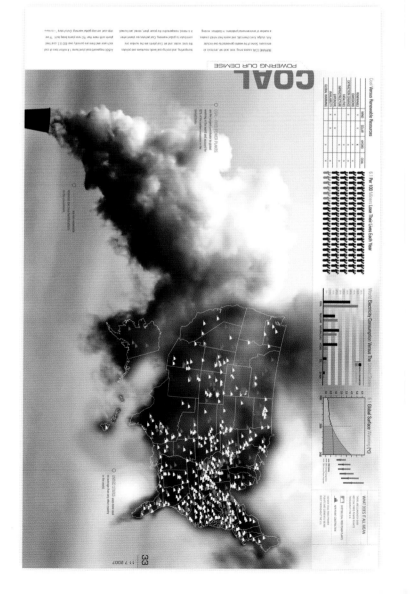

COAL
POWERING OUR DEMISE

World Electricity Consumption Versus The United States

Per 100 Miners Lose Their Lives Each Year

Coal Versus Renewable Resources

Conquering jet lag with melatonin

Melatonin has been shown in studies to correct the out-of-sync effects of jet lag with dosages of 5 to 10 mg, taken 30 to 90 minutes before bedtime on the day of arrival and for as many nights as symptoms exist. These examples display how jet lag differs on various flights. The red dot on the left globe is your body clock, which remains set to home time. The red dot on the right is your body, which has been moved to a new time zone and is now out of sync. The degree of jet lag depends on the minimum number of time zones separating the dots. That is why, regardless of your route from New York to Sydney (east through 15 time zones or west through 9), you will be 9 hours out of sync when you arrive.

DAYS OF JET LAG

	BODY CLOCK TIME	LOCAL TIME

A NEW YORK–LOS ANGELES

⏱ Time zones: 3 ➕ Direction: W

✈ Nonstop flight: 6 hours

Melatonin reduces jet lag to:
1–2 days

NEW YORK 2:39 P.M. / LOS ANGELES 11:39 A.M.

The flight (depart 8:30 A.M., arrive 11:39 A.M.) creates minimal jet lag. On arrival in L.A., you've gained three hours of daylight. Longer daylight suppresses natural melatonin; supplemental melatonin will probably help travelers adjust at one night.

B NEW YORK–LONDON

⏱ Time zones: 5 ➕ Direction: E

✈ Nonstop flight: 7 hours

Melatonin reduces jet lag to:
2–3 days

NEW YORK 4:10 P.M. / LONDON 9:10 P.M.

Sound sleepers can fly overnight and minimize jet lag by staying awake the whole first day in London. But the morning flight (depart 9:30 A.M., arrive 9:10P.M.) delivers you neatly at bed-time. (Although the Concorde is three hours faster, there is no less jet lag, because you still cross five time zones.)

C NEW YORK–SYDNEY

⏱ Time zones: 9 ➕ Direction: W

✈ Direct flight: 21 hours

Melatonin reduces jet lag to:
5–7 days

NEW YORK 5:35 A.M. / SYDNEY 8:35 P.M.

A morning flight departs New York at 9 A.M.; stops in L.A. six hours later, at about noon; and arrives in Sydney 15.5 hours later, at 8:35 P.M. the next day. A night flight leaves New York at 6 P.M. and arrives in Sydney at 6:04 A.M. two days later.

D NEW YORK–DELHI

⏱ Time zones: 10 ➕ Direction: E

✈ Most direct route: 17 hours

Melatonin reduces jet lag to:
6–8 days

NEW YORK 12:45 A.M. / DELHI 11:15 A.M.

A 9:30 A.M. flight out of New York reaches London around 9 P.M. and arrives in Delhi the next day at 11:15 A.M. You reach India as out of sync as you can possibly be: it's noon in Delhi, but 1:30 A.M. in New York—and in your body.

E NEW YORK–LIMA

⏱ Time zones: 0 ➕ Direction: S

✈ Nonstop flight: 10½ hours

❌ No jet lag

NEW YORK 7:20 P.M. / LIMA 7:20 P.M.

There's no jet lag. But think about when you want to fly. If you can spend a day in transit, a 9 A.M. departure gets you to Lima at 7:20 P.M.—just in time for dinner and bed. Or you can catch some sleep on the night flight, which departs JFK at 5 P.M. and arrives in Lima at 3 A.M.

Jet lag: The arithmetic of travel

Each number represents one (simplified) time zone and one day of jet lag. Imagine yourself in New York at noon, your body in sync with eastern standard time. If you fly to London, five time zones east, your body clock remains set to EST for the first day, and it will slowly catch up—at a rate of about one time zone per day—until your body is in sync with Greenwich Mean Time, about five days after you arrive. Most volunteers who used melatonin after long-haul flights reduced that period of adjustment to three days, or even two. The flights shown here and on the facing page demonstrate the differences encountered in flying east vs. west, flying across latitude vs. longitude, taking short flights vs. long flights, and crossing few time zones vs. many.

▼ This information graphic demonstrates how a great deal of data can be packed into one visual. NASA's annual budget data is depicted as a line graph mapped onto a timeline. Associated images connect to points on the graph, and the length of each era is displayed across the bottom.

John Grimwade and Liana Zamora, Condé Nast Publications, United States

▲ Abstract graphics provide new ways of looking at information. These visualizations demonstrate how jet lag affects the body when flying in various directions.

John Grimwade, Condé Nast Publications, United States

The Cognitive Aspect

Space conveys meaning. Abstract graphics are often superior to verbal descriptions because of their effect on cognition. We process them more quickly and easily, particularly compared to reading long explanations or performing numeric calculations. Their tangible quality comes from the meaning we find in the spatial relationships among the graphic's components. We easily derive meaning from spatial relationships because of our familiarity and experience with physical space.

In maps, the spatial relationship among elements is analogous to their geographical locations. We know that if a city map oriented to the north shows a building to the west of where we are standing, the building will be to our left because of this analogous relationship. In diagrams, charts, and graphs, the spatial relationships are metaphorical. When elements are displayed in a hierarchical chart, a spatial metaphor helps us understand that the element in the primary position (usually the top or the left) is the most significant or powerful. When a line graph trends toward the top of the page or screen, we use a spatial metaphor to understand that this means an increase in value.

The order, sequence, and distance between elements also communicate meaning. When two events in a timeline are separated by a large interval, we interpret this to mean the events are far apart in time. These interpretations are grounded in our real-world experience and are thought to be "cognitively natural."[2] Because we can easily interpret the spatial metaphors used in abstract graphics, we make fewer mental transformations to understand them than when we read the same information in text. When a visual explanation is used, fewer cognitive resources are needed to get at the meaning.

Reducing cognitive load. Due to our limited-capacity working memory, we quickly reach our limits when we try to integrate numerous pieces of information. Abstract graphics often alleviate this problem because relationships are explicitly illustrated. A line connects related elements in a diagram, related bars are placed in proximity in a bar graph, and a road connects cities on a map. This explicit depiction of relationships helps viewers process information simultaneously rather than sequentially—as when reading text.

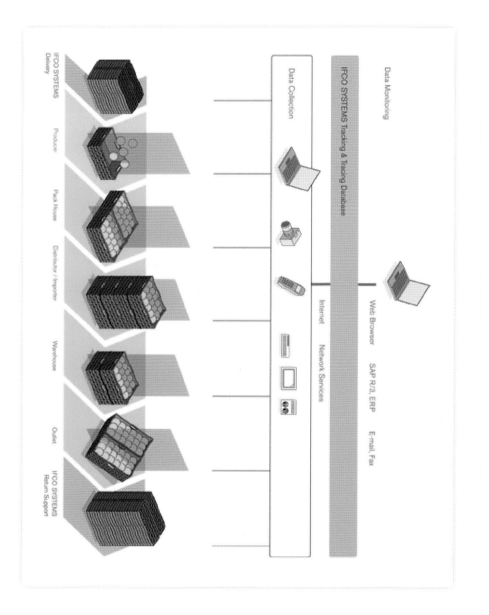

Viewers quickly understand the pattern of a diagram to get an initial sense of its meaning. Here, a database system for tracking and collecting product movement is depicted in a hierarchical format, which makes cognitive sense.

**Franziska Erdle,
Milch Design,** Germany

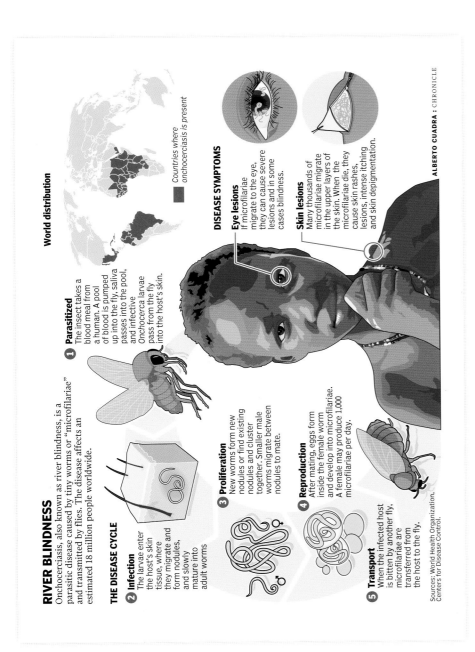

Upon first looking at this cyclical diagram, the viewer gets the gist of the graphic through the illustrations integrated with the circular arrow. The accompanying text explanation fills in the missing pieces.

Alberto Cuadra, Houston Chronicle, *United States*

Improving search efficiency. When we need to locate information, abstract graphics can often improve the efficiency of the search process compared to reading text. To search through text, we typically start at the beginning, skim through headings and paragraphs, try to remember where important information is located, and then return to each of the various locations.

Conversely, abstract graphics are inherently structured so that information is visually linked. When a person searches for and locates the first piece of important information in a diagram, relevant information is typically adjacent to it. This reduces the time and effort involved in acquiring information.[3]

Applying The Principle

The key purpose of a nonrepresentational graphic is to create a visual portrayal that extends the viewer's ability to see, think, and know. To achieve this, the designer can consider which type of mental structure would be most effective to invoke in the viewer. For example, if the goal is to help readers understand how a sequence of actions led to a climactic event, a timeline would facilitate the most effective mental representation. On the other hand, if the intent is to help viewers understand usage patterns on the Internet, then an information visualization that depicts users swarming around Web pages would help the viewer construct the most accurate schemas.

When abstract graphics are complex, designers can enhance them for the automatic processing that occurs in early vision. This shifts more of the cognitive operations to visual perception, reducing the demands on working memory. Based on theories discussed in Principle 1 (Organize for Perception), a graphic can be enhanced for visual perception in several ways. Ensure that similar elements are the same color or shape, so the viewer does not have to unnecessarily discriminate between them. For example, it is easier and quicker to compare the length of bars in a bar graph when they are the same color. When appropriate, cluster similar elements into groups using proximity or bounding lines so the viewer perceives the entities as one unit. Because the size of an object is quickly detected during preattentive vision, use this feature to convey meaning. Make an element half the size of another element if it is of half the value. These techniques will improve the viewer's ability to automatically extract information during early vision.

Each form of abstract graphic has its own unique notation or visual code. We learn these codes through experience and education. For example, we know that a topographical map uses contours to indicate elevation and that line graphs compare two variables. The designer can ensure that the audience understands a particular notational system by following accepted conventions. Viewers infer a great deal from context. Unless the goal is to provide novelty or surprise, remain consistent with what is expected from a notation.

Clarity is an important quality of the abstract graphic, affecting its readability, usefulness, aesthetics, and overall comprehensibility. Take steps to ensure that any visual difference, such as a change in color or texture, is actually intended to convey meaning and remove any unnecessary visual differences. If one arrow in a diagram is larger than the others, for example, this will likely be interpreted as representing an increase in strength or value, even if unintended. Also, avoid ambiguity by making illustrations, icons, and symbols easy to identify and recognize.

Titles, legends, captions, labels, and call-outs add essential information to abstract graphics, making them more substantial and solidifying their meaning. Text often provides redundant information, which creates a second channel for transmitting information. In abstract graphics, ensure that text is legible, brief, and consistent.

These abstract graphics created for a school project effectively use color to convey statistical information about Alzheimer's disease.

Christina Koehn, University of Washington, United States

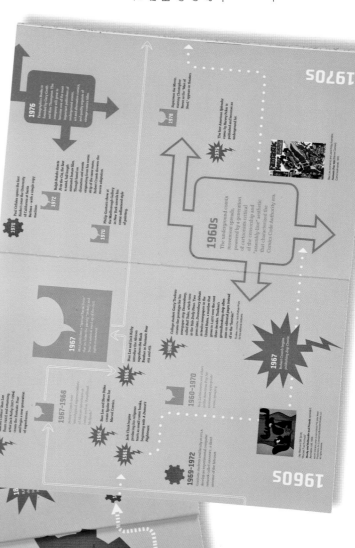

This unusual timeline from the book Strips, Toons, and Bluesies is a small segment of a multipage, chronology of comics and the graphic arts.

Heather Corcoran and Diana Scubert, Plum Studio, United States

Color can provide an additional dimension for conveying meaning. We see this in maps when color is used to indicate road types. Color-coding can also indicate that elements are associated, as when color represents different types of data in a statistical map, such as income or political affiliation. The color-coding of elements and data facilitates information retrieval because color is stored in long-term memory along with associated information.

A final design consideration is whether to represent the features of an abstract graphic as icons, illustrations, geometric shapes, or text. The form of the representation can have a significant effect on the meaning of the graphic. For example, to explain how voice over Internet protocol works, an illustrated diagram that portrays signal transmission between two people on phones clarifies the concept more than if boxes and lines are used to explain the system. The choice of how to represent features not only affects meaning, but also affects the graphic's tone and style.

When graphic designers and illustrators—rather than statisticians or cartographers—produce maps, diagrams, and graphs, a new aesthetic naturally emerges. Designers use the context and purpose of the abstract graphic to communicate on an artistic and emotional level. Through techniques such as textured backgrounds, illustrated or photographed imagery, and unique shapes and patterns, designers are able to convey more than the facts, revealing the indefinable feelings and impressions associated with the content of the graphic.

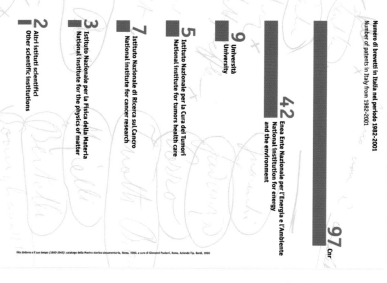

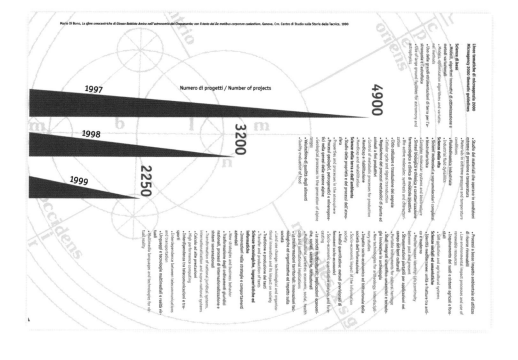

A designer's touch adds a textured and layered look to these graphs created for the National Centre of Research in Italy.

Lorenzo De Tomasi, *Italy*

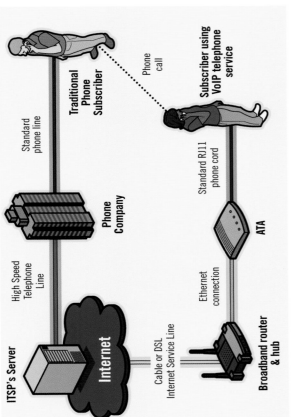

► Diagrams express relationships through spatial layout, as in this abstract graphic depicting a communication system. The schematic style of the symbols, lines, and connectors conveys the precision readers expect from a technical graphic.

Aviad Stark, Graphic Advance, United States

▲ This diagram for Mac-World magazine explains how the voice over Internet protocol works. Schematized illustrations help the viewer understand the system.

Colin Hayes, Colin Hayes Illustrator, United States

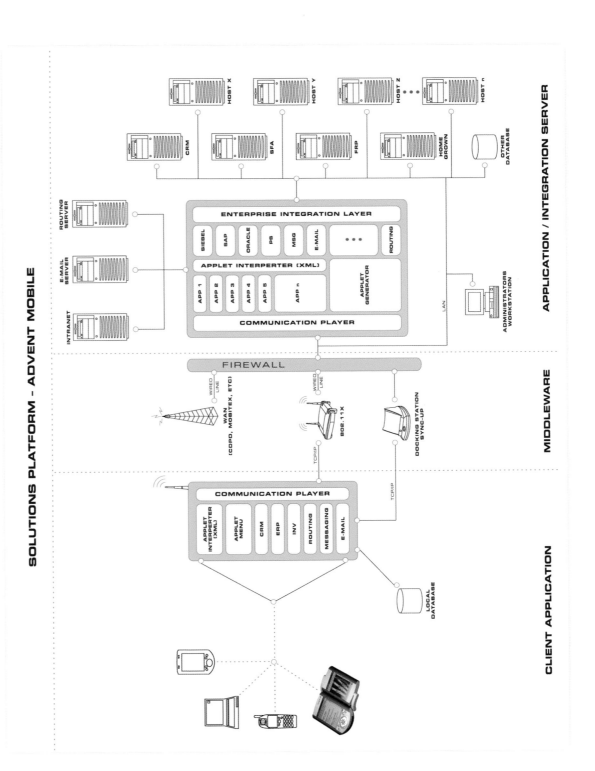

SOLUTIONS PLATFORM – ADVENT MOBILE

CLIENT APPLICATION MIDDLEWARE APPLICATION / INTEGRATION SERVER

BIG-PICTURE VIEWS

There is no common definition for diagrams among people who use, create, and theorize about them. In this book, diagrams refer to a visual explanation that represents a system rather than statistical data. Diagrams are typically composed of a system's elements and their interrelationships. The elements in a diagram vary in their realism, ranging from a representational illustration to iconic symbols or amorphous shapes.

Even though diagrams use spatial organization to convey meaning, the content they represent is not necessarily spatial. Diagrams depict and help us understand the structure, processes, transformations, cycles, and functions of a system. These facets are expressed through the unique arrangements and positioning of the elements and the lines, arrows, and shapes that connect them. As with other abstract graphics, every element in a diagram has a direct relationship with the object to which it refers. The potentially limitless combination of elements contributes to the rich diversity of diagram types, such as the cyclical diagram that represents a recurring process, the hierarchical diagram that illustrates structure and organization, the tree diagram that dissects categories into fine detail, and the flow diagram that explains a process.

In diagrams, arrows point to important content. When arrows are used as connectors, they link elements together and indicate relationships. Arrows also guide the viewer through the flow of a process or events and show a path that is followed. They are effective in depicting the actions that occur in a system, a movement, or a conversion over time. Adjusting the size, shape, color, and emphasis of an arrow are techniques to control what an arrow represents. To signify movement, the arrow might have a jagged, curved, or twisted shaft. Large, emphasized, or contrasting arrows suggest strength and value. Double-headed arrows depict cyclic or reciprocal relationships.

Using arrows can change the meaning of a diagram. In a study that examined how arrows convey meaning, researchers showed students diagrams of mechanical devices with arrows and diagrams of mechanical devices without arrows. The study's participants interpreted the diagram without arrows as depicting the structure of the mechanical device and interpreted the diagrams with arrows as showing cause and effect and functionality.[4]

Viewers derive meaning from a diagram when they detect and recognize its pattern of elements. The pattern creates the diagram's organizational structure. Research shows that this organizational structure affects how information is mentally represented and encoded.[5] Thus, when viewing a diagram with a cyclical structure, a person will construct an internal representation that encodes the diagram's information in some form of circular fashion. The designer can take advantage of this cognitive process to use the most effective structure for communicating information and facilitating its retention.

A viewer can enter a diagram at the global level and see its overall pattern or enter at the local level and focus on the details. This is significant, because the level of entry is where the viewer begins to search for information.[6] In most cases, global precedence is preferred for diagrams, because much of their initial meaning is obtained from the big-picture view. To help viewers enter a graphic at the global level, the elements must be large enough to easily detect the overall pattern. If the elements are overwhelmingly large, however, the viewer will focus only on the element and its detail first.

▼ This graphic depicting the advantages of a commercial software solution tells two stories. The top portion visualizes a sequence of positive customer events along an arrow-based timeline. The bottom portion uses spatial layout and arrows to diagram how the software synchronizes operations.

Drew Crowley, XPLANE,
United States

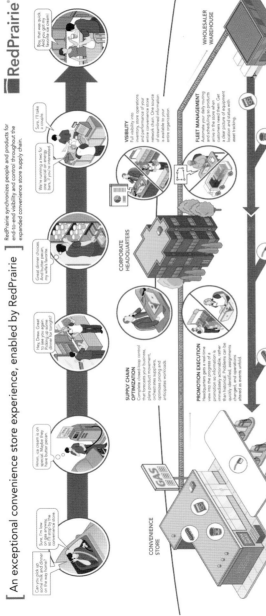

This water cycle diagram for the Chino Creek Wetlands Park uses three different types of arrows to carry much of the information: Large white arrows indicate the cycle's path, dashed arrows represent water, and jagged arrows represent movement.

Claudine Jaenichen and Richard Turner, Jaenichen Studio,
United States

Matthew Luckwitz,
Grafport, United States

▼ Diagrams often provide a holistic view of a system, as depicted in this clever schematic of a bulk email broadcast process portrayed as a circuit board.

▼ This tree diagram illustrates the evolution of commercial imagery through two main trunks—illustration and cartooning. The clean design and color-coding make it easy to follow along a single path.

D. B. Dowd, Mike Costelloe,
Sarah Phares, and
Scott Gericke,
Visual Communications
Research Studio—
Washington University,
United States

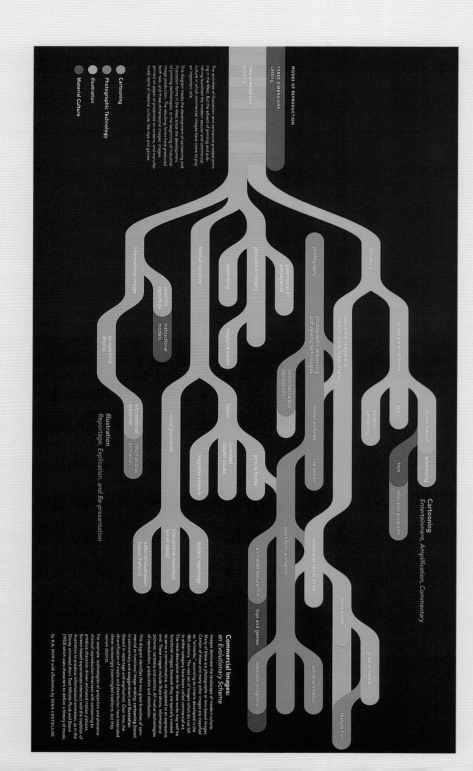

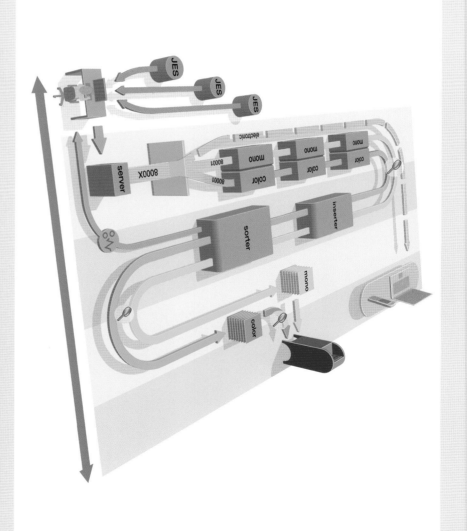

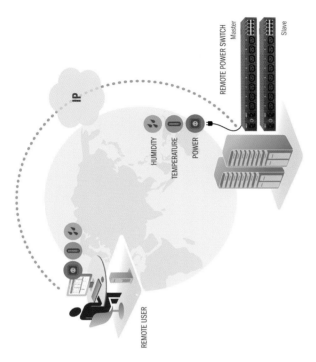

▲ These diagrams visualize the processes of an information technology solution. Dashed lines often convey data transmission.

Ira Ginzburg, B.I.G. Design,
Israel

Dashed Lines

In diagrams, the dashed line is often used with or without the arrowhead to signify transactions, connections, and events that cannot be effectively expressed with a solid line. Because the repeated rectangular shape that forms the dashed line conveys a sense of movement, it is often used to represent a form of invisible energy, such as data transmission. Dashed lines often reflect the tentative or provisional quality of an action. When they indicate a relationship between elements, they often mean that the connection is uncertain or not always present. When dashed lines represent a path, it is often a projected or alternative path that will take place in the future.

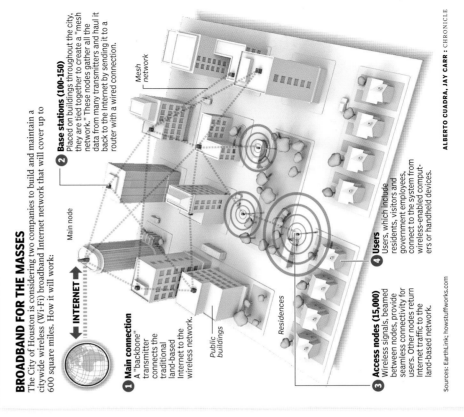

BROADBAND FOR THE MASSES

The City of Houston is considering two companies to build and maintain a citywide wireless (Wi-Fi) broadband Internet network that will cover up to 600 square miles. How it will work:

1 Main connection
A "backbone" transmitter connects the traditional land-based Internet to the wireless network.

2 Base stations (100-150)
Placed on buildings throughout the city, they are tied together to create a "mesh network." These nodes gather all the data from many transmitters and haul it back to the Internet by sending it to a router with a wired connection.

3 Access nodes (15,000)
Wireless signals, beamed between nodes, provide seamless connectivity for users. Other nodes return Internet traffic to the land-based network.

4 Users, which include residents, visitors and government employees, connect to the system from wireless-enabled computers or handheld devices.

Main node

Mesh network

Public buildings

Residences

Sources: EarthLink; howstuffworks.com

ALBERTO CUADRA, JAY CARR : CHRONICLE

▲ In this diagram for the Houston Chronicle, the dashed lines and concentric circles portraying a wireless system enhance the visual explanation.

Alberto Cuadra, Houston Chronicle,
United States

Make the Abstract Concrete   **143**

DATA DISPLAYS

"A child can tell that one-third of a pie is larger than a fourth long before being able to judge that the fraction ⅓ is greater than ¼," writes statistics professor and author Howard Wainer in *Educational Researcher*. In other words, the visual display of numerical data is easier to understand when we can see it in a concrete form, such as in graphs and tables. Information graphics often use a hybrid approach for displaying data, combining representational art with numeric information.

Data displays, such as graphs, visually communicate the relationships hidden in quantitative information and are probably the most common abstract graphic we find in the popular media. It is difficult to pick up a newspaper or news magazine without seeing some type of graph describing business, technical, or scientific data. The simplest and most common graph framework is configured in an L shape, with a horizontal x-axis representing the data being measured and a vertical y-axis representing the type of measurement. Of course, there are numerous other types of graphs for expressing value. Pictographs use icons to represent the quantity of a data type, pie charts express data as a percentage of a whole, statistical maps display the distribution of data across a geographic area, and area graphs use the area of a circle or rectangle to indicate value, just to name a few.

Viewers can quickly get a sense of a graph's meaning by understanding how graphs use space to represent values. In a pie chart it is the size of the slice compared to the whole, in a pictograph it is the length of the row of symbols, and in an area graph it is the size of the region. Graphs also convey meaning through spatial positioning, as when data points are plotted and then connected on a line graph. These conventions provide an immediate preunderstanding before activating more involved cognitive processes.

Of all the forms of abstract graphics, people have the most difficulty understanding graphs. Numerous visual and mental processes are invoked upon studying a graph. Early in the process, the viewer rapidly detects geometric shapes, texture, and color.[7] These represent the graph's code for depicting values. The viewer then must call up graph schemas from long-term memory to derive meaning from the graph's notation. This involves reading the labels and captions, determining the graph's scale, glancing back and forth between entities, and comparing relative magnitudes to each other. Using this information and prior knowledge about the data, the viewer makes inferences and constructs relevant concepts. If a person's graph schemas are incomplete, he or she will have difficulties with one or more of these tasks.

Poor design is a major reason why information is misinterpreted in graphs. Although many data displays are technically accurate, they do not accommodate the strengths and limitations of our information-processing system. Twenty years ago, well-known statistician John Tukey wrote that the main purpose of analyzing numerical data is to describe phenomena rather than to simply present the information. He argued that the phenomena derived from the numbers are of most interest to people.[8] For example, if we are viewing a bar graph that illustrates the rising costs of higher education around the world, we probably won't remember the actual cost of tuition in each location. Through an effective graph, however, we will see and remember how rising tuition prices in one's own country compare with others.

As the popularity of graphs in the media increases, a wider variety of formats is used. The circles in this area graph depict sources of greenhouse gas emissions and appear to be released from a factory smokestack.

Arno Ghelfi, l'atelier starno,
United States

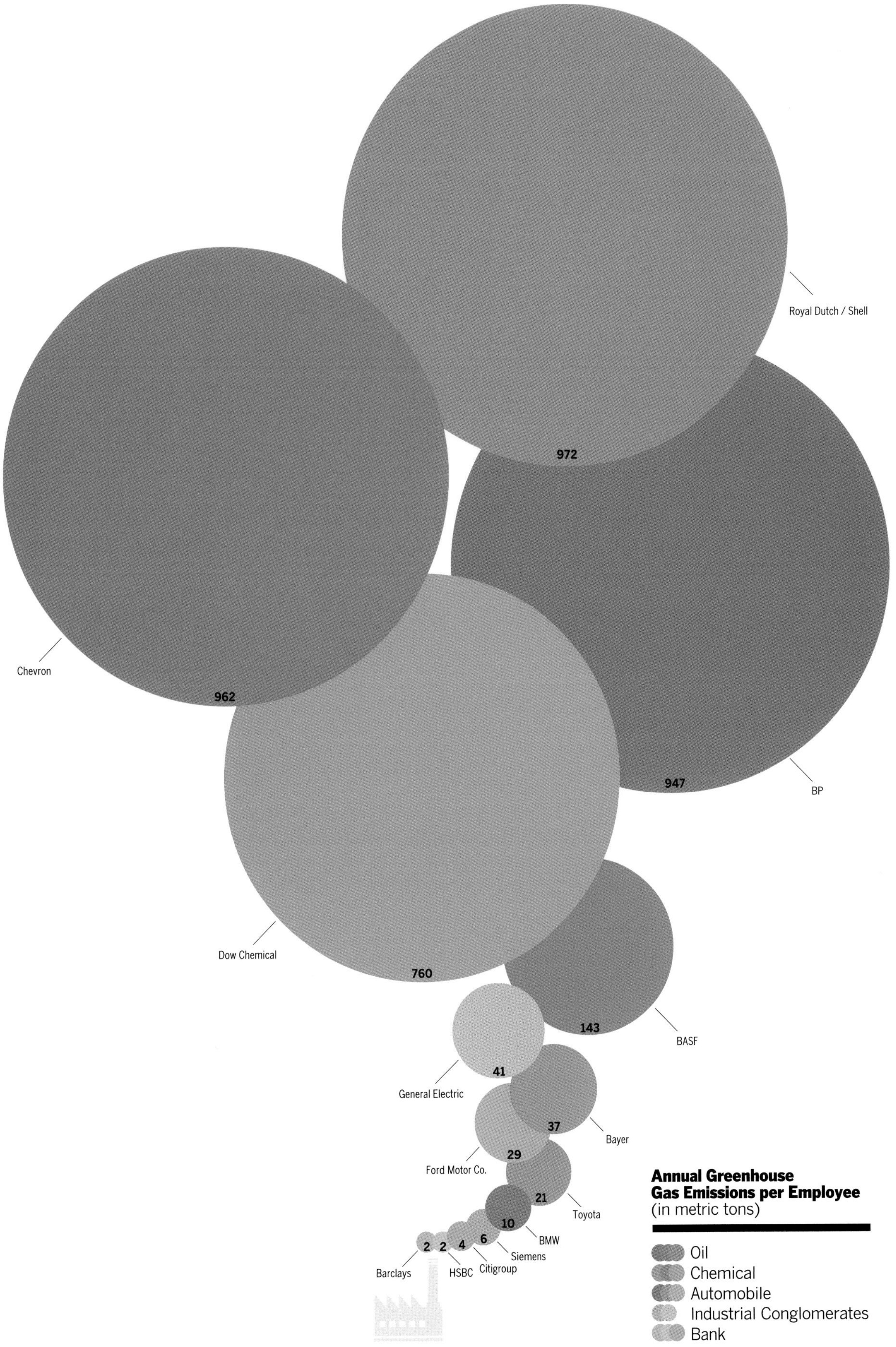

Annual Greenhouse
Gas Emissions per Employee
(in metric tons)

Oil
Chemical
Automobile
Industrial Conglomerates
Bank

Royal Dutch / Shell — 972

BP — 947

Chevron — 962

Dow Chemical — 760

BASF — 143

General Electric — 41

Bayer — 37

Ford Motor Co. — 29

Toyota — 21

BMW — 10

Siemens — 6

Citigroup — 4

HSBC — 2

Barclays — 2

The tasks for which data displays are used—making comparisons, seeing trends, and finding patterns—should ultimately lead to the recognition of phenomena. Tukey emphasized that the foremost quality of an effective graph is to seek impact and immediacy. An effective data display should force the viewer to instantly understand the message. If getting the point is gradual or burdensome, another type of display should be implemented. For instance, if the reader needs to locate individual numerical values, then a table would be more effective than a graph.

In his research on graph design, neuroscientist Stephen Kosslyn expands on several principles of effective data displays to accommodate our visual and cognitive systems. To accommodate the visual system, he notes that all elements in a data display must be large or heavy enough to be detected, and all variations need to be easily discriminated. He also points out the importance of organizing labels and captions so they are grouped with the appropriate visual element. To accommodate the limitations of working memory, Kosslyn recommends restricting displays so there are only four to seven perceptual units. In addition, viewers should not be asked to decompose a display that

is grouped, such as the points on a line. This reverses our automatic tendency to group items that are similar or close together.[9] To meet the expectations and abilities of the audience, provide neither too little nor too much information and consider whether the audience has the appropriate knowledge to understand the display.[10]

A data display is effective if it provides a shortcut to the intended message, promoting visual processing and bypassing the need to make numerical computations. Research has demonstrated that people are better at making comparisons when using bar graphs and better at interpreting trends when using line graphs.[11] When using graphs with an x- and y-axis, minimize numerical computations by using precalculated numbers like percentages and averages for the y-axis rather than raw numerical data.[12] This makes it easier for readers to make quick comparisons. If a designer needs to depict more than two variables, as is common in most graphs in an L framework, use attributes such as color or size to represent the values of additional variables. From a design perspective, imagery can go a long way in conveying the meaning of a graph.

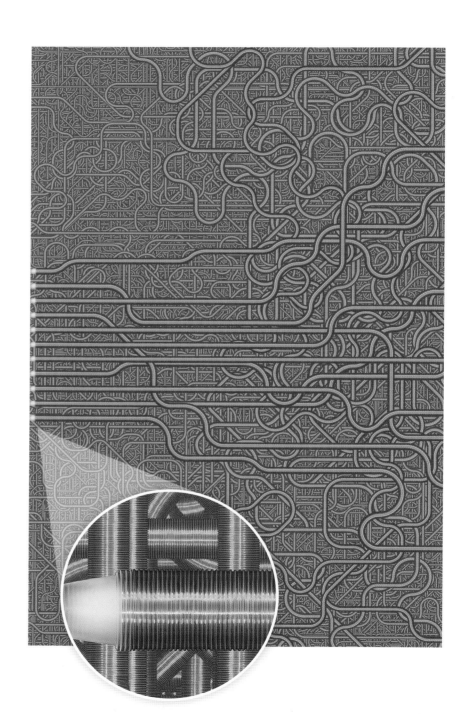

Quantitative depictions can support a social agenda. This display depicts one million plastic cups, which is the number of cups used on airline flights in the United States every six hours.

Chris Jordan, *United States*

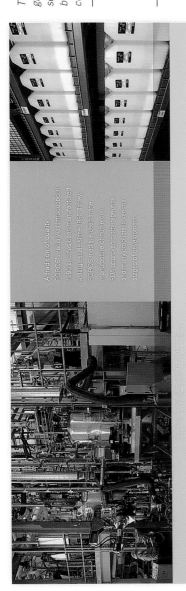

The mix of imagery and graphs helps the viewer see beyond the data in this brochure for a biopharmaceutical company.

**Amy Vest,
Applied Biosystems Brand
& Creative Group,**
United States

A tradition of quality

POROS media was introduced in 1990 and has been manufactured at large-scale since 1995. Today, POROS media is used in the manufacture of numerous FDA-approved biotherapeutics and many products in various stages of development.

High performance on a large scale

PROTEIN PURIFICATION

High performance on a large scale
Product purification involves several critical steps, each one of which must be designed and optimized during research and early stage development, then scaled up for commercial manufacturing. Ideally, purification procedures developed during the early stages of process development can be optimized and scaled up directly to manufacturing levels—without sacrificing performance efficiency.

A selection of selectivities
A broad range of POROS® media are available for production-scale, lab-scale, and quality control applications. All 50-micron POROS products are backed by full regulatory support information and Drug Master Files.

- Protein A Affinity (including new MabCapture A)
- Strong Cation Exchangers
- Strong Anion Exchangers
- Weak Anion Exchangers
- Heparin Affinity
- Reversed Phase
- Metal Chelate

**HighD Capacity at 5%
Breakthrough vs. Linear Velocity**

The new POROS MabCapture A is the highest performance process scale protein A media, providing the highest dynamic binding capacity and capture efficiency over the broadest flow rate range.

Removing scale-up bottlenecks

PROTEIN PURIFICATION

Applied Biosystems POROS® MabCapture™ A Perfusion Chromatography™ Media offer a direct and cost-effective path from lab-scale to production-scale bioseparations. These rigid, robust particles enable high-resolution separations with 2-3X the throughput of conventional fast-flow gels. The unique "throughput" structure of POROS media is designed to provide unmatched dynamic binding capacities and excellent capture efficiencies at high linear velocities, resulting in smaller column volumes, reduced buffer consumption, and faster processing for higher product throughput. With the recent improvements in cell culture technology resulting in higher expression levels, higher capacity process scale media is needed. Applied Biosystems' newest POROS affinity media, POROS MabCapture A, was specifically designed to address this need.

MabCapture A provides up to 136% increased productivity

High Capacity Protein A
New MabCapture A solves the purification bottleneck caused by high expression cell culture.

CHARACTERIZE · PURIFY/ANALYZE · QUALITY CONTROL

People with Diabetes
In millions

Men **7.8** | Women **9.1** | 0 · 5 · 10

Obesity
In millions

Women **33.4** | Men **26.0** | 0 · 10 · 20 · 30

These illustrated bar charts depicting diabetes and obesity statistics appeared in Woman's Day *magazine.*

**Rose Zgodzinski,
Information Graphics,**
Canada

Make the Abstract Concrete **147**

▲ Numerous graph formats depict data regarding trash, recycling, and waste management in the United Kingdom in this information graphic for the Guardian newspapers.

Peter Grundy and Tilly Northedge, United Kingdom

▼ Not all data displays must be in graph form. Here, oversize numbers emphasize academic statistics in this college viewbook.

David Horton and Amy Lebow, Philographica, United States

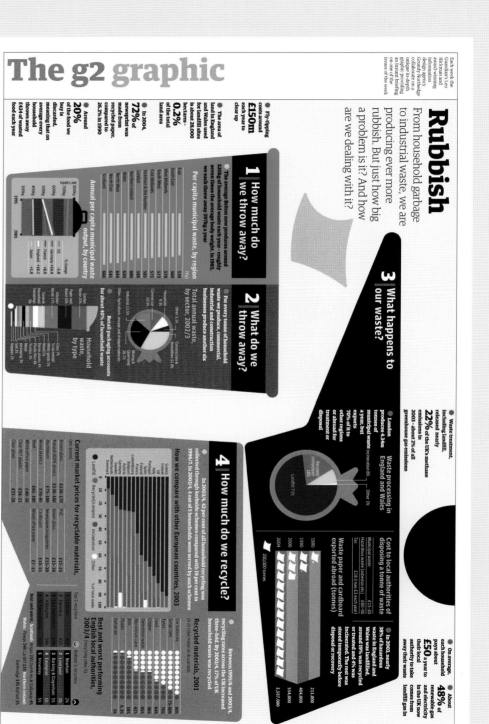

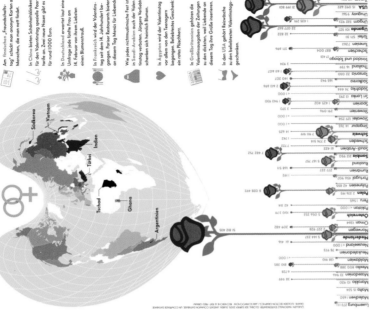

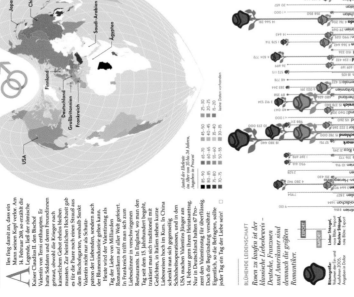

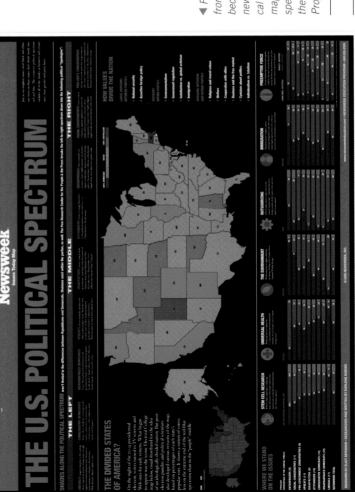

▲ Stemmed roses become bar charts and the globe is heart shaped in this information graphic about Valentine's Day, love, and roses around the world for Vanity Fair, Germany.

Jan Schwochow,
Golden Section Graphics,
Germany

▲ Patterns often emerge from statistical maps because data is grouped in new ways across geographical regions. This statistical map of the U.S. political spectrum was produced for the Newsweek Education Program.

Eliot Bergman, *Japan*

VISUALIZATION OF INFORMATION

In response to the explosion of complex information in many knowledge domains, information visualizations represent and make accessible the structure and intricate relationships found in large sets of data. The information visualization can be thought of as a cognitive tool that expands our ability to comprehend, interpret, and explore data that is too complex for our working memory to manage. It is often a solution for representing information that would otherwise be difficult to comprehend, such as how things change over time or with speed or rotation. Information visualizations are applied to both abstract data and to concrete data about the physical world.[13]

With visualizations, "the important information from more than a million measurements is immediately available. Visualization allows the perception of emergent properties that were not anticipated," notes professor Colin Ware in his book *Information Visualization*. Information visualizations are often generated by a computer and often occur in real time. They provide interactivity and utilize three and often four dimensions. The exploration, rearrangement, and reconstruction of the visualization are a primary means for achieving insight.

Visualizations complement our perceptual and information-processing systems because we are adept at detecting and identifying patterns, we intuitively understand spatial metaphors, and we process information most effectively when it is organized and structured. Most information visualizations use at least two modes of communication: a visual aspect that utilizes space, color, and shape to represent data, and a textual aspect that labels the data.

When computer visualization specialists collaborate with graphic designers, the outcome is more accessible to a wider audience. Perhaps because of this visualization has become increasingly important. In some visualizations, the beauty of the information and the facility of interaction take precedence over their practical use to create artistic works or promote a political or social agenda.

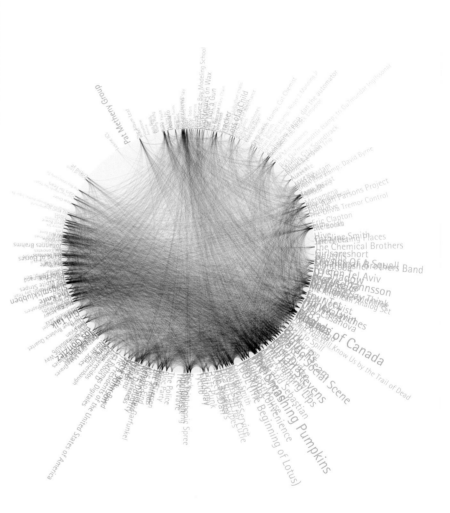

▶ This computer-generated visualization depicts the online music-listening history of a user over an eighteen-month period. The frequency of listening is indicated by text size. Color represents the length of listening time periods.

Lee Byron, *United States*

▼ Visualizations increase our understanding of data by making it tangible. This computer visualization models the aerodynamic forces of a bat in flight. Designed as a joint effort between engineers at Brown University and MIT.

Dave Willis,
Mischa Kostandov,
Dan Riskin, Jaime Peraire,
David H. Laidlaw,
Sharon Swartz,
and Kenny Breuer,
Brown University and MIT
United States

Modeling the flight of a bat

1: A Potential Flow model is used to predict the aerodynamic forces on the bat's wings.

2: The accelerations of the center of gravity are used to determine the aerodynamic forces required to sustain flight.

3: The wake circulation distribution illustrates the flow memory of the force generation during flight.

4: Complex vortex structures are present in the wake as a result of the unsteady force generation during flapping flight.

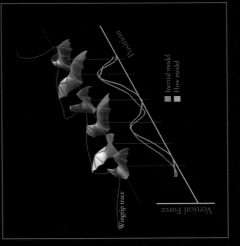

A computer simulation of the unsteady aerodynamics of a bat flying at 3.4 m/s

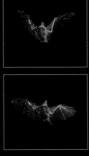

Bats are the only mammals capable of sustained flight. They are highly maneuverable and exploit efficient flight strategies. Today, we are using experiments and computer simulations to understand the details of the invisible air flow around the wings of a flying bat.

To construct a precise time-dependent model of bat flight, state of the art motion capture technology is applied to high speed stereo video of a bat (*Cynopterus brachyotis*) flying in a wind tunnel (above). The three-dimensional positions of the motion capture markers are used to construct the virtual geometry, which is used in the simulations. The surface model is used to compute the aerodynamics forces by applying a boundary element method Potential Flow model as well as a mass distribution inertial model. The vertical forces deduced from the observed accelerations are found to be in good agreement with those predicted by the flow model (right).

Illustrated Visualization

Coinciding with the popularity of computer-generated visualizations is a genre of illustrated visualizations based on smaller data sets. These range from personal data to an analysis of the words and phrases found in literature. Similar to computer-based versions, these human-generated information visualizations are equally fascinating because they present data in a unique format to promote a fresh analysis and perspective.

Effective visualizations of both varieties have specific qualities. They are relatively easy to perceive and interpret, they find novel ways to structure data and information, they are efficient in the way they communicate comparisons and relationships, their movements and interactions (when available) are intuitive and sensible, and their aesthetic qualities attract and engage the viewer.

▶ In this illustrated visualization for a school project, the designer mapped her activities throughout one week of graduate school, focusing on time, category, and hierarchy represented by color, size, and position-ing of type.

Kara Tennant, Carnegie
Mellon University,
United States

▼ This illustrated information visualization represents the complex structure of chapters, paragraphs, sentences, and words in part 1 of Jack Kerouac's On the Road. Each thin line represents a word, which is color-coded according to themes, such as "travel, work and survival, and illegal activities and police encounters."

Stefanie Posavec,
United Kingdom

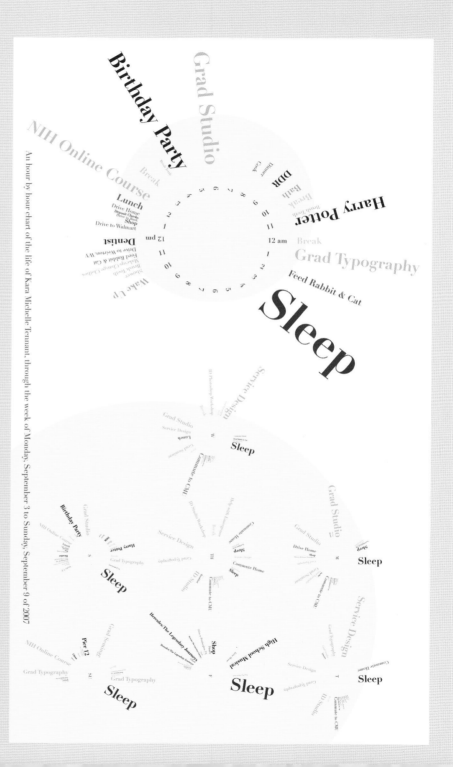

An hour by hour chart of the life of Kara Michelle Tennant, through the week of Monday, September 3 to Sunday, September 9 of 2007

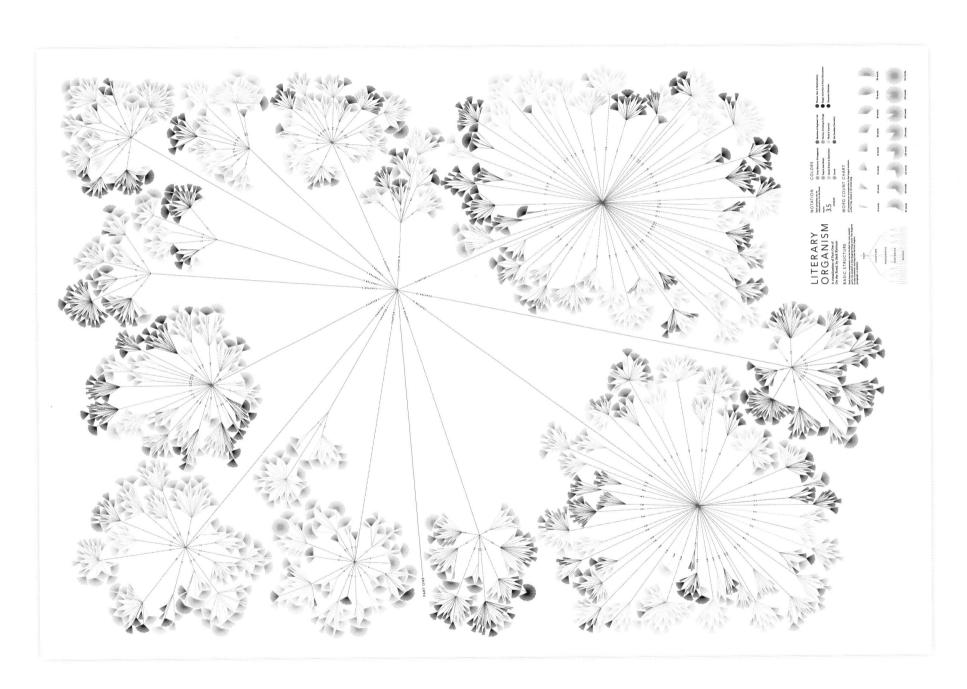

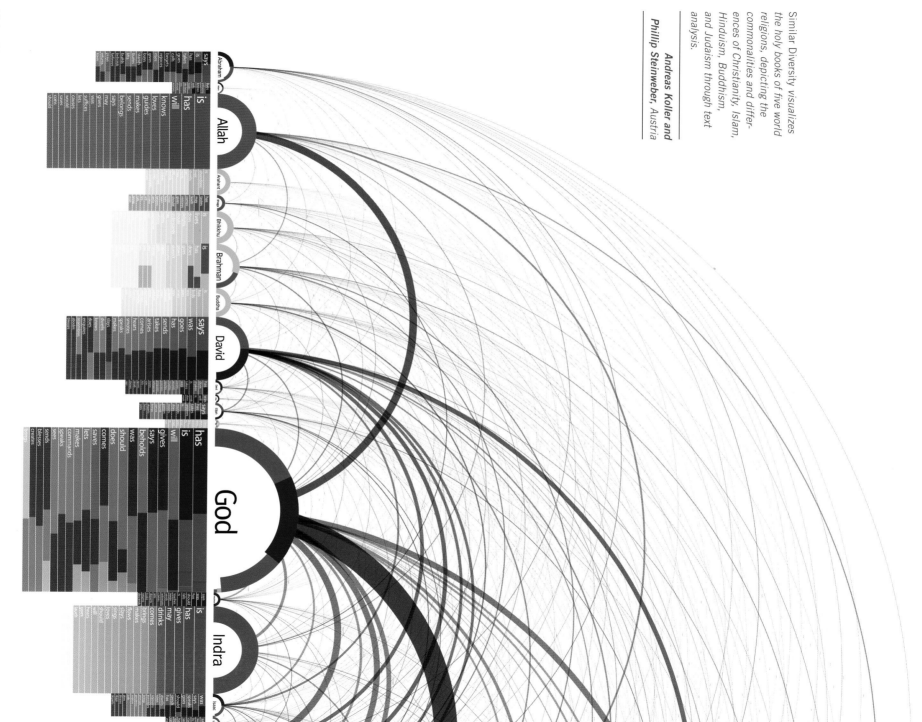

Andreas Koller and Phillip Steinweber, *Austria*

Similar Diversity visualizes the holy books of five world religions, depicting the commonalities and differences of Christianity, Islam, Hinduism, Buddhism, and Judaism through text analysis.

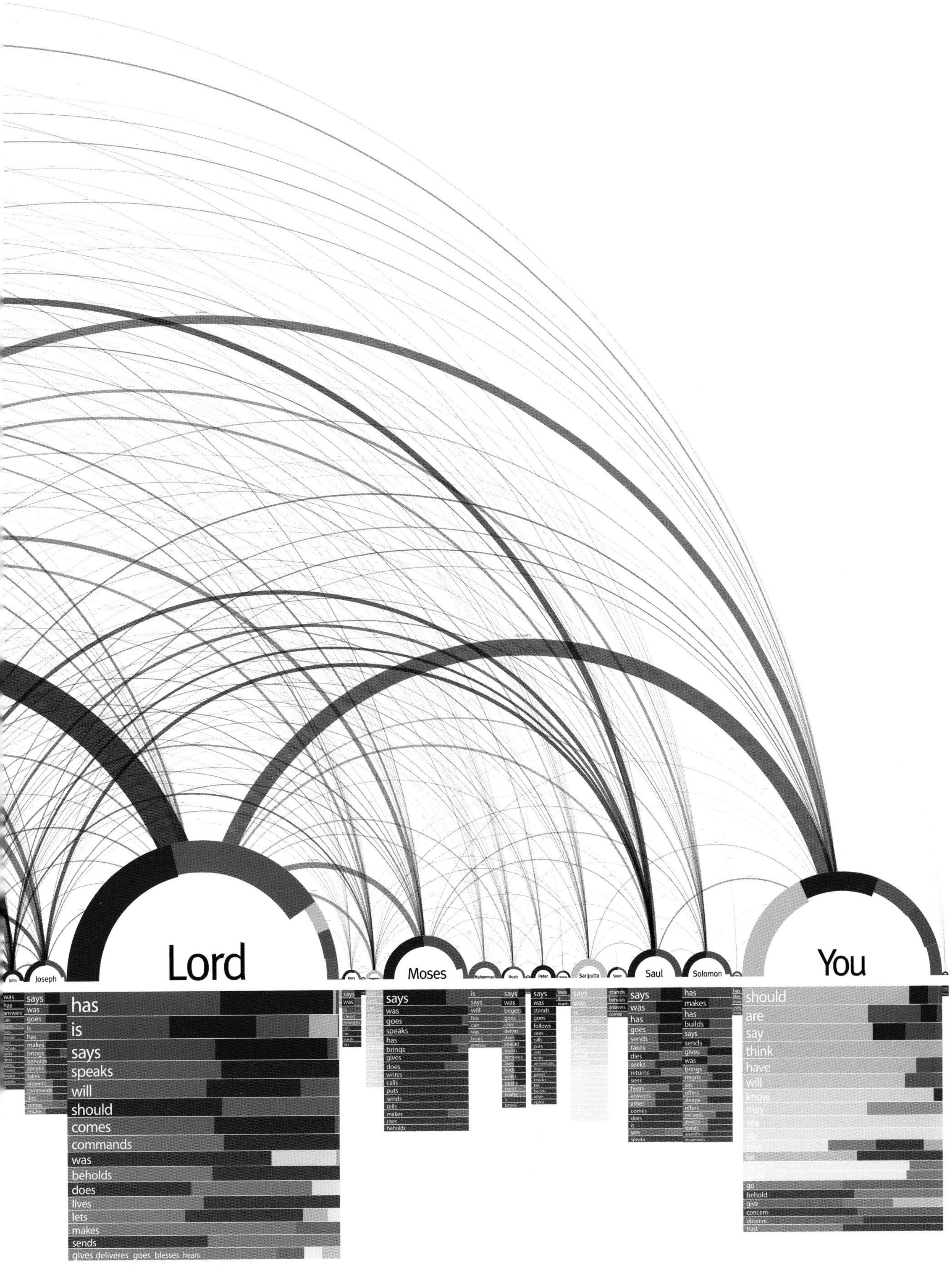
Lord
You
Moses
Saul
Solomon
Joseph
Sariputta
Peter
Noah
has
is
says
speaks
will
should
comes
commands
was
beholds
does
lives
lets
makes
sends
gives deliveres goes blesses hears
should
are
say
think
have
will
know
may
go
behold
give
concern
observe
trust

MORE THAN GEOGRAPHY

Maps record and communicate what we know about an environment and serve as reliable wayfinding tools. They provide a basis for the academic study of many subjects, from geography to history to art. Yet maps also possess a mystical dimension. They tug at the imagination, encouraging us to explore and discover landscapes and cities, people and cultures. They allow us to see and consider the impossible—vast stretches of the planet as well as incredible detail of small regions.

Maps are a reduced version of an analogous space and cannot include everything that is in that same physical space. Thus, a map communicates the features that are important to its purpose. To the extent that one understands how maps are affected by purpose, "one is more likely to avoid the mistaken belief that maps are simply miniaturizations (albeit flattened ones) which show some singular 'reality' or 'truth.' Rather there are infinite 'realities' that can be expressed by maps," writes psychology professor Lynn Liben.[14]

If we were to dissect a map, we would find that it is informative on several levels. One level shows feature information, composed of the map's individual symbols, icons, landmarks, and text along with the attributes detected during preattentive vision, such as size, shape, and color. The second level is the structural information relating to the spatial layout of the map. The structure is composed of the distance between the map's features and the distance between a feature and the map's edge. A third level is the structure the viewer mentally projects onto the map. Research has demonstrated that viewers create additional structures, such as drawing imaginary lines between two mountain peaks or between a landmark and the center of

town. The structure and spatial layout of a map is significant, because it is thought that people perceive a map holistically. In other words, a viewer may mentally hold an intact image of a map in working memory.[15] The fourth level is related to the subjective impression and associations a map invokes. The map's designer may add a scenic route, a friendly illustration, or an artistic spatial perspective. The viewer may respond with emotions triggered by memories of places and people once visited and from a longing to visit new lands.

In general, adults are familiar and comfortable with maps; we have a reliable framework for interpreting maps and we know their conventions. The designer must consider these conventions and decide how they can be aesthetically accommodated. The most obvious convention is the assumption that a map's layout corresponds directly to physical space. Another assumption—which is often incorrect—is that a map will be oriented to the north. This convention is so deeply embedded that when a map has a different orientation, most people will rotate the map so north is at the top in order to process the spatial information. Users also rely on legends to explain the symbols and a grid to provide coordinates if needed.

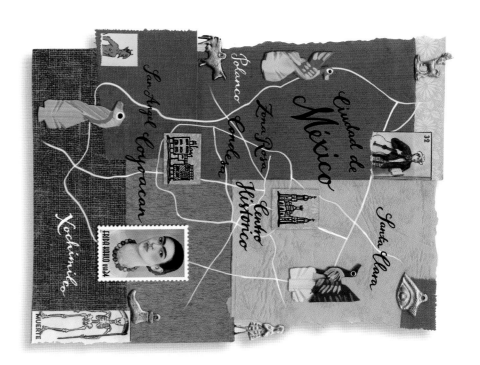

Frida Kahlo's Mexico City captures the personality and geography of the neighborhoods in this map created for Attaché magazine. The illustrator used colors from Kahlo's paintings and iconography from Mexican folklore.

Poul Hans Lange,
Poul Lange Design,
United States

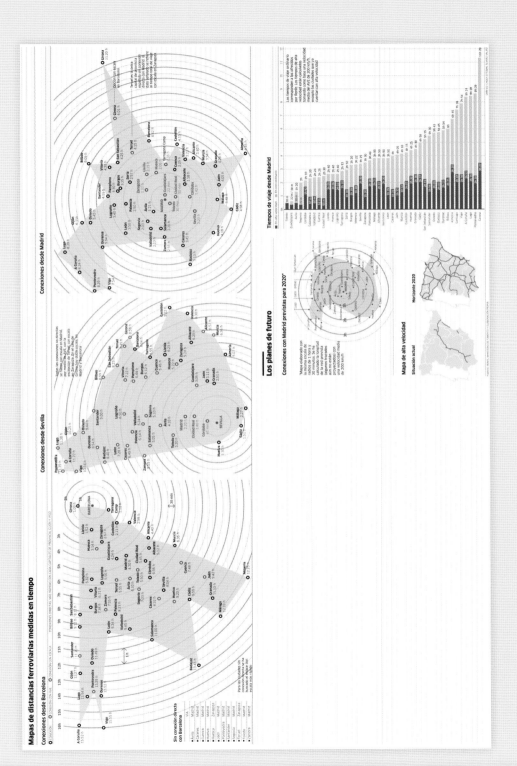

There are an extraordinary number of ways to present map-based information. These travel rail maps, published in the newspaper Público, depict the time it takes to travel to different cities in Spain.

Chiqui Esteban and Álvaro Valiño, Público, Spain

Presenting a bird's-eye view of this farm and garden center's virtual tour helps the viewer immediately understand the layout.

Dermot MacCormack, Patricia McElroy, 21xdesign, United States

Through experience we know that maps are designed within a context, for different purposes and for different people. Although we expect a road map to be drawn accurately to scale, we may not expect precision of scale in a map showing the location of events at a festival. Interestingly, through convention we also know which notations of a map actually represent a physical feature and which are incidental. In a road map, we know that the curves in a line represent the curves of a road, but the thickness of a line does not represent the width of the road.[16]

Graphic designers and illustrators are typically not cartographers. When they engage in map design, it is to make maps simultaneously functional and aesthetically pleasing. Maps can be made more appealing depending on the vantage point that draws in the viewer and the graphics that represent the terrain and relevant imagery. Typefaces can express the personality of an environment, and color and texture can create a rich visual experience for the map viewer. These aspects of map design provide more than aesthetic appeal; they help users interpret and remember the map's features. When map features are visually distinctive and resemble the real objects they represent—such as illustrated landmarks—viewers can more easily recall a map's features than when only text labels are used.[17] Also, minimizing the number of details and using symbols that are familiar and easy to recognize enhance map comprehension.

Bird densities in the New York City region are depicted through vivid colors and imagery in this map created for a student project.

Eli Carrico, *United States*

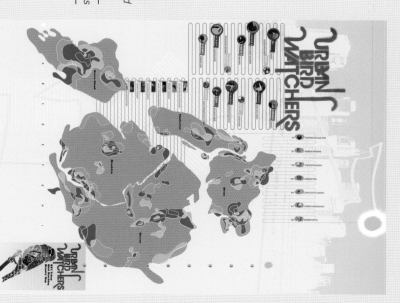

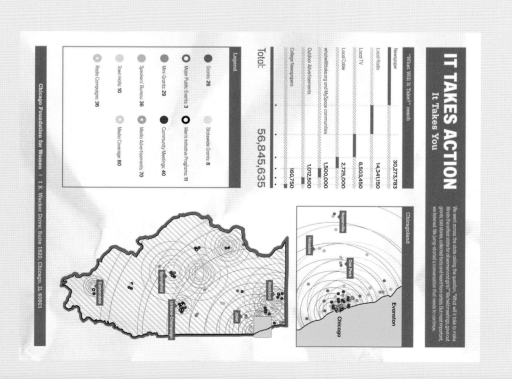

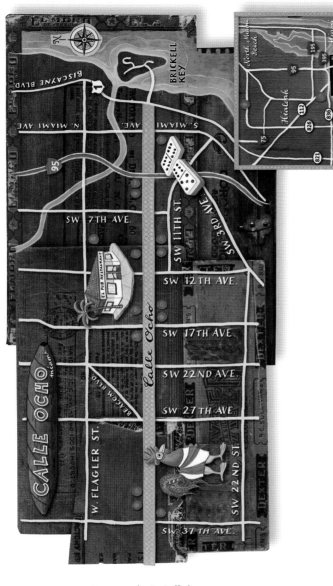

This map of Miami's Cuban neighborhood for Cigar Aficionado magazine incorporates wood from old cigar boxes in the background with paint on top.

Poul Hans Lange, Poul Lange Design, United States

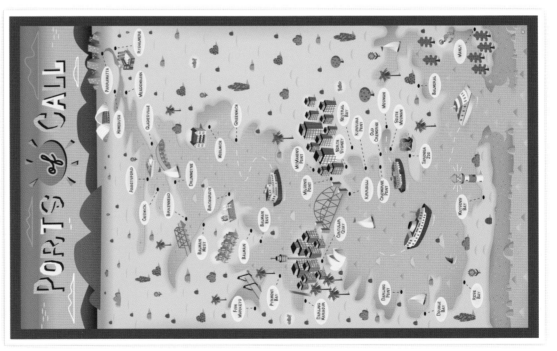

▼ Maps are a natural way to display quantitative information. This one shows summary data related to a statewide antiviolence initiative in Illinois.

Will Miller, Firebelly Design, United States

▲ The illustrated features and clean labels make this ports-of-call map friendly and accessible.

Russell Tate, Russell Tate Illustration, Australia

Franzisca Erdle, Milch Design, Germany

▼ These maps created for an annual report convey the worldwide locations and network of a logistics service provider. The color of the dots indicates the type of center at each site.

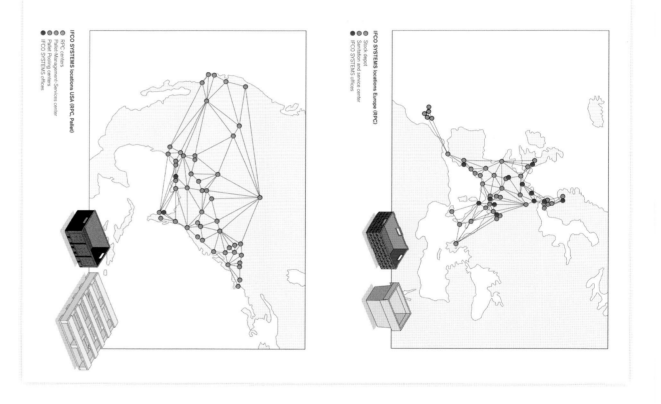

IFCO SYSTEMS locations Europe (RPC)
- Stock depot
- Sanitation and service center
- IFCO SYSTEMS offices

IFCO SYSTEMS locations USA (RPC, Pallet)
- RPC centers
- Pallet-Management-Services center
- Pallet Pooling centers
- IFCO SYSTEMS offices

Angela Edwards, United States

▼ Maps provide a way to communicate more than geography. This map for an art fair printed in the Indianapolis Star is also a comprehensive user guide.

Carlo Giovani, Carlo Giovani Studio, Brazil

▼ This portrait of the San Francisco River in Brazil illustrates the culture, people, animals, and plants along the river from its point of origin to its merging with the ocean.

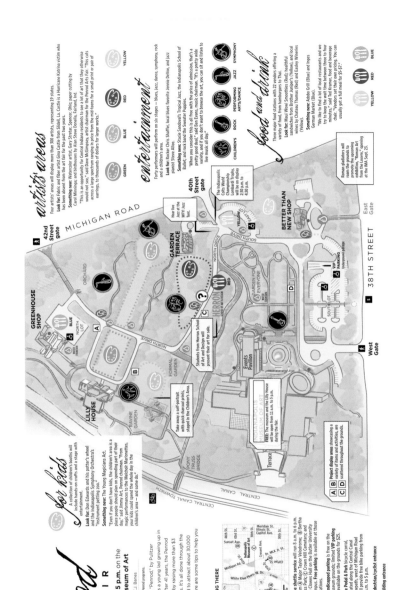

SNAPSHOTS OF TIME

Time has been conceptualized in many ways through history and across different cultures. When we conceive of time, we typically relate it to a spatial metaphor using a horizontal line to move forward. It is also imagined as a cyclical phenomenon that is grounded in natural occurrences, such as the seasons. For some, time is envisioned as a spiral, recurring in the pattern of a helix. In antiquity, scenes were often presented in nonchronological order so that events that were most significant to the artist were placed first. Time is a significant dimension of much information, and it underlies our life experience. Representations of time help us understand relationships and make connections between temporal events.

Of all the graphical forms that depict time, timelines are the most pervasive. Usually, they are depicted in a linear fashion showing time moving forward into the future, perhaps with an arrowhead to indicate direction. It is common to depict an increase in time directionally from left to right or from bottom to top. Timelines are usually structured as a series of fixed temporal events that occur in a chronological sequence. In historical timelines, this may suggest a cause-and-effect relationship between the events.

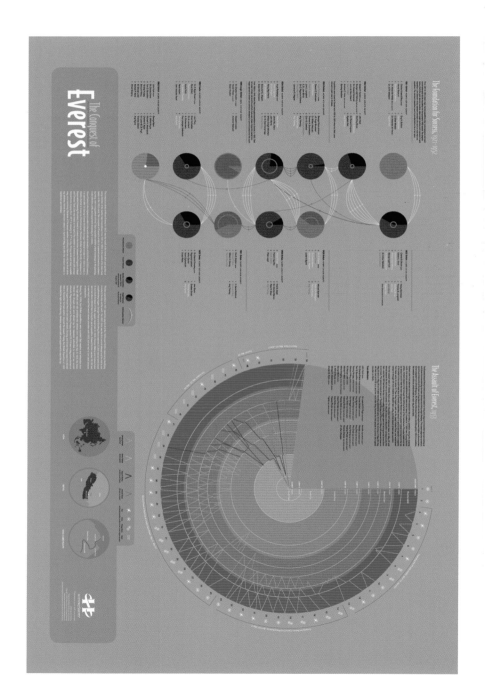

▶ This time-based visualization of the 1953 conquest of Mount Everest maps the ascents and descents of the forty-nine-day expedition on the right. On the left, the history of earlier expeditions and their missions and durations are portrayed.

Larry Gormley, History Shots, and Kimberly Cloutier, White Rhino, United States

▶ In this self-promotional brochure, time is represented in a cyclical zodiac calendar.

Marlena Buczek-Smith, Ensign Graphics, United States

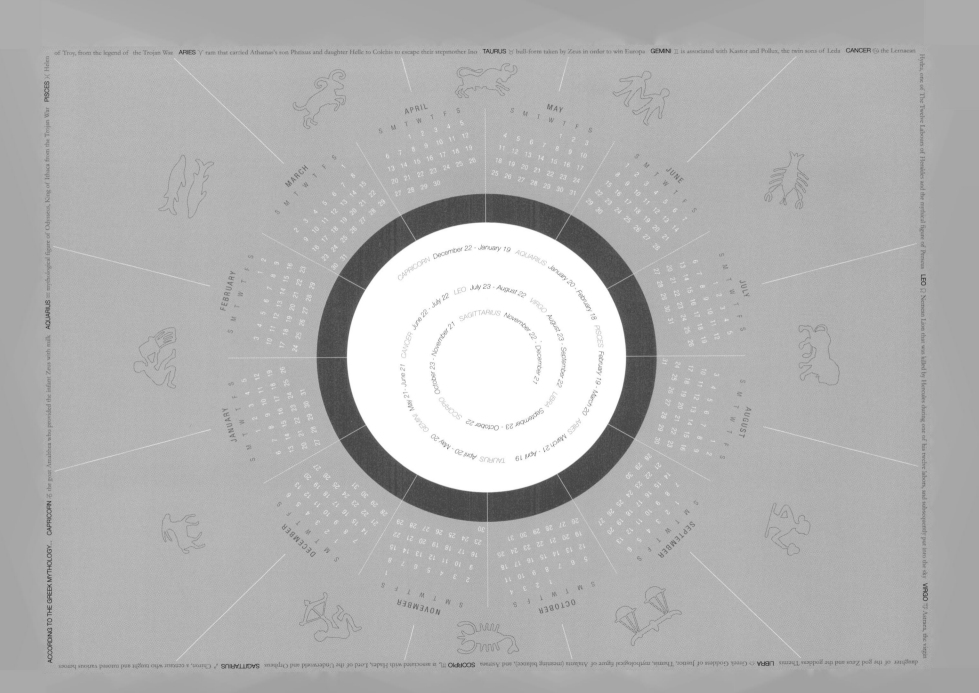

ACCORDING TO THE GREEK MYTHOLOGY... CAPRICORN ♑ the goat Amaltheia who provided the infant Zeus with milk AQUARIUS ♒ mythological figure of Odysseus, King of Ithaca from the Trojan War PISCES ♓ Helen of Troy, from the legend of the Trojan War ARIES ♈ ram that carried Athamas's son Phrixus and daughter Helle to Colchis to escape their stepmother Ino TAURUS ♉ bull-form taken by Zeus in order to win Europa GEMINI ♊ is associated with Kastor and Pollux, the twin sons of Leda CANCER ♋ the Lernaean Hydra, one of The Twelve Labours of Herakles and the mythical figure of Perseus LEO ♌ Nemean Lion that was killed by Hercules during one of his twelve labors, and subsequently put into the sky VIRGO ♍ Astraea, the virgin daughter of the god Zeus and the goddess Themis LIBRA ♎ Greek Goddess of Justice, Themis, mythological figure of Atalanta (meaning balance), and Astraea SCORPIO ♏ is associated with Hades, Lord of the Underworld and Orpheus SAGITTARIUS ♐ Chiron, a centaur who taught and trained various heroes

APRIL
S M T W T F S
1 2 3 4 5
6 7 8 9 10 11 12
13 14 15 16 17 18 19
20 21 22 23 24 25 26
27 28 29 30

MAY
S M T W T F S
1 2 3
4 5 6 7 8 9 10
11 12 13 14 15 16 17
18 19 20 21 22 23 24
25 26 27 28 29 30 31

MARCH
S M T W T F S
1
2 3 4 5 6 7 8
9 10 11 12 13 14 15
16 17 18 19 20 21 22
23 24 25 26 27 28 29
30 31

JUNE
S M T W T F S
1 2 3 4 5 6 7
8 9 10 11 12 13 14
15 16 17 18 19 20 21
22 23 24 25 26 27 28
29 30

FEBRUARY
S M T W T F S
1 2
3 4 5 6 7 8 9
10 11 12 13 14 15 16
17 18 19 20 21 22 23
24 25 26 27 28

JULY
S M T W T F S
1 2 3 4 5
6 7 8 9 10 11 12
13 14 15 16 17 18 19
20 21 22 23 24 25 26
27 28 29 30 31

JANUARY
S M T W T F S
1 2 3 4
5 6 7 8 9 10 11
12 13 14 15 16 17 18
19 20 21 22 23 24 25
26 27 28 29 30 31

AUGUST
S M T W T F S
1 2
3 4 5 6 7 8 9
10 11 12 13 14 15 16
17 18 19 20 21 22 23
24 25 26 27 28 29 30
31

DECEMBER
S M T W T F S
1 2 3 4 5 6
7 8 9 10 11 12 13
14 15 16 17 18 19 20
21 22 23 24 25 26 27
28 29 30 31

SEPTEMBER
S M T W T F S
1 2 3 4 5 6
7 8 9 10 11 12 13
14 15 16 17 18 19 20
21 22 23 24 25 26 27
28 29 30

NOVEMBER
S M T W T F S
1
2 3 4 5 6 7 8
9 10 11 12 13 14 15
16 17 18 19 20 21 22
23 24 25 26 27 28 29
30

OCTOBER
S M T W T F S
1 2 3 4
5 6 7 8 9 10 11
12 13 14 15 16 17 18
19 20 21 22 23 24 25
26 27 28 29 30 31

CAPRICORN December 22 - January 19 AQUARIUS January 20 - February 18 PISCES February 19 - March 20 ARIES March 21 - April 19 TAURUS April 20 - May 20 GEMINI May 21 - June 21 CANCER June 22 - July 22 LEO July 23 - August 22 VIRGO August 23 - September 22 LIBRA September 23 - October 22 SCORPIO October 23 - November 21 SAGITTARIUS November 22 - December 21

In terms of time span, timelines are quite adaptable. They can potentially represent linear time on any scale, running the gamut from personal or organizational time, which would be represented in days, weeks and years, to historical time represented in centuries or eras, to the deep time of geological events based in millions of years. Visualizing relationships and events through time helps us to make sense of the past and allows us to map out the future.

We can find visual depictions of time in numerous types of media. Organizations often use timelines to tout their accomplishments or to explain their narrative. Newspapers and magazines use them to depict newsworthy events or to show how events might affect the future. Textbooks visually represent time for historical purposes in an effort to make intangible events more concrete. In the sciences, timelines convey transformations and cause and effect. More so than verbal communication, visual language provides a flexible way for exploring and portraying time.

A portion of an extensive Olympic timeline published in Superinteressante magazine is shown here. The sepia-toned coloring mixed with old photographs expresses the historical aspect of the timeline.

Juliana Vidigal and Carlo Giovani Giovani, Carlo Giovani Studio, Brazil

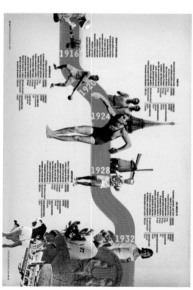

The HISTORY of LIFE on EARTH

This extraordinary portrayal through deep time illustrates the history of life on Earth over the past 600 million years. In intricate detail, it illustrates the rich biodiversity resulting from evolution and gives new meaning to the concept of a timeline.

Brian Finn, Iapetus Press,
United States

This richly textured timeline about the history of
Brazilian popular music is
portrayed on the neck of a
guitar with the frets indicating years. Each string represents a different musical
style.

*Rodrigo Maroja and Carlo
Giovani, Carlo Giovani
Studio, Brazil*

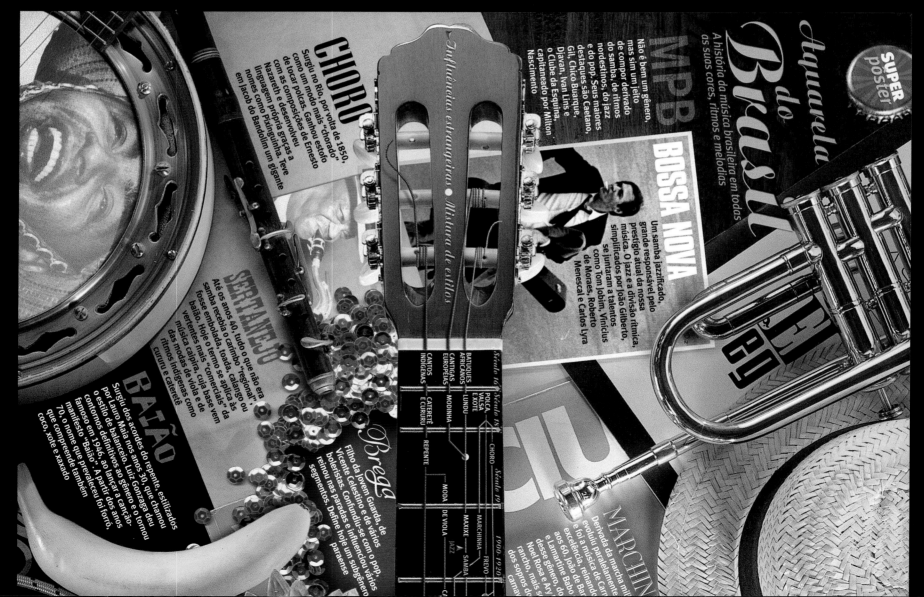

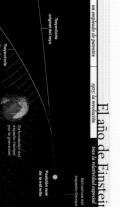

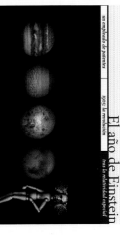

El año de Einstein — 1905: la revolución — tras la relatividad especial — un empleado de patentes

"Complexity isn't what it used to be.
It's more—and different."

YVONNE HANSEN, *Information Design*

Visual complexity is a paradox. On the one hand, complexity is a compelling feature known to capture a viewer's attention and stimulate interest. Rather than looking at an entire picture, viewers tend to look at the informative portions, particularly those with intricate detail, patterns, and occlusions. On the other hand, complexity only arouses curiosity up to a point. When a visual is extremely complex, viewers may tend to avoid it altogether.[1]

Although complexity has always surrounded us, the visual depiction of complex objects, systems, and concepts has become increasingly prevalent. Complex subjects are depicted as infographics in newspapers and magazines; as animated segments in newscasts and documentaries; as exhibits in museums; as instructional graphics in textbooks and online courses; as procedural and assembly instructions in product manuals; and as accompaniments to articles in academic journals.

Objective complexity refers to the properties inherent in a system, information, or task. Systems are considered complex when they have many parts or components that interrelate. Information is complex when it is voluminous, dense, and lacking in structure. Tasks become complex when many cognitive operations and strategies are required to complete them.[2] Task complexity also increases when a person's attention is divided while performing simultaneous operations, like using a cell phone while driving. In these situations, both tasks compete for attention, which is limited in capacity.[3]

On the other hand, subjective complexity is based on individual perception and relates to a person's relevant skills, knowledge, and abilities. "What is highly complex to one person may be much less complex to another person. Rather than a feature of the environment, complexity primarily seems to be in the eye of the beholder," write cognitive researchers Jan Elen and Richard Clark.[4]

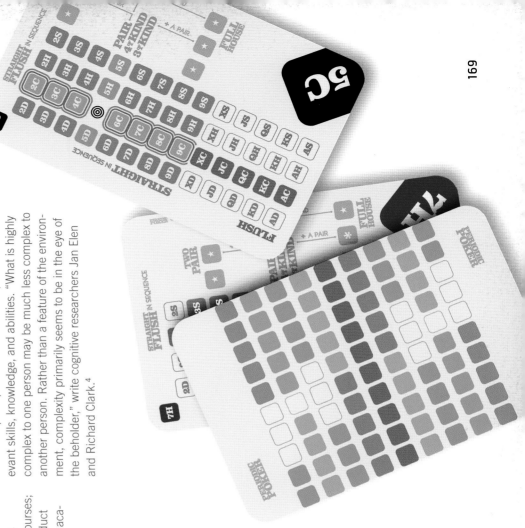

The complexities of poker are clarified with this deck that includes an on-card explanation of the additional cards needed for the best poker hand.

Drew Davies, Oxide Design, *United States*

▼ The frames of this multimedia documentary made for Spain's newspaper El Mundo explain Albert Einstein's landmark discoveries from 1905. Breaking complex concepts into small segments can help viewers understand complexity.

Alberto Cairo, United States

Explaining Complex Concepts

The explanation of complex concepts often results in visually complex graphics. Complex graphics are information rich, conveying meaning through an increased use of detail, patterns, shapes, text, color, density, and diversity of elements. Viewers may have difficulty with these visuals because there are a greater number of pictorial stimuli to discriminate, identify, and process. Also, it takes longer to search through and to locate relevant information when a graphic is complex. One eye-tracking study found that visually complex Web pages produce a more scattered and disordered eye-scanning path than Web pages with fewer elements.[5]

The challenge for visual communicators is to provide a full and complete graphical explanation while accommodating the limits and strengths of human cognitive architecture. It is most effective when designers use techniques to clarify information rather than to simplify it. Although simplification is highly effective for many communication needs, some concepts and systems are too deep and too rich to pare down. As Evelyn Goldsmith writes in her book *Research into Illustration*, "Just as a verbal exposition sometimes needs to consider a number of issues in order to present an argument in its true perspective, so a drawing can lose much of its communicative value if in an attempt at simplicity it is denied an appropriate context."

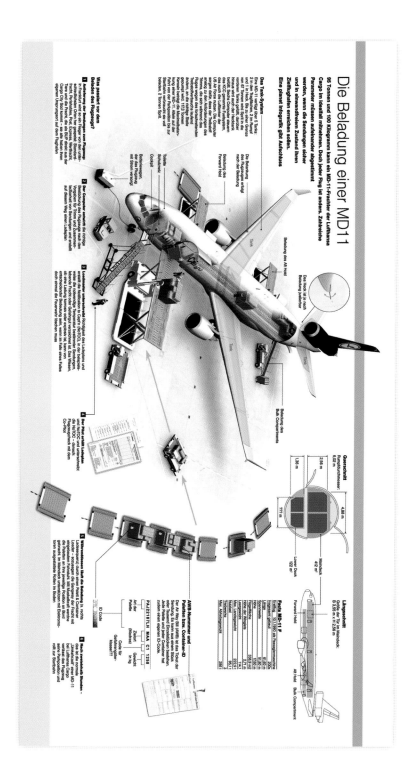

▲ A complex explanation requires a visually complex graphic, as shown in these depictions of the import process at Frankfurt Airport for Planet magazine.

Jan Schwochow,
Golden Section Graphics,
Germany

▼ The features of the high-energy-performance Condé Nast Building are illustrated through call-outs and spot enlargements to make the explanation more effective.

Mathew Luckwitz, grafPort,
United States

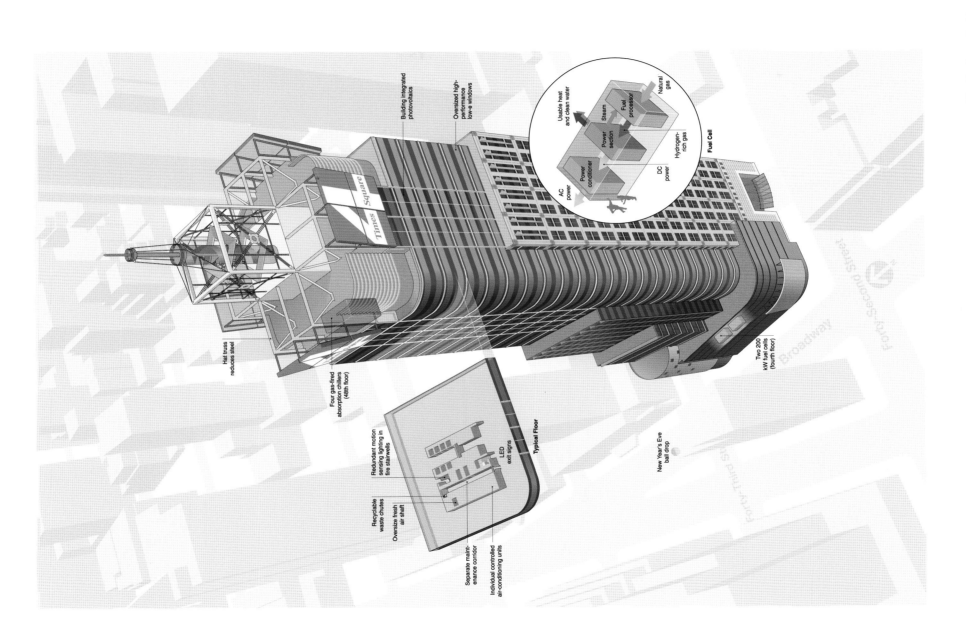

Hat truss
reduces steel

Four gas-fired
absorption chillers
(48th floor)

Building integrated
photovoltaics

Oversized high-
performance
low-e windows

Times Square

Usable heat
and clean water

Steam

Fuel
processor

Natural
gas

Power
section

Power
conditioner

Hydrogen-
rich gas

AC
power

DC
power

Fuel Cell

Broadway

Two 200
kW fuel cells
(fourth floor)

New Year's Eve
ball drop

Recyclable
waste chutes

Oversize fresh
air shaft

Redundant motion
sensing lighting in
fire stairwells

LED
exit signs

Typical Floor

Separate maint-
enance corridor

Individual controlled
air-conditioning units

Forty-Second Street

Forty-third Street

Cognition and Complexity

In a complex world, we are bound to seek all kinds of explanations to better understand it. We rely on previous knowledge, which is structured in mental representations or schemas, to perform cognitive tasks and to assimilate new information. Our schemas are often fuzzy and incomplete. Explanations help us refine them so they are more accurate. Our schemas may have conflicting and illogical concepts. Explanations help dissolve cognitive dissonance.

Regardless of whether it is visual or verbal, a complex explanation places a great demand on working memory. The more the informational components of an explanation interact, the greater the cognitive load. This is because understanding an interdependent system is more difficult than understanding elements in isolation.[6] For example, cognitive load is greater in trying to understand how an entire computer network operates than in trying to understand how one component, such as a router, functions.

Fortunately, our cognitive architecture is equipped to handle complex information. When we come upon something new and complex, it is theorized that we gradually build up schemas into large entities in working memory in order to have more information simultaneously available.[7] This ensures that the limited capacity of working memory will not be strained, as it can only accommodate a few entities at a time.

We also construct mental models to help us understand complex systems. Mental models, which are based on schemas, are broader representations of how different aspects of the world operate. They integrate what is common about a particular type of system or phenomena. For instance, a person who has an accurate mental model of how computer printers work will be able to use this mental model to operate almost any printer. While studying an explanatory graphic, viewers will construct a network of knowledge to understand it and will enhance their mental models with this new information.

Two important contributors to building accurate mental representations are coherency and context. Coherency refers to the consistent logic that makes an explanation meaningful. Coherent explanations might involve understanding cause and effect or the steps of a process. They contain a structure that makes sense. Just as verbal explanations require coherency, so do visual ones. Designers can ensure graphical explanations are coherent by ensuring that the order for viewing information is clear, extraneous information is limited, and the graphic is visually unified and logical.

The context of an explanation is the framework within which new information is assimilated. In picture comprehension, context is a constraining feature that determines what objects to expect and what not to expect in a particular type of visual. As a result, context helps to guide the viewer's attention and influences how a picture is interpreted. It so strongly influences meaning that when something is perceived as out of context, it often does not make sense. Providing context in a complex visual explanation, such as showing the big-picture view and the detail in an inset, goes a long way in helping a viewer understand a concept.

▼ *This visually coherent information graphic explains the causes of obesity in the United States as compared to Japan.*

Alan Lau, *United States*

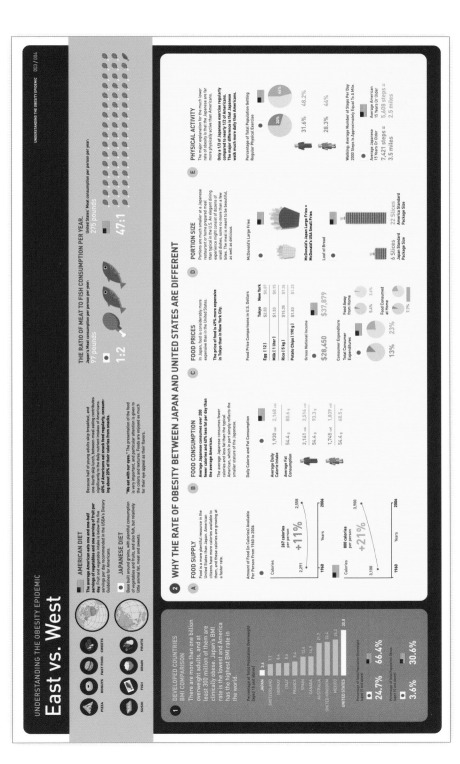

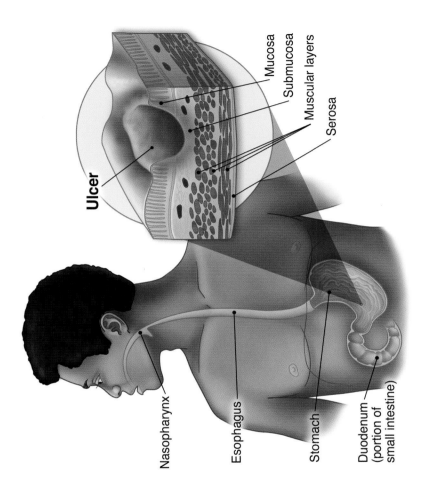

Nasopharynx

Esophagus

Stomach

Duodenum
(portion of
small intestine)

Ulcer

Mucosa

Submucosa

Muscular layers

Serosa

▲ In this medical illustration for online patient-
education materials, pre-
senting the visual context
of the stomach provides a
reference for the viewer to
understand the detail.

Joanne Haderer Müller,
Haderer & Müller
Biomedical, *United States*

Lo más parecido a una mano verdadera

La gran ventaja de esta prótesis con respecto a sus antecesoras es la variedad de movimientos que permite y la posibilidad de darle un aspecto casi real

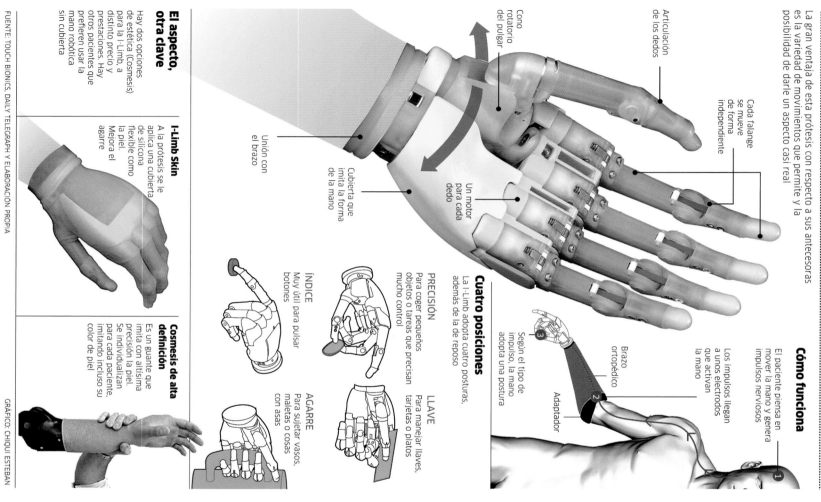

Articulación de los dedos

Cada falange se mueve de forma independiente

Cono rotatorio del pulgar

Unión con el brazo

Cubierta que imita la forma de la mano

Un motor para cada dedo

Cómo funciona

El paciente piensa en mover la mano y genera impulsos nerviosos

Los impulsos llegan a unos electrodos que activan la mano

Brazo ortopédico

Según el tipo de impulso, la mano adopta una postura

Adaptador

Cuatro posiciones

La I-Limb adopta cuatro posturas, además de la de reposo

PRECISIÓN
Para coger pequeños objetos o tareas que precisan mucho control

LLAVE
Para manejar llaves, tarjetas o platos

ÍNDICE
Muy útil para pulsar botones

AGARRE
Para sujetar vasos, maletas o cosas con asas

El aspecto, otra clave

I-Limb Skin
A la prótesis se le aplica una cubierta flexible como la piel. Mejora el agarre

Cosmesis de alta definición
Es un guante que imita con altísima precisión la piel. Se individualizan para cada paciente, imitando incluso su color de piel

Hay dos opciones de estética (Cosmesis) para la I-Limb, a distinto precio y prestaciones. Hay otros pacientes que prefieren usar la mano robótica sin cubierta

FUENTE: TOUCH BIONICS, DAILY TELEGRAPH Y ELABORACIÓN PROPIA

GRÁFICO: CHIQUI ESTEBAN

In this explanation of how a mechanical hand works for the Público newspaper, the main illustration with call-outs provides the context for the smaller explanatory segments that surround it.

Chiqui Esteban, Público,
Spain

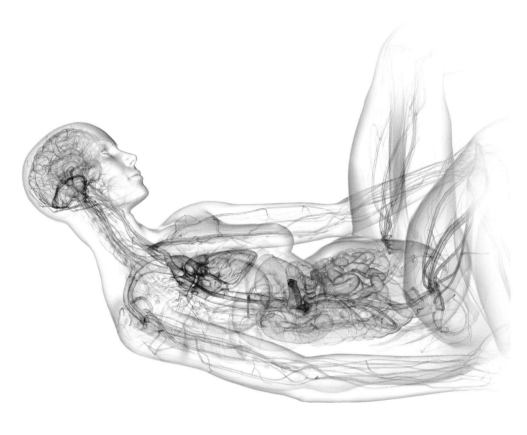

Applying The Principle

It is well known that viewers have an easier time understanding simpler graphics than complex ones. Increased complexity can interfere with the viewer's ability to decode and interpret a visual. Thus, designers must find effective ways to clearly convey meaning without overwhelming the audience. A complex visual explanation does not require extraneous and distracting detail. It does, however, require the detail necessary for providing a coherent explanation.

Several visual approaches can facilitate building accurate schemas and appropriate mental models without overloading the audience. One is to segment complex content into smaller units to minimize the amount of information processed at one time. Organizing information into smaller chunks allows schemas to slowly build up so that content can be gradually understood and ultimately integrated into one whole. Segmenting can take many forms. A designer can present simpler visuals first and then progressively reveal more complex components. Or a complex task can be broken down into simpler steps that form a chronological sequence. Alternately, information can be divided into frames and animated. Any of these approaches can potentially decrease the cognitive demands placed on the viewer.

A second approach to clarifying complexity is to expose parts and components that are normally concealed. This can include a straightforward portrayal of what is normally hidden from sight, creating a variety of interior views, such as cutaways and cross sections or using pictorial devices to show movement. These approaches reveal the inner form of an object or system, conveying new meaning about how things are structured and how they function.

A third technique for clarifying complexity is to reveal the inherent structure of the information, which conveys its organizing principle. Inherent structure is based on an intuitive understanding of how information is ordered. For example, in a calendar, information is structured in months and days. In a graphic about soil, information is structured in layers. This cognitively natural approach provides a somewhat abstract path to facilitating comprehension. When a graphic is visually organized so that it makes conceptual sense, it helps viewers get the message.

The success of creating a complex visual explanation depends on whether the visual techniques meet the goal for which the graphic is created and accommodate the prior knowledge of the viewer. When clarifying complexity, designers and illustrators must balance the cognitive requirement for detail with the knowledge that viewers can become overwhelmed with too much visual information.

In this poignant rendering of a woman with diabetes for the New York Times, *a transparent view portrays the organs thought to be associated with the disease.*

**Bryan Christie,
Bryan Christie Design,**
United States

▼ These Christmas Cheat Sheets (one for male and one for female) were created to provide a person's clothing sizes to potential gift givers. The form is organized by the inherent structure of the information.

Simon Cook,
United Kingdom

▼ Text and images in this information graphic are sequenced to pace the information presentation of the ethanol manufacturing process.

Nivedita Ramesh,
University of Washington,
United States

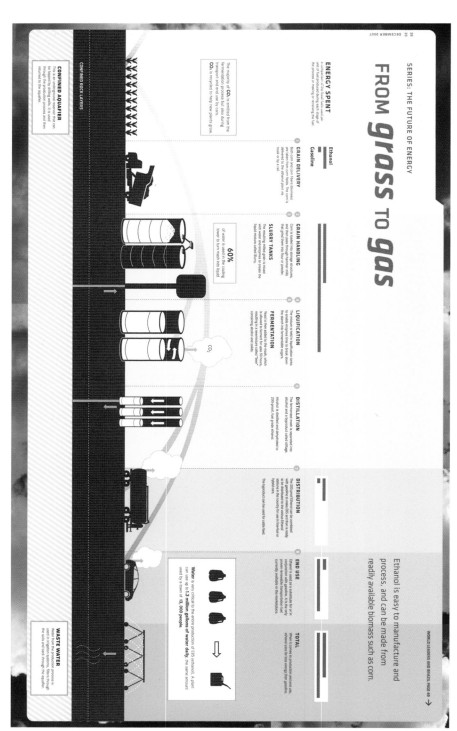

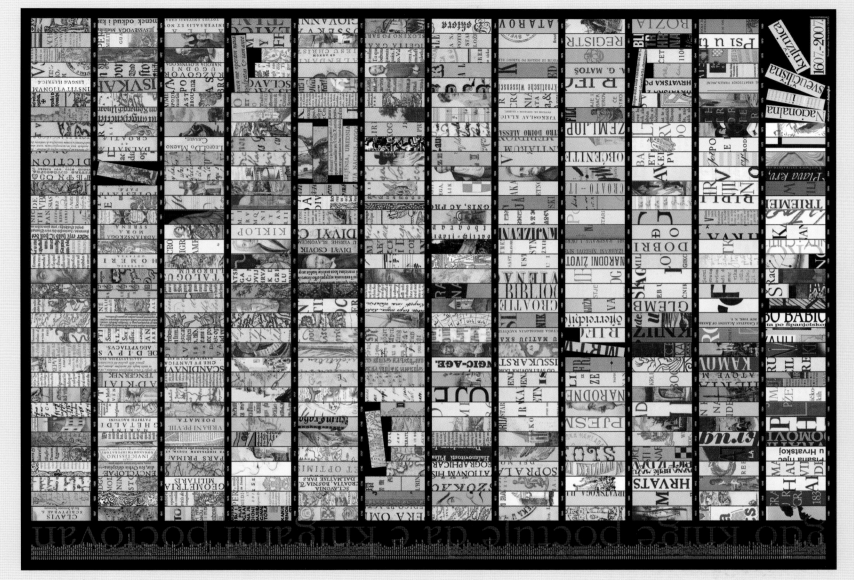

Information has an inherent structure. A poster celebrating a library's 400-year anniversary is structured out of 400 books.

**Boris Ljubicic,
Studio International,**
Croatia

SEGMENTS AND SEQUENCES

Providing a complex visual explanation in one spatial layout can result in a cluttered composition of disorganized ideas. It takes thoughtful restraint and controlled logic to pace an explanation or to organize it into a sequence with a beginning, middle, and end.

Research has shown that when the entirety of an explanation is presented all at once, people are less likely to comprehend it.[8] In particular, people feel overwhelmed when confronted with complex information for which they have little prior knowledge. Essentially, the amount of processing required to understand the information exceeds what the person can hold in working memory. One effective way designers can avoid creating cognitive overload is to segment information into digestible pieces.

Information segmentation is particularly effective because it is a natural cognitive strategy we use to decompose our world into smaller units. Babies segment sounds when they learn to speak; authors segment books into chapters and topics; designers segment graphics into dominant and subordinate elements; and songwriters segment songs into verse and chorus. We routinely use segments to internally manage our world. As we experience the activities in our life, we naturally parse them into temporal segments and think of them as separate events. We do this because when information is in smaller entities, it is easier to manage in working memory and easier to fit into existing schemas for future storage and retrieval.[9]

In this explanation of how to use Netflix for Stanford magazine, dividing the visual into small chrono-logical steps helps to avoid cognitive overload.

Nigel Holmes,
United States

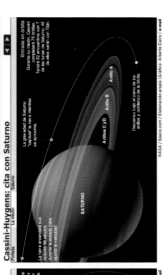

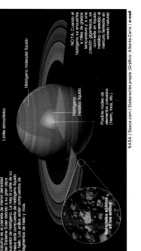
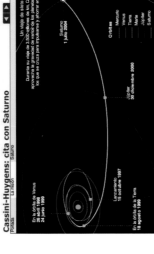

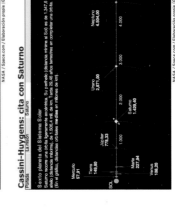

NASA's Cassini-Huygens mission to explore Saturn is a complex online explanation created for El Mundo. Breaking it into interactive segments controls the pace of the presentation, which helps viewers slowly build their comprehension.

Alberto Cairo, United States

Graphic designers can segment information by dividing a visual into small but meaningful units. Each unit groups conceptually related information. Segmenting slows the pace at which information is introduced, allowing viewers to take the time to process a minimal number of concepts before moving on to the next one. People understand and learn more deeply when information is presented in smaller segments rather than larger ones.

Segmenting is a risk when a viewer cannot combine the individual segments into one coherent mental model. The segment must be maintained in working memory until the person views the next portion of the graphic. Some viewers may be unable to integrate across units of information when a composition is visually fragmented. To avoid this, ensure that the viewer gets the holistic view of a concept or system while studying the smaller segments. This can be achieved in several ways: depicting the big-picture view to provide context; introducing the overriding concept at the start; providing visual continuity to the information; and slowly building on previous concepts. In addition, the designer should ensure that a segmented visual connects elements by directing the viewer's eyes

using the compositional techniques or pictorial devices discussed in Principle 2, Direct the Eyes.

Sequencing is a special type of segmenting that presents information in a chronological order, similar to how it would occur in the real world. This is an effective approach for explaining a procedure, a set of steps, cause and effect, or a complex idea where one principle builds on the next. When creating a sequence, prioritize the information to determine its logical order and display it from left to right or top to bottom. Ensure that the relevant details are displayed for each step, avoiding too much simplification so that information associated with the concept or task does not get lost.

An advantage to sequencing is that it groups important visual information together, often through proximity, a connecting line, or a visual boundary. When items are perceptually organized into a group, they are represented together in visual working memory. This enhances the probability that the information will be encoded as one group into long-term memory.[10] Sequential presentations are also processed faster and tend to increase comprehension.[11]

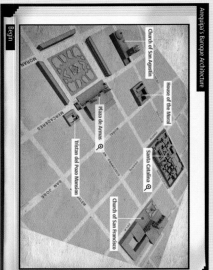

▶ *Renderings and descriptions of the architecture in Arequipa, Peru, are presented in multiple interactive segments to gradually present the information.*

**Vu Nguyen,
Biofusion Design,**
United States

▶ *In this visualization of how nuclear power is generated, the procedure is clearly sequenced to make a complex process comprehensible.*

Kimberly Fulton, University of Washington,
United States

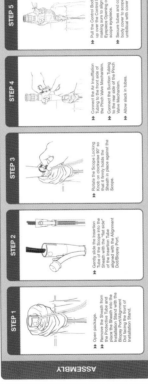

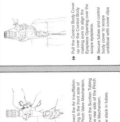

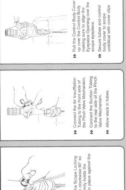

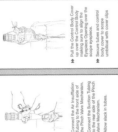
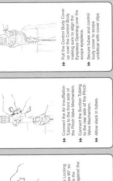

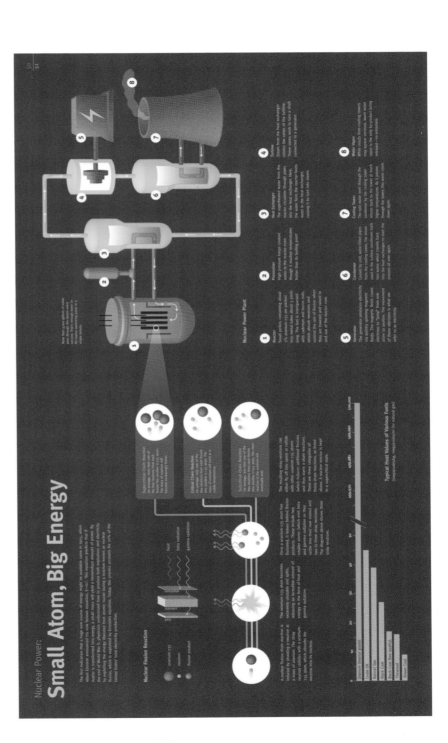

This visual guide breaks down the assembly and disassembly of a medical device into a sequence of clear and discrete steps. This approach facilitates comprehension, allowing working memory to process one step at a time.

Aviad Stark,
Graphic Advance, *United States*

Nuclear Power:
Small Atom, Big Energy

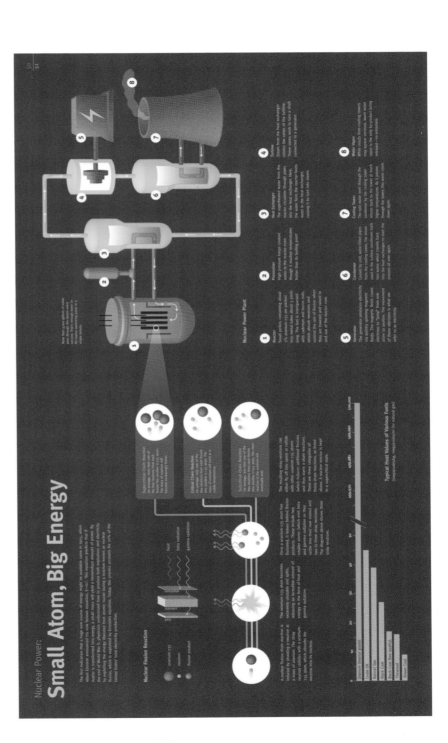

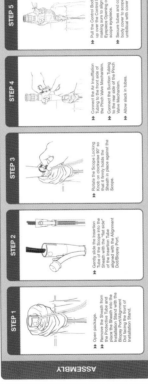

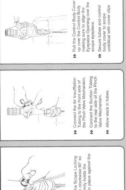

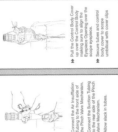

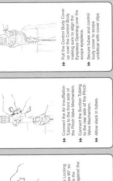

An explanation of Einstein's theory of special relativity for Discover magazine is incrementally presented in small segments so one concept can build on the next.

Nigel Holmes with Michio Kaku, United States

Special Relativity

Special relativity unlocked the secret of the stars and revealed the untold energy stored deep inside the atom. But the seed of relativity was planted when Einstein was only 16 years old, when he asked himself a children's question: what would a beam of light look like if you could race along side?

According to Newton, you could catch up to any speeding object if you moved fast enough. Catching up to a light wave, it would look like a wave frozen in time. But even as a child, Einstein knew that no one had ever seen a frozen wave before.

When Einstein studied Maxwell's theory of light, he found something that others missed, that the speed of light was always constant, no matter how fast you moved. He then boldly formulated the principle of special relativity: the speed of light is a constant in all inertial frames (frames which move at constant velocity).

No longer were space and time absolutes, as Newton thought. Clocks beat at different rates throughout the universe. This is a profound departure from the Newtonian world.

Previously, physicists believed in "ether," a mysterious substance which pervaded the universe an provided the absolute reference frame for all motions. But the Michelson-Morely experiment measured the "ether wind" of th earth as it moved around the su and it was zero. Either the earth motionless... or the meter sticks experiment had somehow short... In desperation to save Newtonia physics, some believed the atoms in meter sticks were mechanically compressed by the force of the ether wind. Einstei showed that the ether theory w totally unnecessary, that space i contracted and time slowed dow as you moved near the speed of light...

186,282 miles per second

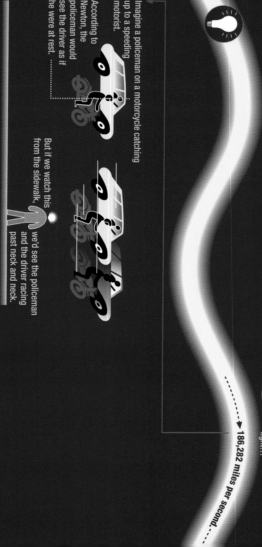

Imagine a policeman on a motorcycle catching up to a speeding motorist.

According to Newton, the policeman would see the driver as if he were at rest.

But if we watch this from the sidewalk, we'd see the policeman and the driver racing past neck and neck.

Now replace the motorist with a light beam.

From the sidewalk, we see the policeman racing right alongside the light beam. But later, if you talked to the policeman, he would shake his head and say that no matter how fast he accelerated, the light beam raced ahead at the speed of light, leaving him in the dust.

But how can the policeman's story differ so much from what we just saw from the sidewalk with our own eyes? Einstein was stunned when he found the answer: **time itself had slowed down for everything on the policeman's motorcycle.**

To **Newton**, time was uniform throughout the universe. One second on Mars was the same as one second on earth. One o'clock on earth was the same as one o'clock on Mars.

But to **Einstein**, time beats at different rates. The faster you travel, the slower time beats. There is no such thing as absolute time. When you say that it is one o'clock on earth, it's not necessarily one o'clock throughout the universe.

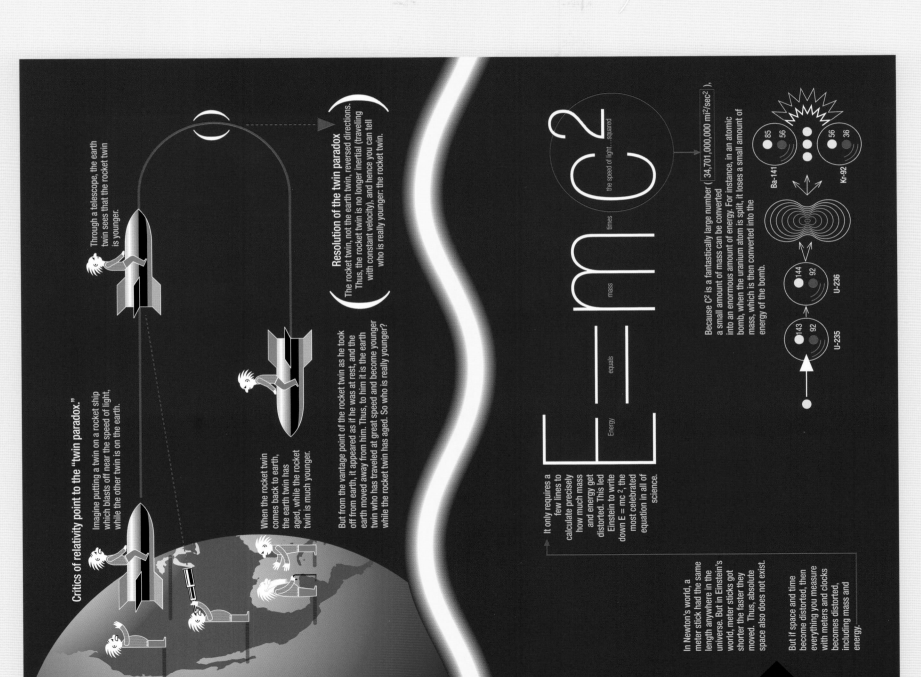

SPECIALIZED VIEWS

Although our visual system is remarkably intelligent, it does have its physical limitations. Many structures and mechanisms are invisible to the unaided eye, and many processes can only be seen through their outcomes. Revealing what is physically hidden and depicting unobservable phenomena through special forms of representations and pictorial devices are effective ways to portray complex systems. Cutaways, magnifications, and other interior views work well for depicting structural information. Techniques that depict movement are valuable for communicating functional information.

Specialized views comprise any technique that allows a person to see through the obstructions of the surface and beyond tightly assembled components. These types of graphics are based on the conventions of technical illustration, defined as "a technique used to graphically present complex parts and assemblies so that professional and lay people alike can understand their form and functionality."[12] As graphic designers and generalist illustrators increasingly create explanatory graphics, they find ways to make complex content more accessible and engaging.

To break through the complexity barrier, designers must keep in mind that novices use different cognitive strategies than experts. "Experts are expert not only because they know more but critically because they know differently," write David Evans and Cindy Gadd in *Cognitive Science in Medicine*. When learning about physical systems, the internal representations of a novice focus on the static physical structures with minimal understanding of how things function and operate. Experts have a more integrated model that incorporates the structure, functions, and behaviors of a system.[13]

Contrary to many of the recommendations in this book, increased realism in a graphic may be more effective than highly schematized drawings when viewers will need to apply their knowledge about a physical system to a real system. In this case, highly schematized drawings that omit too much detail can lead to misunderstandings.[14] These findings validate the principle that clarifying rather than simplifying complexity is most effective.

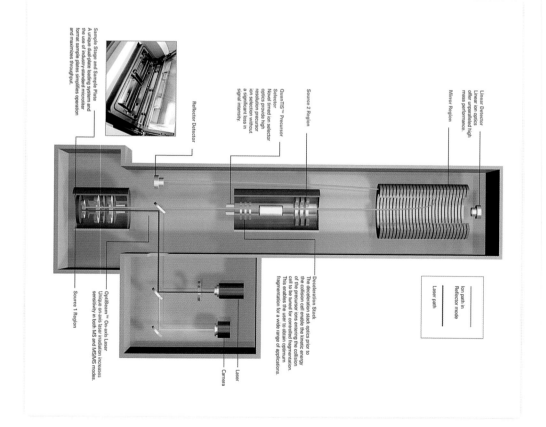

Linear Detector
Linear ion optics offer unparalleled high mass performance.

Mirror Region

Source 2 Region

Deceleration Stack
The deceleration stack optics prior to the collision cell enable the kinetic energy of the precursor ions entering the collision cell to be tuned for controlled fragmentation. This enables the user to obtain optimum fragmentation for a wide range of applications.

QuanTIS™ Precursor Selector
Novel timed ion selector optics provide high resolution precursor ion selection without a significant loss in signal intensity.

Reflector Detector

OptiBeam™ On-axis Laser
Unique on-axis laser irradiation increases sensitivity in both MS and MS/MS modes.

Sample Stage and Sample Plate
A unique dual-plate loading system and the use of industry-standard microtiter format sample plates simplifies operation and maximizes throughput.

Source 1 Region

Laser

Camera

Ion path in Reflector mode

Laser path

▲ In promotional materials for a scientific device used for protein analysis, the interior view and call-outs help clarify the optics technology inside.

Amy Vest,
Applied Biosystems Brand & Creative Group, United States

▼ The explanations of physical objects and systems often require specialized views because we can often only see the tip of the iceberg, as illustrated here for Scientific American.

David Fierstein,
David Fierstein Illustration, Animation & Design, United States

Interior Views

Cutaways, cross sections, and transparent views are established ways of portraying the interior structure of a system. Complex objects and systems are difficult to imagine when their parts are obscured. Cutaways usually remove around one-fourth of the surface so a particular interior region is visible. The view inside is often rendered through a window or tear. As a convention, a jagged or rough edge along the viewing window conveys that a cut has been made, and its inner texture often conveys the quality of the enclosing skin. Interiors are often shown as cross sections, which depict an object cut off at right angles to its axis. Even more revealing are transparent or phantom views that make the exterior surface of an object invisible so the full internal structure is exposed.

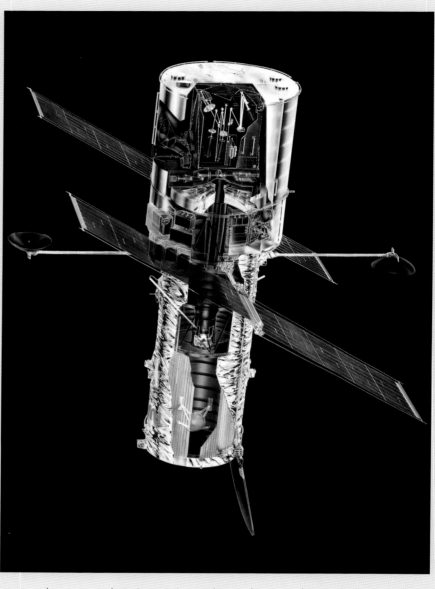

▲ Cutaway views help people understand a system's components and how they are configured, as shown in this intricately detailed rendering of the Hubble Space Telescope created for NASA.

**George Ladas,
Base24 Design Systems,**
United States

▼ This visual depiction of an ankle sprain for patient-education materials reveals and magnifies a targeted area of the skeletal system to clarify a complex concept.

**Joanne Haderer Müller,
Haderer & Müller
Biomedical Art,**
United States

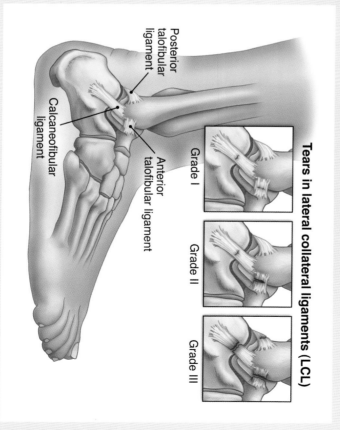

Tears in lateral collateral ligaments (LCL)

Posterior talofibular ligament

Calcaneofibular ligament

Anterior talofibular ligament

Grade I

Grade II

Grade III

In this virtual anatomy presentation, a transparent view of the human body enables physicians to visually explain the progression of breast cancer to their patients.

Nicola Landucci,
CCGMetamedia,
United States

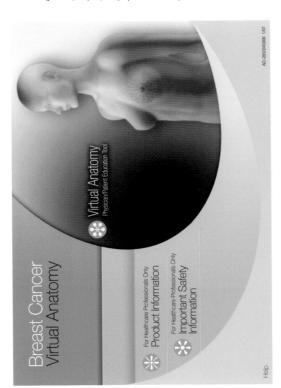

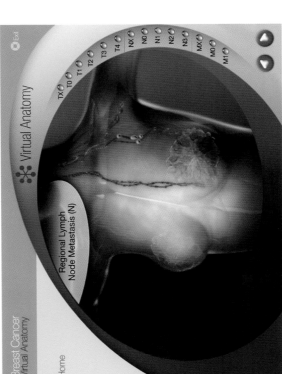

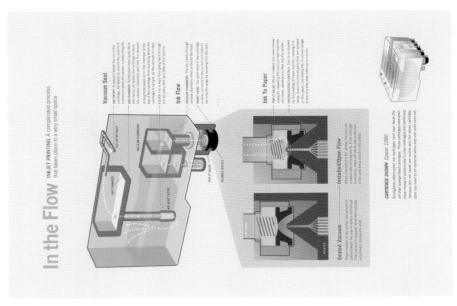

This explanation of the inkjet printing process is shown through several specialized views that will help a viewer build a correct mental model. The transparent view portrays the system and how it functions. Cross-sectional views provide details about how a cartridge operates.

Jacob Halton,
Illinois Institute of Art,
United States

Exploded Views

When a machine, architectural structure, or organism has hidden parts that cannot be fully seen with a standard interior view, an exploded version can provide even greater clarification. Exploded views show the components of an object in their correct arrangement, though slightly separated and spread along a common axis, to reveal how they fit together. This is one way to show both the details of the individual parts, their relationships, and the order in which they are assembled.

If the proportions of the exploded pictorial graphic do not fit within the constraints of the layout, the parts may be moved out of alignment. Flow lines can then indicate where the parts fit into the assembly. Call outs are helpful for naming the parts that may be referenced in a verbal explanation. Although exploded views typically convey structure, the drawing can also convey function with the addition of arrows to indicate movement.

Depending on the purpose of the graphic and the qualities of the object, exploded views do not necessarily require a realistic rendering. It is not uncommon for the parts of a device to be portrayed as a line drawing because the components are recognizable by shape. This type of simplification may be helpful when the graphic is used for the purposes of assembly or disassembly. When exploded views are rendered for homes and buildings, increased realistic detail is often appealing. Because exploded views usually eliminate any type of occlusion, viewers get a better understanding of structure.

▶ Pictorial graphics that show how the parts of an object are assembled, as in this exploded view of a classical guitar, provide a greater understanding of a system's structure.

George Ladas, Base24 Design Systems, United States

▼ The exploded view in this information graphic about the mechanical alarm clock clarifies its internal structure and how the gears move.

MaryClare M. Crabtree, Illinois Institute of Art, United States

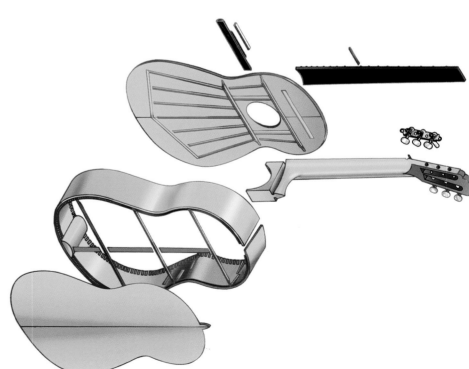

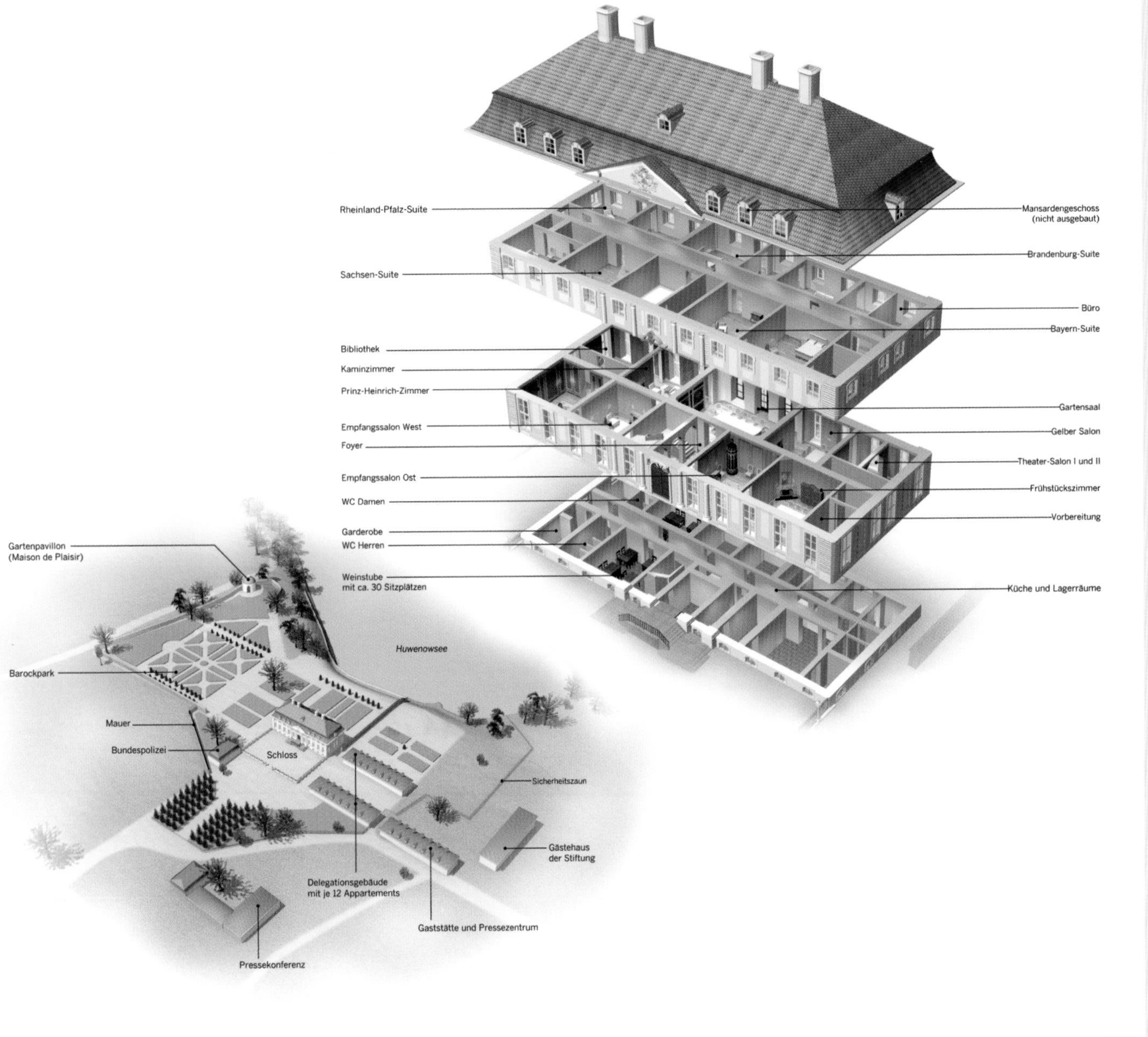

Mansardengeschoss
(nicht ausgebaut)

Brandenburg-Suite

Büro

Bayern-Suite

Gartensaal

Gelber Salon

Theater-Salon I und II

Frühstückszimmer

Vorbereitung

Küche und Lagerräume

Rheinland-Pfalz-Suite

Sachsen-Suite

Bibliothek

Kaminzimmer

Prinz-Heinrich-Zimmer

Empfangssalon West

Foyer

Empfangssalon Ost

WC Damen

Garderobe

WC Herren

Weinstube
mit ca. 30 Sitzplätzen

Gartenpavillon
(Maison de Plaisir)

Barockpark

Mauer

Bundespolizei

Delegationsgebäude
mit je 12 Appartements

Huwenowsee

Schloss

Sicherheitszaun

Gästehaus
der Stiftung

Gaststätte und Pressezentrum

Pressekonferenz

An exploded view of Castle
Meseburg for the German
Sunday paper Welt am
Sonntag allows for an
extremely detailed view
of the interior.

*Jan Schwochow, Katrin
Lamm, Juliana Köneke,
Jaroslaw K. Kaschtalinski,
Golden Section Graphics,*
Germany

MAGNIFICATION

Magnification or zoom-ins portray a level of detail that offers a fine-tuned perception of an object. Increasing the level of detail is valuable for focusing on the crucial aspects of a device or system. Usually, the detail is enlarged and arranged as an inset or in a shape of a contrasting color. To highlight the detail, the magnified area can be pulled away from the main illustration but remain connected with lines, arrows, or a zoom effect. An advantage to enlarging individual areas of an object is that the main illustration provides the needed reference for context. This provides a holistic view before the viewer delves into the details.

Detailed areas of skin are magnified to better explain how skin retracts as a result of liposuction.

Travis Vermilye,
Travis Vermilye Medical &
Biological Illustration,
United States

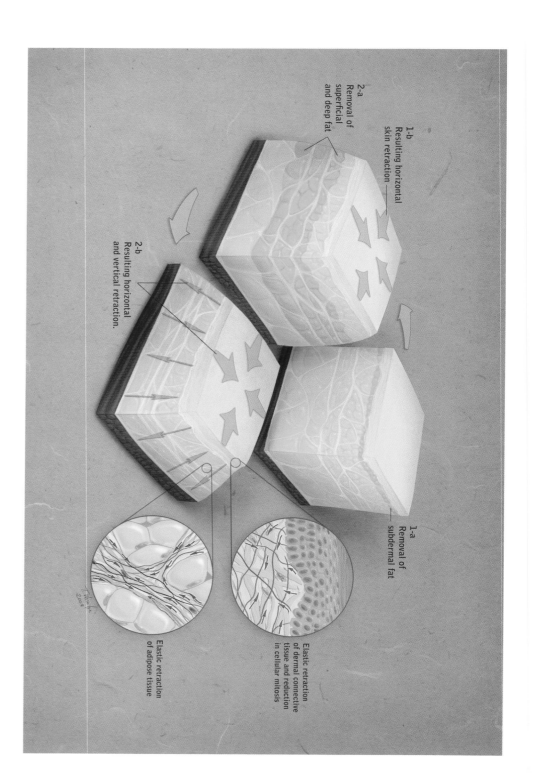

1-b
Resulting horizontal
skin retraction

2-a
Removal of
superficial
and deep fat

2-b
Resulting horizontal
and vertical retraction.

1-a
Removal of
subdermal fat

Elastic retraction
of adipose tissue

Elastic retraction
of dermal connective
tissue and reduction
in cellular mitosis

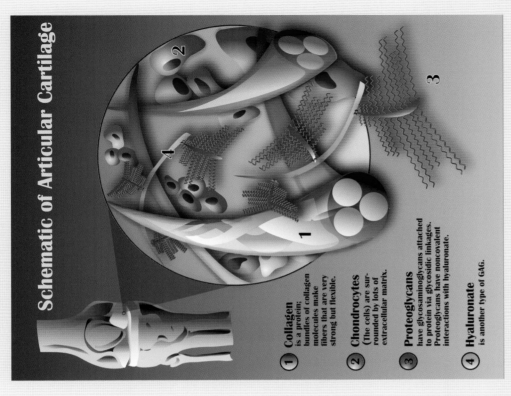

Schematic of Articular Cartilage

(1) **Collagen**
is a protein; bundles of collagen molecules make fibers that are very strong but flexible.

(2) **Chondrocytes**
(The cells) are surrounded by lots of extracellular matrix.

(3) **Proteoglycans**
have glycosaminoglycans attached to protein via glycosidic linkages. Proteoglycans have noncovalent interactions with hyaluronate.

(4) **Hyaluronate**
is another type of GAG.

This visual explanation of articular cartilage uses a stylized approach to depict the magnified area of the illustration.

Melisa Beveridge,
Natural History Illustration,
United States

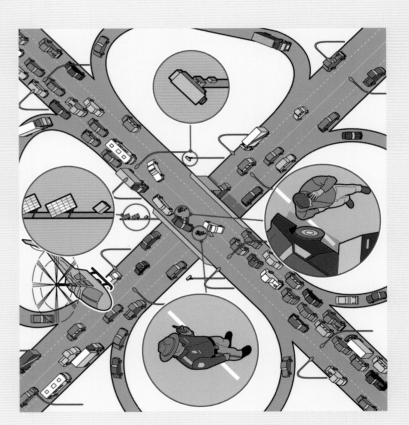

In this overview of how a traffic accident is reported for CIO Insight magazine, the significant areas of the graphic are magnified to help the audience understand the explanation.

Colin Hayes, Illustrator,
United States

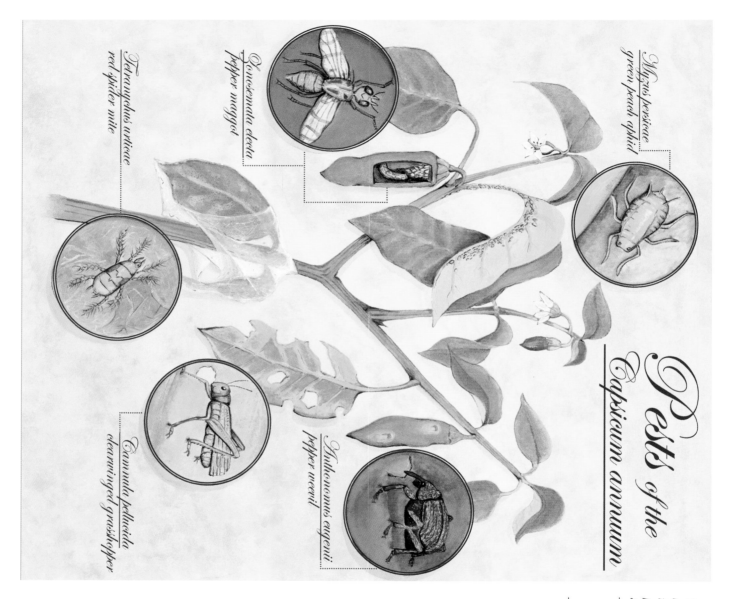

Pests of the
Capsicum annuum

Myzus persicae
green peach aphid

Senosemata electa
pepper maggot

Tetranychus urticae
red spider mite

Anthonomus eugenii
pepper weevil

Gammata pellucida
clearwinged grasshopper

This elegant illustration uses magnification to show the pests of the pepper plant along with the damage they cause.

Melisa Beveridge, Natural History Illustration, United States

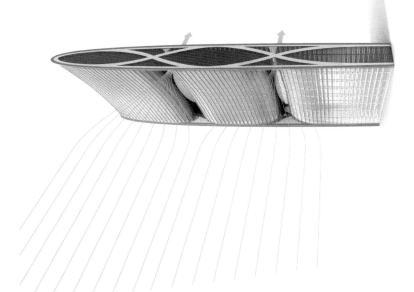

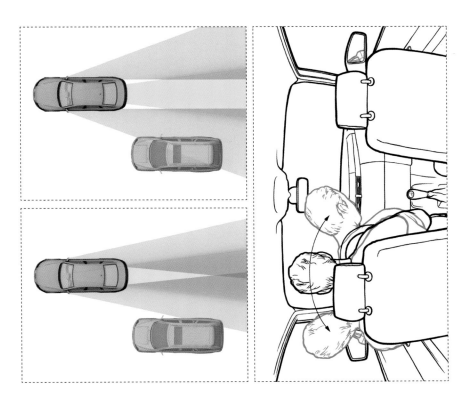

▲ Arrows convey the correct
approach for using side
mirrors while passing a car
in a graphic for Popular
Mechanics magazine.

Jaroslaw Kaschtalinski,
Golden Section Graphics,
Germany

▲ Arrows demonstrate
the ventilation in an eco
building—the Pearl River
Tower in China.

Bryan Christie,
Bryan Christie Design,
United States

IMPLIED MOTION

Although static interior views are effective at showing structure, they don't clarify the dynamic aspects of a system or concept. Representing motion is important, however, for explaining the workings of a machine, the assembly of a product, human movement, and the dynamics of unseen forces. They clarify the ambiguity that might occur from a structural view and help a viewer to build a dynamic mental model that represents how something moves. Several powerful techniques can create the mental impression of movement. These include motion lines, stroboscopic movement, action arrows, and motion blur.

Motion lines are the set of streaking lines placed behind an object or person to suggest speed. Several studies that examined motion lines found this technique to be quite successful at conveying the impression of quick movement and the direction of motion.[15] Stroboscopic movement, on the other hand, simulates motion by depicting a progression of images that are similar in size and shape but differ in their position or pose. The difference between each image creates the rhythm of the motion. A ghosting technique that creates a transparent object or person makes the transition between images seem even smoother.

A common way to depict motion and its direction in scientific and technical illustrations is with arrows. The arrows are often curved to convey a sense of action. Because the arrow symbol seems to have limitless uses, action arrows often depend on context to be understood. Another technique for showing movement is motion blur. This is often depicted in photographs. A disadvantage to blur is that much of the object's detail can be lost with this approach.

Rafi Margalit – Five Works

This CD packaging for cel-
list Rila Margalit communicates the complex notion of
virtuoso ability through the
expressive use of motion
lines.

Ira Ginzburg, B.I.G. Design,
Israel

Viewers understand that the
curvature of arrows depicts
movement in the context of
an explanatory graphic, as
in this one about a robotic
arm for Popular Science
magazine.

Kevin Hand, United States

The use of ghosted stroboscopic movement deftly simulates the action of a snowboard move.

Kevin Hand, *United States*

INHERENT STRUCTURE

An inherent structure underlies information just as the spokes of an umbrella underlie its covering. Visual communication depends upon structure, and viewers rely on it as a feature that conveys the nature of a graphic. In the radial structure of the genome map shown, the organizing principle transmits a sense of energy, of a biological or mathematical form—a basis for life. The lack of visual hierarchy conveys that all chromosomes have equal importance and are generated from the same source. Thus, the sensory impression of the graphic's structure helps us interpret its meaning.

Our visual and cognitive systems make sense of the world by understanding structure, which is based on the relationships between entities. Phillip Paratore describes this in his book Art and Design: "Meaning emerges from relationships. Nothing exists or is perceived in isolation. A design acquires its form and meaning from the relationships on which it is based.

In pictorial design, this is called composition; in music, orchestration; in nature, ecology. The process of developing meaning through the organization of relationships is analogous in all fields, in all media and for all artists."

Memory for content improves whenever information is organized. The theory behind this is that spatial and physical features of the visual structure may be encoded along with the semantic structure of the information. Consequently, when information in memory is well organized, it is thought to be easier to retrieve and to integrate with new information. Researchers have found that memory improves dramatically when people apply hierarchical organization to large amounts of information.[17] This is the basis for the learning strategy known as information mapping, in which people are taught to represent concepts in spatially constructed diagrams to improve their memory of it.

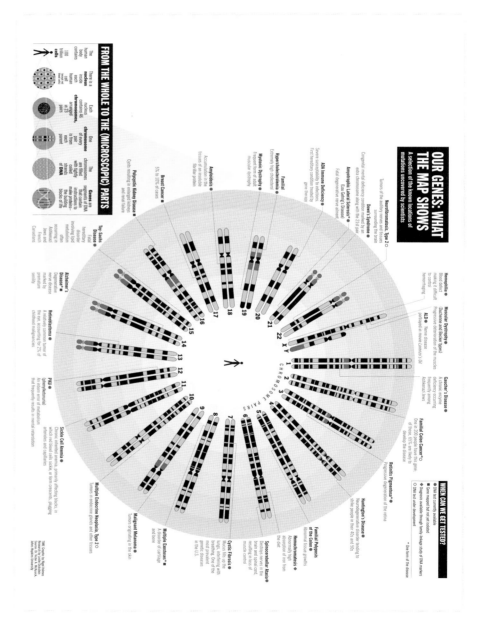

Vivien Chow, Edmund Li,
Fang-Pin Lee, Pauline
Dolovich, Tony Reich, and
Stephen Petri, Reich +
Petch, Canada

▲ A radial structure, which seems to reflect life itself, is used to map some of the known mutations in the human genome in this information graphic for Time magazine.

*Nigel Holmes,
United States*

▼ The structures of these exhibit displays, showing the coevolution of butterflies and plants, are based on organic shapes and seemingly random arrangements to emphasize the diversity of nature generated by evolution.

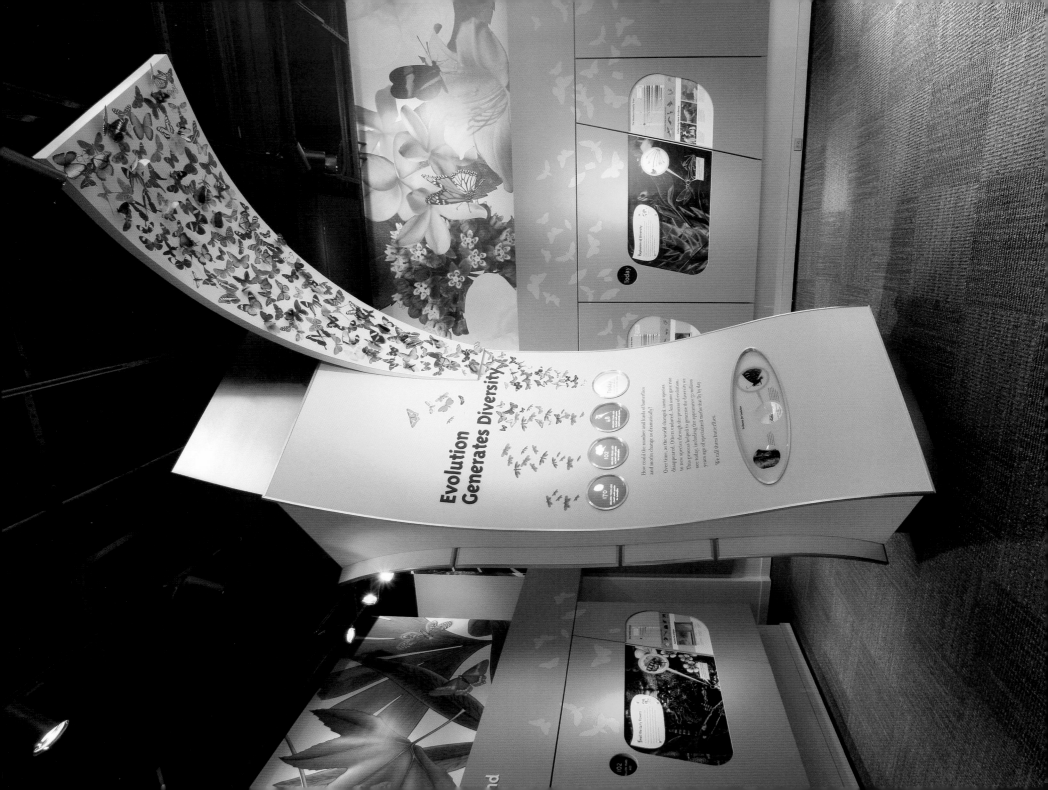

Evolution Generates Diversity

How could the number and kinds of butterflies and moths change so dramatically?

Over time, as the world changed, some species disappeared. Others endured. And some gave rise to new species through the process of evolution. This process helped to generate the diversity we see today, including the appearance 50 million years ago of specialized moths that fly by day.

We call them butterflies.

tor, many mammals

From one ancestor, many mammals

In this exhibit portraying
biological evolution for the
Smithsonian Institution, the
evolutionary relationships
of mammals are conveyed
by their placement on the
double-helix structure of
the DNA molecule.

Vivien Chow, Edmund Li,
Fang-Pin Lee, Pauline
Dolovich, Tony Reich, and
Stephen Petri, Reich +
Petch, Canada

The layered visual structure of this exhibit signage mirrors the actual structure of the subsurface wetlands that it explains.

Claudine Jaenichen and Richard Turner, Jaenichen Studio, United States

Sub-surface Wetlands

What you can't see beneath the gravel in front of you is a thick mat of plant roots and thousands of tiny organisms swimming through the water located underground. The series below shows what it would look like if you dug a hole down to check it out.

Wetland in early growth stage, Chino, CA

Subsurface wetlands may not look very wet, but beneath their surface there exists a flurry of aquatic activity

Subsurface rocks helps sedimentation

Roots act as screening mechanism

Subsurface wetlands naturally occur when groundwater comes close enough to the surface that aquatic plants can grow their roots down and "tap" into the water supply below. Instead of forming from rainfall or flooding, subsurface wetlands are created by underground water channels.

Establishing structure usually involves more than just ordering elements in an aesthetic arrangement. It entails finding the conceptual basis of the graphic's meaning and expressing this through visual language. Visual structures are as varied as there are types of information. For example, the designers of an exhibit that explains mammal evolution and diversity used the structure of the DNA molecule as the organizing principle.

Some information is best organized by physical attributes, when the conceptual purpose is to help viewers discriminate between visual forms, as in field guides. When a set of varied forms are arranged in proximity to one another, the viewer can make comparisons and understand the similarities and differences between objects. It is one way that viewers can build knowledge through inference.

Structuring visual elements according to their organizing principle can have a profound effect on how someone perceives information. In his book *Information Anxiety 2*, Saul Wurman writes, "Each way of organizing permits a different understanding; each lends itself to different kinds of information; and each has certain reassuring limitations that will help make the choices of how the information is presented easier."

Graphic designers may find Wurman's approach to information architecture useful. Known by the acronym LATCH, his recommendation is to order information by location, alphabet, time, category, and hierarchy. Wurman states that this organizational system is the basis for almost all of the structured information we encounter, from telephone directories to entire libraries. Many of these organizational structures are so embedded in our cognitive strategies, we use them without much thought, as when we alphabetize a filing system.

The LATCH system is particularly helpful when considering how to organize large amounts of information. For example, a catalog of retail goods can be sorted by alphabetical order or category of item. A brochure of seasonal performances can be ordered by performance category, season of event, or a hierarchy ranging from the most popular to the least known. For designers, the essence of this approach is to translate the organizing principle into an effective visual form.

EAU PROPRE =
BONNE SANTÉ

In this informational poster about the proper uses of water, the information is arranged in a droplet structure. This enables viewers to quickly get the gist of the visual, promoting a preunderstanding of the message.

Nathanaël Hamon, Slang, and Jaana Davidjants, Wiyumi, *Germany*

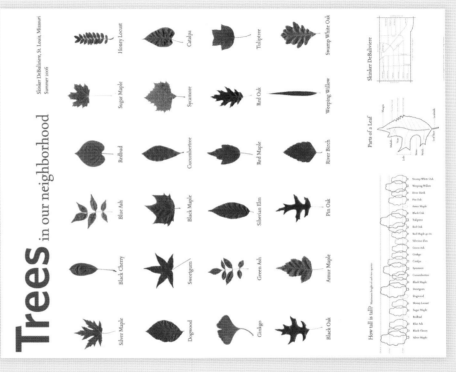

▲ When information is organized into logical categories, as in this paper catalog, it enhances the perception of the products.

Wing Chan, Wing Chan Design, *United States*

▲ This simple arrangement for a poster depicting the leaves of common trees in a St. Louis neighborhood offers a wealth of information by enabling viewers to compare and discriminate the shapes, structures, and textures of leaves.

Heather Corcoran, Plum Studios, *United States*

PRINCIPLE 6

CHARGE IT UP

"The brain states and bodily responses are the fundamental facts of an emotion, and the conscious feelings are the frills that have added icing to the emotional cake."

JOSEPH LEDOUX, *The Emotional Brain*

What raises the voltage level of a graphic and gives it a charge? Why do visuals with that special spark grab attention and sustain interest? Some viewers find the compositional aesthetic compelling. Others may be moved by a poignant image or visual symbolism filled with personal meaning. Some are amused by humorous and entertaining pictures. One thing is certain— good design creates an emotional response.

The common assumption that art evokes emotion is reliably supported through brain research. When viewers look at both pleasant and unpleasant pictures, they consistently demonstrate an emotional reaction indicated by pronounced brain activity that does not occur when they look at neutral pictures. Even with repeated showings of the same affective picture—up to ninety repetitions in one study—viewers continued to elicit a marked emotional response.[1] Viewers also spend more time looking at affective pictures than neutral pictures.

Although by definition emotions are nonverbal, cognitive psychologists have no difficulty finding the words to describe the components of affect. They define emotion as a powerful, usually short-lived experience that is a reaction to a specific stimulus. Emotions result from a rapid appraisal of an object or event's significance in order to prepare us for action. They help us cope with changes in the environment. This is in contrast to feelings, which are the subjective and internal experiences of emotion. Another component of affect is mood, which refers to a longer-lasting, generalized experience that is milder than emotion.

Emotion also has a physical component. Everyone is familiar with the body states associated with emotion, such as the pounding heart, tightened muscles, and sweaty palms that accompany fear or the light-headed, energized sensations of romantic love. On a daily basis, we may not generate particularly powerful emotions, but they do affect us in many ways. For example, emotions often motivate us to pursue goals, like learning a new graphics program or finding a new job.

Viewers have a preference for imagery that evokes emotions. A sensual photograph, such as this one for an arts and culture brochure, will grab a viewer's attention.

CG Lemere, Campbell Fisher Design,
United States

Emotive graphics inform at an immediate, visceral level. Whether they amuse, entertain, sadden, anger, or frighten, emotional graphics arouse an audience. Affective pictures capture attention before the audience processes the content of the message, circumventing many rational and cognitive processes. When this occurs, emotional graphics influence how a message is subsequently perceived and interpreted.

When a potential viewer is distracted, busy, or just plain cynical, aiming at the emotions is a designer's best chance for arousing interest. "Messages which adopt creative, unusual, complex, intense, explicit, unconventional, or fast-paced message strategies can help to overcome boredom and disinterest," writes information design professor Judy Gregory.[2] Grabbing attention gets viewers involved, stimulates interest, and motivates them to decode the rest of the message.

Another reason for emotional appeals is to promote attitude change. This is often the case in social issue promotions, public service announcements, and political campaigns. Some of these appeals use stirring imagery, such as innocent animals in the wild, as a way to trigger emotional responses and persuade

viewers to adopt a particular viewpoint or contribute to a cause. On the other end of the spectrum are the campaigns that evoke fear in order to persuade. In public health promotions, for example, messages based on the fear of harmful consequences from risky behaviors are often used to sway attitudes. In political campaigns, images that evoke fear are used to influence voter opinion. Empirical evidence shows that the experience of fear is effective at persuasion.[3]

Emotion-laden images are a well-known influence on decision making, from voting choices to laundry soap. Advertising specialists provide emotional messages in an effort to bypass cognitive analysis and shorten the decision-making cycle. They often concentrate on positive associations and symbolism to generate a pleasant feeling toward a product or an idea. In her essay "Thinking Positively," communications researcher Jennifer Monahan writes, "The appeal of positive affect for commercial advertisers is simple: Research consistently shows advertisements that arouse positive emotions result in more positive feelings toward the product and greater intent to comply with the message."

1 OF 4 WEAPONS USED DAILY IN DARFUR

This poster is designed with bullet shells to raise awareness that rape is used as a weapon of war in Darfur.

Greg Bennett, Siquis,
United States

▲ Combining the imagery of sugar and slavery in a poster for the Museum of London Docklands creates an emotional reminder of this dark period in the United Kingdom's history.

Cog Design,
United Kingdom

▼ Copy and image provide emotional impact for this Native American antismoking campaign.

Dale Sprague, Canyon Creative, United States

Emotion and the Information-Processing System

Emotion and cognition. Contrary to the widespread belief that emotion and cognition are opposites, they are now thought to be distinct but inseparable functions. The interplay of emotion and cognition contributes to how we think, feel, and act. Emotion is known to affect mental processes, such as attention, perception, and memory. For example, emotive images can lead to biased perceptions when a persuasive symbol is paired with a neutral object or person. A good example is when news programs consistently pair people of a particular race or religion with images of guns and violence. The negative feelings evoked from the images tend to transfer to individuals of that race or religion.

Emotions also affect how information is processed and encoded into long-term memory. A growing body of research indicates that unpleasant memories fade more quickly than pleasant ones. Furthermore, pleasant phenomena—whether words, images, or events—are processed more efficiently and accurately and recalled more quickly.[4]

Emotions have a powerful impact on our personal life and history. The narrative of our life's experiences is thought to be stored in episodic memory, which is autobiographical. Episodic memory automatically captures the time, place, events, and emotions of our personal story. When we view a picture, autobiographical memories are often triggered by images, symbolism, and compositional elements that convey emotional content. When this connection occurs, the emotional component of a visual message becomes personal and meaningful.

Emotion and attention. Graphics with meaningful emotional content capture attention and interest because they generate a state of arousal, which is a cognitive and biologically energized state. As a general rule, most people find monotony and boredom to be an unpleasant experience and stimulation and activation to be a pleasant experience. Many psychologists theorize that although individuals vary in their need for stimulation, most people want to maintain an optimal state of activation. They seek "newness, change, sensation, or inconsistency" in moderate amounts.[5] Emotional experiences help people achieve and maintain this optimal state of arousal. When a graphic generates a satisfactory level of stimulation, viewers will stay with a message and process it. When a message is considered boring, the viewer will look elsewhere for activation.

The emotional imagery of a dancing skeleton implores viewers to celebrate the Day of the Dead festival.

Lars Lawson, Timber Design Company, *United States*

DAY OF THE DEAD
A FREE CELEBRATION, SATURDAY October 27
ALTARS & SHRINES · TRADITIONAL FOOD · DANCE · MUSIC · ART ACTIVITIES

LOVE LIFE

DIA DE LOS MUERTOS

LIFE IS FRAGIL
LOVE IT OR LEAVE IT

INDIANAPOLIS ART CENTER
820 EAST 67TH STREET, BROAD RIPPLE

3:00 ~
8:00 PM

Applying the Principle

Affective visuals generate attention either through an emotional reflex that occurs beneath conscious awareness or through conscious selective attention. In either case, visual language triggers autobiographical memories, arouses curiosity and interest, and enhances the viewer's involvement. Some effective strategies for producing charged graphics are to convey emotional salience, provide a thematic narrative, make use of visual metaphors, and incorporate novelty and humor.

When a graphic has emotional salience, affective appeal is its prominent characteristic. It transmits emotional content in a compelling way. Designers can achieve this by composing with design elements and imagery that have significance for the audience. Graphics with emotional salience take viewers beyond a literal interpretation to one that connects with their feelings.

The visual narrative form also transmits emotion. Narratives are a cognitively and emotionally natural way for people to communicate. Telling a story or tying visuals to a coherent theme draws viewers to the message. Narratives allow designers to create an underlying emotional track that runs through the visual.

The visual metaphor is another effective vehicles for conveying emotion. Metaphors resonate with the non-verbal quality of emotions. Because they result from a synthesis of ideas, visual metaphors are often imaginative and captivating.

A pervasive strategy for evoking emotion is to startle an audience with an innovative and unexpected approach. Not only do viewers enjoy surprise, but novelty arouses curiosity, which sustains audience attention. This includes using humor to shock, entertain, or amuse, as is appropriate with the content of the message.

An important consideration of the emotionally charged graphic is its potential effect on an audience. Emotions are often multifaceted, so a viewer may respond with a mix of conflicting feelings. This can result in an unintended reaction. A good example comes from a study that examined persuasive public service messages to prevent the transmission of AIDS. The research found that when a message evoked fear, the viewer was likely to comply with it. When the message evoked anger along with fear, the persuasive effect of the message was lost.[6] Designers should carefully analyze whether their visual approach will obtain the reaction they desire. For many purposes, a simple emotional response might be the most effective.

▶ *Visual metaphors are a potent way to express emotion, as in this deluge of bits and bytes.*

Erin Cubert, *United States*

▶ *The symbolic image in this poster is effective for a conference on gender and violence in the indigenous communities of Ecuador.*

Antonio Mena,
Antonio Mena Design,
Ecuador

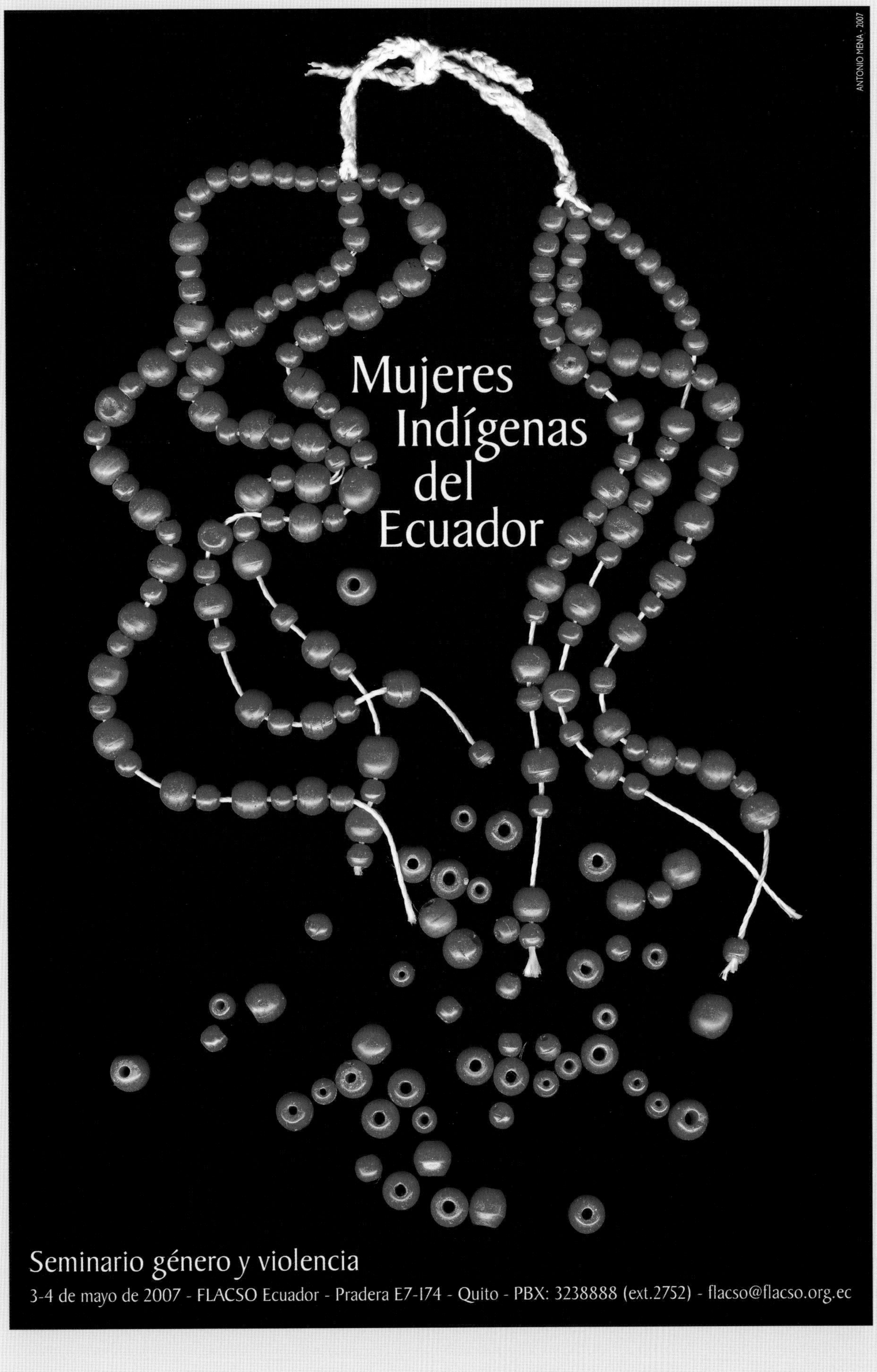

ANTONIO MENA · 2007

Mujeres
Indígenas
del
Ecuador

Seminario género y violencia
3-4 de mayo de 2007 - FLACSO Ecuador - Pradera E7-174 - Quito - PBX: 3238888 (ext.2752) - flacso@flacso.org.ec

EMOTIONAL SALIENCE

The English language has an estimated 400 words to express emotional states, but with visuals the ways are infinite. For a graphic to communicate and evoke emotion, it must be charged with personal meaning and significance. It must appeal to both the eyes and the affect. This motivates a person to attend to and to process a visual message.

Just as salient features such as color and shape pop out from the visual field during preattentive processing, emotional salience stands out against a sea of neutral graphics. People seem to preattentively pick up visual emotional signals, possibly to avoid threatening situations. People also have a tendency to place increased attention on the source of the emotional signal. Emotionally arousing events narrow a person's cognitive focus to concentrate on the causal circumstance. Similarly, emotionally salient graphics almost compel a person to pay attention and engage with the picture.

Moreover, research shows that people prefer emotional pictures to neutral ones. One study that measured emotional responses to advertisements found that successful ads evoke a strong emotional response. "Clearly the level and quality of emotional response is a critical differentiator between the best and the worst advertisements in this sample," concluded the study's author.[7]

vidual taste, cultural context, and gender. Yet cognitive research has found rather consistent associations between a color and its emotional and physical effects. A group of studies substantiated that cool colors tend to have a sedating effect and warm colors invoke more energetic feelings. Generally, green and blue colors evoke feelings of calmness and decreased anxiety. In contrast, red was found to be exciting, stimulating, and highly emotive. In a continuum from red to yellow, participants associated positive and cheery emotions with the colors that were closer to yellow.[8]

Other aspects of color that can evoke an emotional response are saturation and value. For example, highly saturated colors are more intensely felt than soft, pale, and neutral colors. Lighter colors are associated with more positive feelings and darker colors with more negative feelings.[9] Some researchers claim that saturation and value have a greater effect on emotion than hue. Color combinations with variations of value and saturation are an effective way to communicate emotional content and to convey meaning.

Designing for Emotion

Of all the basic design elements, color seems to have the most potential to evoke emotion. This is reflected in English language metaphors, which refer to a veritable rainbow of feelings, such as rose-colored glasses, feeling blue, green with envy, and red with anger. In addition to metaphorical usage, people tend to associate many aspects of color with emotions. These reactions may be influenced by personal experience, individual taste, cultural context, and gender.

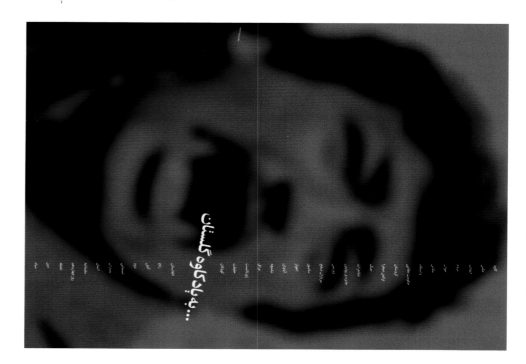

▶ Through color and pained imagery, In Memoriam of Kaveh Golestan expresses the grief felt by the death of the renowned photojournalist killed by a land mine in Iraq.

Majid Abassi,
Did Graphics, Iran

▶ In this promotional graphic for a poster exhibition, an intriguing, obscured photograph is an effective way to express emotion.

Majid Abbasi,
Did Graphics, Iran

Compositional effects are also powerful ways to express and evoke emotion. To generate a disquieting and disturbing experience, designers can take advantage of the audience's need to resolve tension. Tension can be generated through ambiguity—using shapes and forms that are indistinct, obstructed, and difficult to recognize and identify. Tension may also result from exaggeration, when forms, colors, and textures are obviously overstated. In addition, distortion can arouse emotion because viewers expect objects and people to have a natural or conventional shape. Any effect that prevents cognitive closure can potentially create an unsettling experience.

Powerful imagery increases emotional salience, particularly photographs and drawings of the face. Our brains are especially attuned to appraising facial expressions and following eye gaze. The rapid and efficient detection of facial emotion appears to be another biological mechanism on which designers can rely to increase a message's impact. Incorporating facial gestures that express emotional intensity will capture attention and make a graphic memorable.

Symbolism plays a critical role in visual communication and provides an eloquent way to communicate emotional content to represent abstract and often profound ideas. The diversity of objects and signs that work as visual symbols is enormous, providing designers with a large vocabulary to shape meaning. Through experience, people learn to associate the symbols of their culture with societal values and themes. In this process, many symbols acquire emotional meaning. Religion, nationalism, societal status, oppression, and justice are some of the diverse concepts that can be communicated with symbols.

Symbolism associated with New Orleans and the devastation from Hurricane Katrina creates a stirring poster used in a fund-raising effort for victims.

Greg Bennett, Siquis,
United States

WE'LL BE PARENTS SOMEDAY
For now we're using condoms.

PLANNED PARENTHOOD
1-800-800-PLAN www.ppnyc.org

Planning *is Power.*

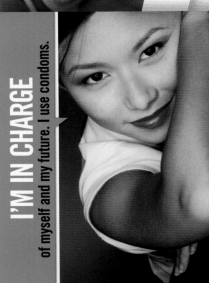

I'M IN CHARGE
of myself and my future. I use condoms.

PLANNED PARENTHOOD
1-800-800-PLAN www.ppnyc.org

Planning *is Power.*

▲ The calming colors, appealing images, and thoughtful message promote the benefits of mature decision making.

*Arno Ghelfi,
Katie Kleinsasser,
Public Media Center,*
United States

▼ The poignant imagery used in this brochure creates a touching narrative of the people that benefit from the organization.

*Niall O'Kelly, Schwartz
Brand Group, United States*

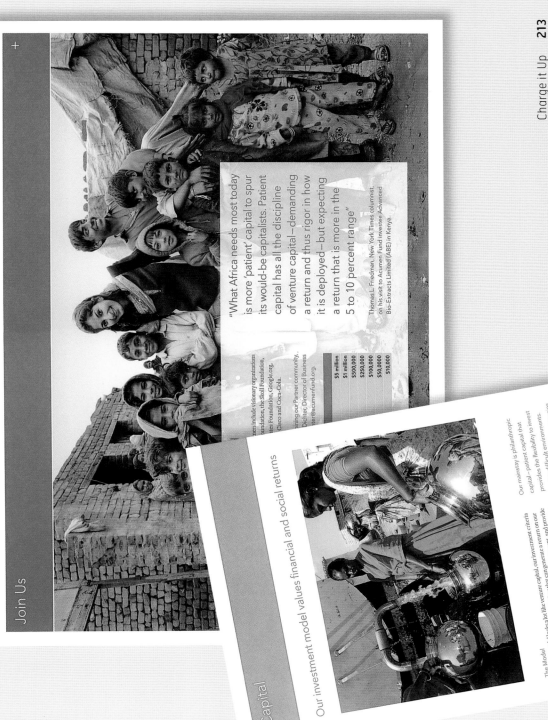

Join Us

"What Africa needs most today is more 'patient' capital to spur its would-be capitalists. Patient capital has all the discipline of venture capital—demanding a return and thus rigor in how it is deployed—but expecting a return that is more in the 5 to 10 percent range"

Thomas L. Friedman, New York Times columnist, on his visit to Acumen Fund investee Advanced Bio-Extracts Limited (ABE) in Kenya.

$5 million	
$1 million	
$500,000	
$250,000	
$100,000	
$50,0000	
$10,000	

...ces include visionary organizations
...oundation, the Skoll Foundation,
...tes Foundation, Google.org,
...Cisco and Coca-Cola.

...ining our Partner community.
...bichler, Director of Business
...ter@acumenfund.org.

Capital

Our investment model values financial and social returns

The Model
While our model looks a lot like venture capital, our investment criteria are different. We invest in enterprises that can generate a return on our capital, grow by a factor of ten in the fields of health, water, housing, and energy. breakthrough insights in the fields of health, water, housing, and energy. ...business models reach consumers in new ways with ... for low-income people. We invest where there ...people, high, and where there

Our mainstay is philanthropic capital—patient capital that provides the flexibility to invest in very difficult environments. We typically invest in companies with a 2–3 year operating history, an established business model, ...nd revenue stream. We give ...rt support to

NARRATIVES

People are powerfully drawn to stories and use them to naturally organize their own and others' experiences. Through this familiarity and comfort with the structure and emotion of the narrative, people often have a vicarious experience while reading or watching a story. Because of this cognitive and emotional readiness, visual narratives are an excellent way to generate an emotional resonance with the audience.

In books, film, theater, and television, we may find stories with a clever plot to be interesting, but it is their emotional impact that is most attractive. It is not uncommon to continue to watch a show or film with a thin plot and poor acting only to realize it is the magnetism of the emotional drama that sustains our interest. A significant feature of the narrative is that it has the power to captivate an audience regardless of whether it is based on experience or is completely fictional. It is the dramatic and emotional aspect of people's lives—their desires and achievements, their disappointments and sufferings—that is common to a narrative, whether it is fact or fantasy.

The emotional response to narratives has been substantiated in brain research. In a study where subjects listened to a script and were told to imagine their involvement in the scenes, the narratives triggered areas of the brain that emotionally prepared the participants to take physical action.[10] In other words, the brain reacted as though the story was occurring in the physical environment.

Graphic designers can use this natural human affinity for stories in imaginative ways. The crucial point is to create an absorbing visual narrative—a sequence of events and actions tied together with emotional and conceptual continuity. Visual narratives often follow a formal structure with an obvious beginning, middle, and end. Photographic documentaries, animated stories, graphic novels, and comic book formats achieve this because a sequence of images is understood to describe a succession of events. When pictures are placed in a temporal order, viewers will mentally fill in any gaps, such as actions needed to maintain continuity.[11]

In addition to this more structured approach, implicit narratives are also compelling. For example, promotional materials, annual reports, and brochures often embody a narrative that is implied on every page. For some, the narrative might follow the development and history of an organization. Others implicitly suggest a coherent emotional theme through image and type.

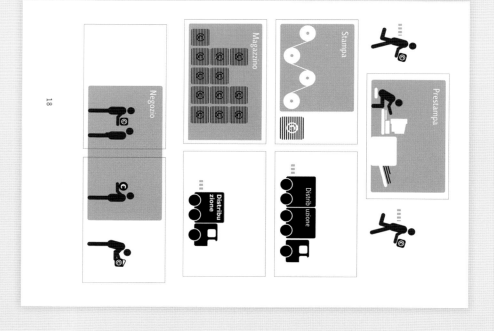

18

▶ A wordless narrative is used here to explain the traditional publishing process. Implementing this as a story adds to its interest.

Lorenzo De Tomasi, Italy

▶ A dramatic story line is illustrated to demonstrate the use of a new device that relays information on the status and location of wounded soldiers.

**Colin Hayes,
Colin Hayes Illustrator,**
United States

Narratives can emerge from timelines. Here, the history of MIT's Urban Studies and Planning Department is described through images and words.

Erica Gregg Howe, Philographica, *United States*

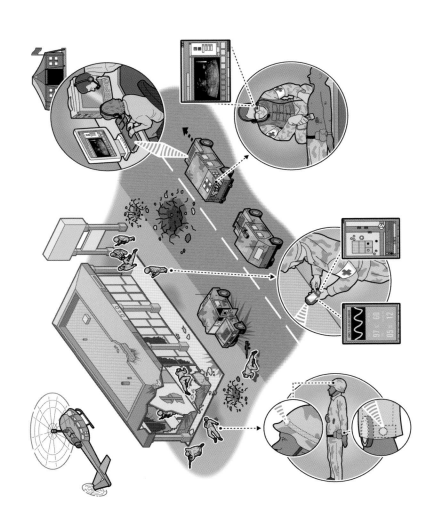

Dixie Albertson and Jeri Bowers, Darning Pixels, United States

Used as an employee-training tool, these illustrations employ a story-based approach to explain the causes of resistance to coaching and change.

Misunderstanding and lack of trust

No idea on first steps

NEW APPROACH
DIRECTIONS

1 Insert logs

2 Roll forward

3 Bring logs back to front

Resistance to Coaching and Change :

MAIN DRIVERS

▲ The story of movie piracy, from recording to distribution, is effectively described in narrative form for Sound & Vision magazine.

Colin Hayes,
Colin Hayes Illustrator, United States

▼ In this viewbook for a school of engineering, "Listen to our story" presents the advantages of the school in a narrative by its graduates. The narrative is completed through photographs of animated and engaged faculty.

Christine Kenney, IE Design + Communications, United States

Marc Bostian and Cameron
Eagle, S Design,
United States

Part of this report about
careers in the petroleum
industry uses an appealing
narrative in comic book
format to add interest.

The visual narrative in this college prospectus focuses on a nostalgic photographic journey leading to the present.

David Horton and Ian Koenig, Philographica, United States

We treasure the classic liberal arts tradition.

What we do at Kenyon emanates from integrity and a sense of self. We know who we are and what we believe.

We are Kenyon.

"When I wrote my name in the Matriculation Book, I felt connected not only with generations of Kenyon students, but with an unbroken chain of learning that leads back to antiquity. Even as a first-year student, I knew this was serious business."

Kemaru Nsokainiema, Class of 2005

...aspirations, there is no end in other ways with evidence that is some ways like that—obliged to do so with evidence that is some ways like. And we are always obliged to do—it suggestive, fragmentary, and difficult to interpret."

Iames r Bowsovec McGry-Bost One Distinguished Teaching Professor and Associate Professor of History

The only thing that can finally save the world is education. The only thing we could invest in that will yield more. There is nothing more.

VISUAL METAPHORS

Our cognitive system often relies on metaphors and analogies to think and imagine. It is how we understand things for which we have no specific knowledge. We use metaphors to transfer the properties of one object to another or to conceptualize an idea in terms of another. For example, in her book *Design for Communication*, Elisabeth Resnick describes the metaphor she uses to teach typography. "I describe typography as two-dimensional architecture upon which a foundation of visual communication can be built. Letterforms become the building blocks that create the structure to convey an idea or deliver a message."

We often use metaphors to describe phenomena that are difficult to verbalize, such as emotions. When emotions seem ambiguous and ethereal, metaphors help make them explicit and tangible. Pictorial metaphors can be vivid and imaginative when they compare or combine two previously unconnected objects or ideas. Designers often use emotionally charged imagery in metaphors to create impact. One effective way to bring a metaphor to life is to combine the qualities of two images. An example is a public health advertisement that combines a cooking mushroom with a nuclear mushroom cloud to communicate the potential dangers of food-borne illness.

Another approach is to juxtapose two images in the same graphic, implying that they should be compared; the properties of one image are intended to transfer to the second. Juxtaposing an image of a sleek computer with a racing panther, for example, implies that the computer has fast processing power. Visual metaphors can also stand on their own, as in this information graphic about the history of money explained on a Monopoly board.

When a visual metaphor succeeds, it synthesizes two objects or concepts to reveal a new connection or a deeper meaning. But to understand a metaphor requires knowledge of its cultural context and the ability to make the correct inferences. The viewer must be able to interpret a metaphor's figurative rather than literal meaning. Thus, the metaphor should accommodate the viewer's abilities, using recognizable objects and familiar concepts.

▶ *The history of money is explained in this information graphic for* Superinteressante *magazine that uses a Monopoly board as a metaphor.*

**Adriano Sambugaro,
Carlo Giovani Studio,** *Brazil*

▶ *The clever visual metaphor and clear copy send a straightforward message in this health sanitation campaign.*

**Tonatiuh Arturo Gómez,
AW Nazca Saatchi &
Saatchi,** *Venezuela*

La Santé

AN UNWASHED VEGETABLE CAN BECOME A DEADLY WEAPON

ALWAYS WASH YOUR VEGETABLES IN ORDER TO WIN THE BATTLE AGAINST FOODBORNE ILLNESS SUCH AS AMOEBIASIS, DISENTERY AND CHOLERA. THIS IS A HEALTHY MESSAGE FROM THE GASTRIC AND ANTIBACTERIAL THERAPY DIVISIONS OF ELTER DRUGS.

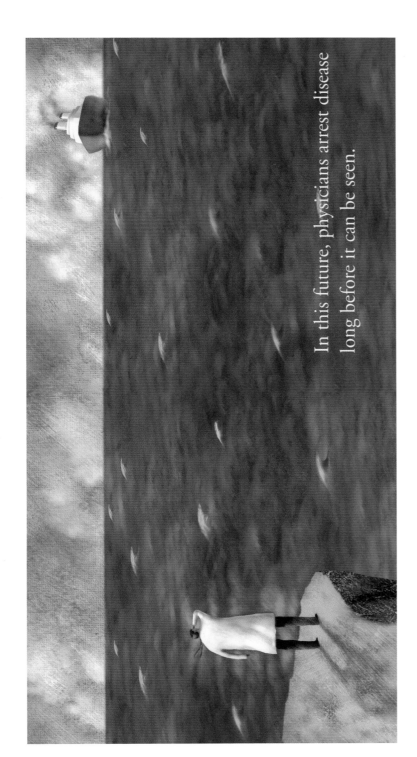

In this future, physicians arrest disease long before it can be seen.

▲ Metaphors can generate an emotional response if they speak to the imagination. This illustration expresses a future promise to arrest disease in an informational brochure about a children's hospital.

Erica Gregg Howe and Amy Lebow, Philographica, United States

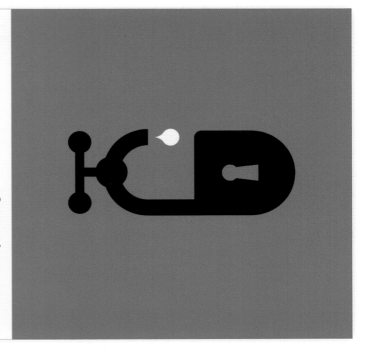

UN DP

Human Development Report **2006**

Water and human development
The 21st century challenge

▼ This metaphor used for the cover graphic of a United Nations report on water and human development aptly demonstrates the coming challenges of the global water crisis.

Peter Grundy and Tilly Northedge, United Kingdom

▼ This editorial piece on memory loss demonstrates how metaphors emotionally connect with the audience.

Travis Vermilye, Travis Vermilye Medical and Biological Illustration, United States

NOVELTY AND HUMOR

In the midst of ubiquitous visual communications, novelty can be riveting. A graphic with an unusual twist invokes an emotional reaction—surprise, astonishment, or possibly, shock. Unusual graphics reliably grab attention and arouse curiosity because they cross into unfamiliar territory, a place that challenges one's visual memory. Novelty tends to be amusing, but it can also tackle serious topics as well. It simply must defy convention and create visual surprise.

Research has found that any novel object triggers an orienting response. Distinctive objects, which are unfamiliar or out of context, create an emotional reaction that triggers attention and heightened interest. Perhaps we think that anything unusual could potentially be threatening, or this reaction may be a natural result of human curiosity. The intensity of the emotional reaction and the significance of the object contribute to the degree of interest that is aroused.

Novelty sustains attention because it doesn't match the associated schemas activated in long-term memory. When there are inconsistencies, such as when something is unexpected or unusual, additional visual attention and processing is required to comprehend the discrepancy.[12] This means that a person spends more time examining a novel graphic to resolve its inconsistencies.

Novelty arises from unusual juxtapositions or from seeing objects in unconventional perspectives. It results when unexpected themes are brought together and when type and image seem to oppose each other. The extent to which a graphic uses novelty affects the audience's emotional reaction. Moderate incongruities seem to generate the most favorable reactions among viewers. Extreme incongruities create confusion.

Humor is another form of novelty that, when properly implemented, evokes amusement and enjoyment. Messages with humor are often considered more interesting than serious messages. Unexpected events and entertaining graphics can generate a positive effect. Humor is usually related to deviating from normal expectations, from incongruity that can be resolved, and from contrasts between the everyday and the unanticipated. People also find humor in surprise and inconsistency. Simply processing and resolving discrepant information can result in humor. As with all forms of novelty, humorous strategies must be implemented with taste. Most people do not find it appropriate to see a light-hearted treatment of a very serious topic. This strategy can reduce the effectiveness of a message.

▶ Retro graphics and humorous copy appeal to young mobile travelers in this flyer advertising accommodations for backpackers visiting New Zealand.

Alexander Lloyd, Lloyds Graphic Design,
New Zealand

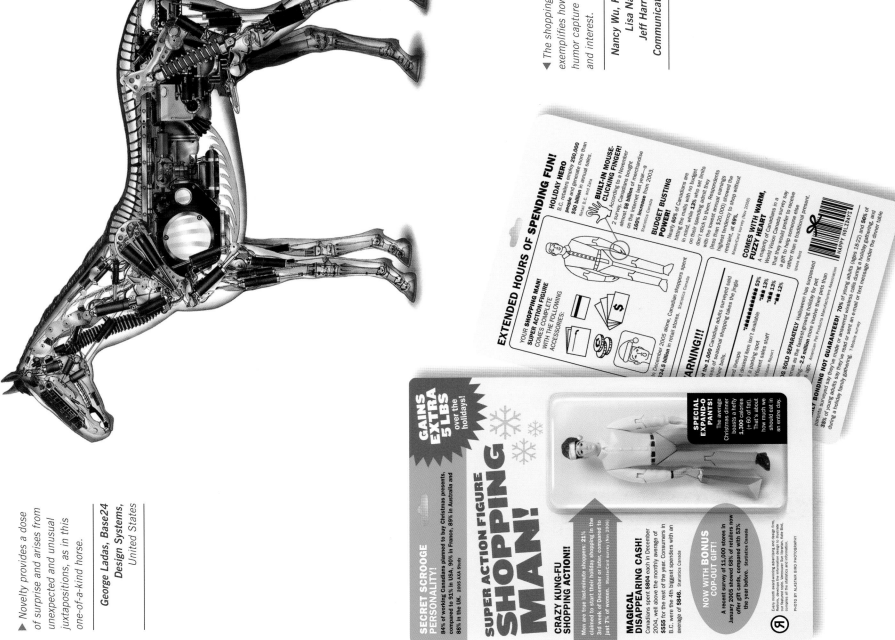

▲ Novelty provides a dose of surprise and arises from unexpected and unusual juxtapositions, as in this one-of-a-kind horse.

George Ladas, Base24 Design Systems, United States

▼ The shopping man doll exemplifies how novelty and humor capture attention and interest.

Nancy Wu, Kim Rigewell, Lisa Nakamura, and Jeff Harrison, Rethink Communications, Canada

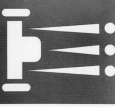

▼ Viewers will spend time reconciling the unusual juxtaposition of objects in this image for a theatrical brochure.

Francheska Guerrero,
Unfolding Terrain,
United States

▼ An unexpected end view of two pigs provides humor for the play Pig Farm in a theater festival brochure.

Francheska Guerrero,
Unfolding Terrain,
United States

PIG FARM

a play by GREG KOTIS

"You may hate the federal government, Tina. But the federal government loves you. At least, it could. If you'd let it."

From Greg Kotis, Tony-winning writer of the hit musical satire "Urinetown," comes a cliché-skewering comedy about Pig Farming where men are men, women are women, and pigs are everywhere. The feds want the snouts accurately counted;

Tom yearns to farm freely, and his wife just wants a baby. Their love is big as all outdoors — and so is their pig farm.

STICKFLY

a play by
Lydia R. Diamond

"... someone fell in love with someone they weren't supposed to . . . "

Funny and deeply passionate, Chicago writer Lydia R. Diamond's play is a probing family drama and an up-to-the-minute consideration of privilege and perception. When an elite African American family reunites on Martha's Vineyard, incendiary dialogues ignite about race and class, the desire to break free and the need to belong.

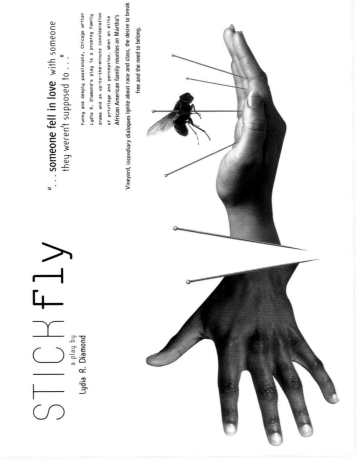

▼ This amusing idea for a self-promotional poster consists of designs on perforated cards that break apart and fit into a small juice box, which just happens to reflect this company's name.

Jay Smith, Juicebox De-
signs, United States

BIBLIOGRAPHY

Arnheim, Rudolf. Art and Visual Perception (Berkeley: University of California Press, 1974).

Bateson, Gregory. Steps to an Ecology of Mind: Collected Essays in Anthropology, Psychiatry, Evolution, and Epistemology (Chicago: University of Chicago Press, 2000).

Card, Stuart, Jock Mackinlay, and Ben Shneiderman. Readings in Information Visualization: Using Vision to Think (San Francisco: Morgan Kaufman, 1999).

Deregowski, Jan B. Distortion in Art (London: Routledge & Kegan Paul, 1984).

Evans, David, and Cindy Gadd. "Managing Coherence and Context in Medical Problem-Solving Discourse," in Cognitive Science in Medicine, ed. David Evans and Vimla Patel (Cambridge: MIT Press, 1989).

Evelyn Goldsmith, Research into Illustration: An Approach and a Review (Cambridge: Cambridge University Press, 1984).

Holmes, Nigel. Designing Pictorial Symbols (New York: Watson Guptill, 1985).

Kosslyn, Stephen. Clear and to the Point (Oxford: Oxford University Press, 2007).

Kress, Gunther, and Theo van Leeuwen. Reading Images: The Grammar of Visual Design. (London: Routledge, 1996).

Massironi, Manfredo. The Psychology of Graphic Images (Mahwah, NJ: Lawrence Erlbaum, 2001), 70.

Mayer, Richard E., ed., The Cambridge Handbook of Multimedia Learning (New York: Cambridge University Press, 2005).

Monahan, Jennifer. "Thinking Positively," in Designing Health Messages, ed. E. Maibach and R. Parrott (Thousand Oaks, CA: Sage, 1995), 81–98.

Norman, Donald A. Things That Make Us Smart: Defending Human Attributes in the Age of the Machine (London: Perseus Books, 1993), 41.

Paratore, Philip Carlo. Art and Design (Upper Saddle River, NJ: Prentice Hall, 1985).

Resnick, Elizabeth. Design for Communication: Conceptual Graphic Design Basics (Hoboken, NJ: Wiley, 2003).

Waimer, Howard. "Understanding Graphs and Tables," Educational Researcher 21 (1992).

Ware, Colin. Information Visualization: Perception for Design (San Francisco: Morgan Kaufmann, 2004).

Wurman, Saul. Information Anxiety 2 (Indianapolis: Que, 2001).

Zelanski, Paul, and Mary Pat Fisher. Design Principles and Problems (Fort Worth, Texas: Harcourt Brace College Publishers, 1996).

GLOSSARY OF TERMS

Bottom-up visual processing: visual awareness that is driven by an external stimulus

Cognitive load: the total amount of mental demand imposed on working memory at a given moment

Cognitive science: the multidisciplinary study of mind and intelligence

Dual coding: the theory that states verbal and visual information are processed through separate channels

Fovea: the region of the retina that gives us sharpness of vision

Long-term memory: a component of memory that provides relatively permanent storage

Mental model: broad conceptualization or representation about how things work in the real world

Schemas: the theoretical underlying structures of memory

Sensory memory: the immediate brief recording of information brought in by the senses that persists after the original stimulus has ceased

Top-down visual processing: visual awareness that is influenced by memories, expectations, and intentions

Working memory: the temporary storage of information while mental work is performed (sometimes known as short-term memory)

INTRODUCTION

1. Michael S. Beauchamp, e-mail message to author, March 19, 2008.

2. Lionel Standing, Jerry Conzeio, and Ralph Norman Haber, "Perception and Memory for Pictures: Single-Trial Learning of 2500 Visual Stimuli," Psychonomic Science 19 (1970): 73–74.

3. Kepes, Gyorgy. Language of Vision (Mineola, NY: Dover, 1995).

4. Dino Karabeg, "Designing Information Design," Information Design Journal 11 (2003): 82–90.

SECTION 1: GETTING GRAPHICS

1. Elizabeth Boling, et al., "Instructional Illustrations: Intended Meanings and Learner Interpretations," Journal of Visual Literacy 24 (2004): 189.

2. Joydeep Bhattacharya and Hellmuth Petsche, "Shadows of Artistry: Cortical Synchrony during Perception and Imagery of Visual Art," Cognitive Brain Research 13 (2002): 170–186.

3. C. F. Noide, P. J. Locher, and E. A. Krupinski, "The Role of Format Art Training on Perception and Aesthetic Judgment of Art Compositions," Leonardo 26 (1993): 219–227.

4. Jorge Frascara, "Graphic Design: Fine Art or Social Science?" in Design Studies: Theory and Research in Graphic Design, ed. Audrey Bennett and Steven Heller (Princeton: Princeton Architectural Press, 2006), 28.

5. Robert Solso, Cognition and the Visual Arts (Cambridge: MIT Press, 1994).

6. Martin Graziano and Mariano Sigman, "The Dynamics of Sensory Buffer: Geometric, Spatial and Experience-Dependent Shaping of Iconic Memory," Journal of Vision 8 (2008): 1–13.

7. Nelson Cowan, "The Magical Number 4 in Short-Term Memory: A Reconsideration of Mental Storage Capacity," Behavioral and Brain Sciences 24 (2000): 87–185.

8. Akira Miyake and Priti Shah, "Models of Working Memory: An Introduction," in Models of Working Memory: Mechanisms of Active Maintenance and Executive Control, ed. Akira Miyake and Priti Shah (Cambridge: Cambridge University Press, 1999), 1–27.

9. Lynn Hasher, Cindy Lustig, and Rose Zacks, "Inhibitory Mechanisms and the Control of Attention," in Variation in Working Memory, ed. Andrew R. A. Conway et al. (New York: Oxford University Press, 2007), 227–249.

10. Milton J. Dehn, Working Memory and Academic Learning: Assessment and Intervention (Hoboken, NJ: Wiley, 2008).

11. John Sweller, "Visualisation and Instructional Design," International Workshop on Dynamic Visualizations and Learning, 2002, www.iwm-kmrc.de/workshops/visualization.

12. Robert A. Bjork and Elizabeth Ligon Bjork, "A New Theory of Disuse and an Old Theory of Stimulus Fluctuation," in From Learning Processes to Cognitive Processes: Essays in Honor of William K. Estes, Volume 2, ed. Alice F. Healy (Mahwah, NJ: Lawrence Erlbaum, 1992), 36.

13. Ibid.

14. Jim Sweller, "Implications of Cognitive Load Theory for Multimedia Learning," in The Cambridge Handbook of Multimedia Learning, ed. Richard E. Mayer (New York: Cambridge University Press, 2005), 19–30.

15. William Winn, "Cognitive Perspectives in Psychology," in Handbook of Research on Educational Communications and Technology, ed. David H. Jonassen and Phillip Harris (Mahwah, NJ: Lawrence Erlbaum, 2003).

16. Joan Peeck, "Increasing Picture Effects in Learning from Illustrated Text," Learning and Instruction 3 (1993): 227–238.

PRINCIPLE 1: ORGANIZE FOR PERCEPTION

1. Anne Treisman, "Preattentive Processing in Vision," Computer Vision, Graphics, and Image Processing 31 (1985): 156.

2. Anne Treisman and Stephen Gormican, "Feature Analysis in Early Vision: Evidence from Search Asymmetries," Psychological Review 95 (1988).

3. Colin Ware, Information Visualization: Perception for Design (San Francisco: Morgan-Kauffman, 2004).

4. William Winn, "Contributions of Perceptual and Cognitive Processes to the Comprehension of Graphics" in Comprehension of Graphics, ed. Wolfgang Schnotz and Raymond W. Kulhavy (Amsterdam: North Holland, 1994), 12.

5. Jeremy M. Wolfe and Todd S. Horowitz, "What Attributes Guide the Deployment of Visual Attention and How Do They Do It?" Nature Reviews Neuroscience 5 (2004): 1–7.

6. Anne Treisman, "Preattentive Processing in Vision," Computer Vision, Graphics, and Image Processing 31 (1985): 156–177.

7. James J. Gibson, The Ecological Approach to Visual Perception (Mahwah, NJ: Lawrence Erlbaum, 1986), 116.

8. Timothy P. McNamara, "Mental Representations of Spatial Relations," Cognitive Psychology 18 (1986): 87–121.

9. Stephen Palmer and Irvin Rock, "Rethinking Perceptual Organization: The Role of Uniform Connectedness," Psychonomic Bulletin & Review 1 (1994): 29–55.

PRINCIPLE 2: DIRECT THE EYES

1. J. P. Hansen and M. Støvring, "Udfordringer er Blikfang," Hrymfaxe 3 (1988): 28–31 in ed. Arne John Glenstrup and Theo Engell-Nielsen, Eye Controlled Media: Present and Future State, University of Copenhagen Institute of Computer Science, 1995, www.diku.dk/~panic/eyegaze/node17.html.

2. Eric Jamet, Monica Gavota, and Christophe Quaireau, "Attention Guiding in Multimedia Learning," Learning and Instruction 18 (2008): 135–145.

3. Jason Tipples, "Eye Gaze Is Not Unique: Automatic Orienting in Response to Uninformative Arrows," Psy-

chonomic Bulletin & Review 9 (2002): 314–318.

4. Michael J. Posner, "Orienting of Attention," Quarterly Journal of Experimental Psychology 32 (1980): 3–25.

5. Jan Theeuwes, "Irrelevant Singletons Capture Attention," in Neurobiology of Attention, ed. Laurent Itti, Geraint Rees, and John K. Tsotsos (Burlington, MA: Elsevier Academic Press, 2005), 418–427.

6. Eric Jamet, Monica Gavota, and Christophe Quaireau, "Attention Guiding in Multimedia Learning," Learning and Instruction 18 (2008): 135–145.

7. Walter Niekamp, "An Exploratory Investigation into Factors Affecting Visual Balance," Educational Communications and Technology 29 (1981): 37–48.

8. Ibid.

9. Evelyn Goldsmith, Research into Illustration: An Approach and a Review (Cambridge: Cambridge University Press, 1984).

10. Rudolf Arnheim, Art and Visual Perception (Berkeley: University of California Press, 1974).

11. Jeannette A. M. Lortejie et al., "Delayed Response to Animate Implied Motion in Human Motion Processing Areas," Journal of Cognitive Neuroscience 18 (2006): 158–168.

12. Andrea R. Halpern and Michael H. Kelly, "Memory Biases in Left Versus Right Implied Motion," Journal of Experimental Psychology: Learning, Memory, and Cognition 19 (1993): 471–484.

13. Noam Sagive and Shlomo Bentin, "Structural Encoding of Human and Schematic Faces: Holistic and Part-Based Processes," Journal of Cognitive Neuroscience 13 (2001): 937–951.

14. Shlomo Bentin et al., "Electrophysiological Studies of Face Perception in Humans," Journal of Cognitive Neuroscience 8 (1996): 551–565.

15. Jason Tipples, "Eye Gaze Is Not Unique: Automatic Orienting in Response to Uninformative Arrows," Psychonomic Bulletin & Review 9 (2002): 314–318.

16. Stephen Langton and Vicki Bruce, "You Must See the Point: Automatic Processing of Cues to the Direction of Social Attention," Journal of Experimental Psychology: Human Perception and Performance 26 (2000): 755.

17. Bruce Hood, Douglas Willen, and John Driver, "Adult's Eyes Trigger Shifts of Visual Attention in Human Infants," Psychological Science 9 (1998): 131-134.

18. Patricia D. Mautone and Richard E. Mayer, "Signaling as a Cognitive Guide in Multimedia Learning," Journal of Educational Psychology 93 (2001): 377-389.

19. David E. Irwin, "Fixation Location and Fixation Duration as Indices of Cognitive Processing" in The Interface of Language, Vision, and Action ed. John M. Henderson and Fernanda Ferreira (New York: Psychology Press, 2004), 105-134.

20. Richard J. Lamberski and Francis M. Dwyer, "The Instructional Effect of Coding (Color and Black and White) on Information Acquisition and Retrieval," Educational Communications and Technology Journal 31 (1993): 9-21.

PRINCIPLE 3: REDUCE REALISM

1. Christopher Chabris and Stephen Kosslyn, "Representational Correspondence as a Basic Principle of Diagram Design" in Knowledge and Information Visualization, Searching for Synergies, ed. Sigmar-Olaf Tergan and Tanja Keller (New York: Springer, 2005), 36-57.

2. Joe Savrock, "Visual Aids in Instruction and Their Relationship to Student Achievement" (E-Bridges, Penn State College of Education News), www.ed.psu.edu/.

3. Gary Anglin, Hossein Vaez, and Kathryn Cunningham, "Visual Representations and Learning: the Role of Static and Animated Graphics," in Handbook of Research for Educational Communications and Technology, ed. David H. Jonassen (Mahwah, NJ: Lawrence Erlbaum, 2004).

4. Paul Rademacher et al. "Measuring the Perception of Visual Realism in Images," 2001, http://research.microsoft.com/.

5. Gavriel Solomon, Interaction of Media, Cognition and Learning (Mahwah, NJ: Lawrence Erlbaum, 1994).

6. Peter Longhurst, Patrick Ledda, and Alan Calmers. "Psychophysically Based Artistic Techniques for Increased Perceived Realism of Virtual Environments," in Proceedings of the 2nd International Conference on Computer Graphics, Virtual Reality, Visualisation and Interaction in Africa, February 2003, http://portal.acm.org/.

7. Yvonne Rogers, "Icons at the Interface: Their Usefulness," Interacting with Computers 1 (1989): 105-117.

8. See Note 3: 867.

9. Stephen Doheny-Farina, Effective Documentation: What We Have Learned from Research, (Cambridge: MIT Press, 1988).

10. Janette Atkinson, Fergus Campbell, and Marcus Francis, "The Magic Number 4 ± 0: A New Look at Visual Numerosity Judgments," Perception 5 (1976): 327-334.

PRINCIPLE 4: MAKE THE ABSTRACT CONCRETE

1. Jacques Bertin, Semiology of Graphics (Madison: University of Wisconsin Press, 1984).

2. Barbara Tversky, "Some Ways that Graphics Communicate," in Working with Words and Images, ed. Nancy Allen (New York: Ablex Publishing, 2002).

3. William Winn, "How Readers Search for Information in Diagrams," Contemporary Educational Psychology 18 (1993): 162-185

4. Julie Heiser and Barbara Tversky, "Arrows in Comprehending and Producing Mechanical Diagrams," Cognitive Science 30 (2006): 581-592.

5. William Winn, "Cognitive Perspectives in Psychology," in Handbook of Research on Educational Communications and Technology, ed. David H. Jonassen and Phillip Harris (Mahwah, NJ: Lawrence Erlbaum, 2003).

6. William Winn, "How Readers Search for Information in Diagrams," Contemporary Educational Psychology 18 (1993): 162–185.

7. William S. Cleveland and Robert McGill, "Graphical Perception: The Visual Decoding of Quantitative Information on Graphical Displays of Data," Journal of the Royal Statistical Society 150 (1987): 192–199.

8. John W. Tukey, "Data-Based Graphics: Visual Display in the Decades to Come," Statistical Science 5 (1990): 327–339.

9. Stephen M. Kosslyn, "Understanding Charts and Graphs," Applied Cognitive Psychology 3 (1989): 185–226.

10. Stephen M. Kosslyn, Elements of Graph Design (New York: W. H. Freeman and Company, 1994).

11. Jeff Zacks and Barbara Tversky, "Bars and Lines: A Study of Graphic Communication," Memory and Cognition 27 (1999): 1073–1079.

12. Priti Shah, Richard E. Mayer, and Mary Hegarty, "Graphs as Aids to Knowledge Construction: Signaling Techniques for Guiding the Process of Graph Comprehension," Journal of Educational Psychology 91 (1999): 690–702.

13. Stuart K. Card, Jock D. Mackinlay, and Ben Shneiderman, Readings in Information Visualization: Using Vision to Think (San Francisco: Morgan Kaufmann, 1999), 7.

14. Lynn S. Liben, "Thinking through Maps," in Spatial Schemas and Abstract Thought, Merideth Gattis ed. (Cambridge: Massachusetts Institute of Technology, 2001), 50.

15. Michael P. Verdi and Raymond W. Kulhavey, "Learning with Maps and Texts: An Overview," Educational Psychology Review 14 (2002): 27–46.

16. Lynn S. Liben, "Thinking through Maps," in Spatial Schemas and Abstract Thought, ed. Merideth Gattis (Cambridge: Massachusetts Institute of Technology, 2001) 45–78.

17. William A. Kealy and James M. Webb, "Contextual Influences of Maps and Diagrams on Learning," Contemporary Educational Psychology 20 (1995): 340–358.

PRINCIPLE 5: CLARIFY COMPLEXITY

1. Larry Nesbit, "Relationship between Eye Movement, Learning, and Picture Complexity," Educational Communications and Technology Journal, 29 (1981): 109–116.

2. Richard Clark, Keith Howard, and Sean Early, "Motivational Challenges Experienced in Highly Complex Learning Environments," in Handling Complexity in Learning Environments, ed. Jan Elen, Richard Clark, and Joost Lowcyck (Oxford: Elsevier, 2006), 27–42.

3. David Strayer and Frank Drews, "Attention," in Handbook of Applied Cognition, ed. Francis Durso (Hoboken, NJ: Wiley & Sons, 2007), 29–54.

4. Jan Elen and Richard E. Clark, "Setting the Scene: Complexity and Learning Environments," in Handling Complexity in Learning Environments: Theory and Research (Oxford: Elsevier, 2006), 2.

5. Eleni Michailidou, "ViCRAM: Visual Complexity Rankings and Accessibility Metrics," Accessibility and Computing 86 (2006).

6. John Sweller, "How the Human Cognitive System Deals with Complexity," in Handling Complexity in Learning Environments: Theory and Research, ed. Jan Elen and Richard E. Clark (Oxford: Elsevier, 2006), 13–25.

7. Ibid.

8. E. Pollick, P. Chandler, and J. Sweller, "Assimilating Complex Information," Learning and Instruction 12 (2002): 61–86.

9. Christopher Kurby and Jeffrey Zacks, "Segmentation in the Perception and Memory of Events," Trends in Cognitive Sciences 12 (2007): 72–79.

10. Woodman et al., "Perceptual Organization Influences Visual Working Memory," Psychonomic Bulletin & Review 10 (2003): 80–87.

11. Eric Jamet, Monica Gavota, and Chrisophe Quaireau, "Attention Guiding in Multimedia Learning," Learning and Instruction 18 (2008): 135–145.

12. Gary Bertoline et al., Technical Graphics Communication (Boston: McGraw-Hill, 1997), 995.

13. Cindy Hmelo-Silver and Merav Pfeffer, "Comparing Expert and Novice Understanding of a Complex System," Cognitive Science 28 (2004): 127–138.

14. Mary Hegarty, "Multimedia Learning about Physical Systems," in Cambridge Handbook of Multimedia Learning, ed. Richard E. Mayer (New York: Cambridge University Press, 2005), 447–466.

15. Takahiro Kawabe and Kayo Miura, "New Motion Illusion Caused by Pictorial Motion Lines," Experimental Psychology 55 (2008): 228–234.

16. William Winn, "Cognitive Perspectives in Psychology," in Handbook of Research on Educational Communications and Technology, ed. David H. Jonassen and Phillip Harris (Mahwah, NJ: Lawrence Erlbaum, 2003).

17. Lawrence W. Barsalou, Cognitive Psychology: An Overview for Cognitive Scientists, (Mahwah, NJ: Lawrence Erlbaum, 1992).

PRINCIPLE 6: CHARGE IT UP

1. Maurizio Codispoti, Vera Ferrari, and Margaret M. Bradley, "Repetition and Event-Related Potentials," Journal of Cognitive Neuroscience 19 (2007): 577–586.

2. Judy Gregory, "Social Issues Infotainment," Information Design Journal 11 (2003): 67–81.

3. Dillard et al., "The Multiple Affective Outcome of AIDS PSAs," Communication Research 23 (1996): 44–72.

4. Margaret Matlin, Cognition (Hoboken, NJ: John Wiley and Sons, 2005).

5. Lewis Donohes, Philip Palmgreen, and Jack Duncan, "An Activation Model of Exposure," Communication Monographs 47 (1980): 295–303.

6. Dillard et al., "The Multiple Affective Outcome of AIDS PSAs," Communication Research 23 (1996): 44–72.

7. Bruce F. Hall, "On Measuring the Power of Communications," Journal of Advertising Research 44 (2004): 181–187.

8. Tom Clarke and Alan Costall, "The Emotional Connotations of Color: A Qualitative Investigation," COLOR Research and Application 33 (2008): 406–410.

9. Ibid.

10. Dean Sabatinelli et al., "The Neural Basis of Narrative Imagery: Emotion and Action," Progress in Brain Research 156 (2006): 93–103.

11. Patricia Baggett, "Memory for Explicit and Implicit Information in Picture Stories," Journal of Verbal Learning and Verbal Behavior 14 (1975): 538–548.

12. G. R. Loftus and N. H. Mackworth, "Cognitive Determinants of Fixation Location during Picture Viewing," Journal of Experimental Psychology: Human Perception and Performance 4 (1978): 565–572.

Majid Abbasi
Did Graphics, Inc.
Tehran, Iran
didgraphics.com
Page 56, 210, 211

Dixie Albertson and Jeri Bowers
Darning Pixels, Inc.
Waterloo, IA USA
darningpixels.com
Page 216

Jonathan Avery
University of North Carolina
Morganton, NC USA
averyj@email.unc.edu
Page 102

Jonas Banker and Ida Wessel
BankerWessel
Stockholm, Sweden
bankerwessel.com
Page 82, 93, 106

Stephen J. Beard
Stephen J. Beard Infographics
Fishers, IN USA
stephenjbeard.com
Page 91

Sorin Bechira
X3 Studios
Timisoara, Romania
x3studios.com
Page 86, 204, 212

Greg Bennett
Siquis
Baltimore, MD USA
siquis.com
Page 57, 82

Eliot Bergman
Shinjuku-ku, Tokyo Japan
ebergman.com
Page 28, 96, 112, 149

Drew Berry
The Walter and Eliza Hall Institute of
Medical Research
Parkville, Victoria Australia
wehi.edu.au
Page 51

Melisa Beveridge
Natural History Illustration
Brooklyn, NY USA
naturalhistoryillustration.com
Page 99, 191, 192

Annie Bissett
Northampton, MA USA
anniebisset.com
Page 25

Rhonald Blommestijn
Amersfoort, Netherlands
blommestijn.com
Page 18, 29, 34

Mark Boediman
Clif Bar & Company
Berkeley, CA USA
clifbar.com
Page 50

Marc Bostian and Cameron Eagle
s design, inc.
Oklahoma City, OK USA
sdesigninc.com
Page 218

Marlena Buczek-Smith
Ensign Graphics
Wallington, NJ USA
ensigngraphics.net
Page 163

Lee Byron
Pittsburgh, PA USA
lee@megamu.com
leebyron.com
Page 150

Alberto Cairo
University of North Carolina
Chapel Hill, NC USA
albertocairo.com
Page 168, 179

Eli Carrico
Los Angeles, CA USA
modulate.net
Page 158

Ninian Carter
ninian.net
Page 39

Sarah Cazee
Miami, FL USA
iamsarahcazee.com
Page 124

Wing Chan
Wing Chan Design, Inc.
New York, NY USA
wingchandesign.com
Page 121, 201

Vivien Chow, Edmund Li, Fang-Pin Lee,
Pauline Dolovich, Tony Reich, and
Stephen Petri
Reich + Petch
Toronto, ON Canada
reich-petch.com
Page 197, 198

Bryan Christie
Bryan Christie Design
Maplewood, NJ USA
bryanchristiedesign.com
Page 53, 101, 175, 193

Gordon Cieplak
Schwartz Brand Group
New York, NY USA
ms-ds.com
Page 32

Kristin Clute
University of Washington
Seattle, WA USA
kristinclute@gmail.com
Page 38

Cog Design
London, UK
cogdesign.com
Page 80, 115, 205

Simon Cook
London, UK
made-in-england.org
Page 176

Heather Corcoran
Plum Studio
St. Louis, MO USA
sweetplum.com
Page 201

Heather Corcoran and Diana Scubert
Plum Studio
St. Louis, MO USA
sweetplum.com
Page 137

Heather Corcoran, Colleen Conrado,
Jennifer Saltzman, and Anna Donovan
Plum Studio and Visual Communications
Research Studio
St. Louis, MO USA
sweetplum.com
Page 116

Mike Costelloe and D.B. Dowd
Visual Communications Research Studio
(VCRS) at Washington University
St. Louis, MO USA
Page 142

MaryClare M. Crabtree
Illinois Institute of Art
Chicago, IL USA
crabtreemc@gmail.com
Page 188

Drew Crowley
XPLANE
St. Louis, MO USA
xplane.com
Page 141

Alberto Cuadra
The Houston Chronicle
Richmond, TX USA
acuadra.com
Page 111, 135, 143

Erin Cubert
Nashville, TN USA
erincubert@gmail.com
Page 208

Jaana Davidjants
Wiyumi
Berlin, Germany
wiyumi.com
Page 200

Drew Davies
Oxide Design Co.
Omaha, NE USA
oxidedesign.com
cherubino.com
Page 169

Lorenzo De Tomasi
Sesto Calende, VA Italy
isotype.org
Page 78, 138, 214

Sudarshan Dheer and Ashoomi Dholakia
Graphic Communication Concepts
Mumbai, India
gccgrd.com
Page 72

Greg Dietzenbach
McCullough Creative
Dubuque, IA USA
shootforthemoon.com
Page 37

Sean Douglass
Sammamish, WA USA
colossalhand.com
Page 132

Jean-Manuel Duvivier
Jean-Manuel Duvivier Illustration
Brussels, Belgium
jmduvivier.com
Page 6, 42, 85, 95, 120

Angela Edwards
Indianapolis, IN USA
angelaedwards.com
Page 69, 161

Chronopoulou Ekaterini
La Cambre School of Visual Art
Brussels, Belgium
catcontact@gmail.com
Page 73

Franziska Erdle
Milch Design
Munich, Germany
milch-design.de
Page 134, 160

Chiqui Esteban
Público
Madrid, Spain
infografistas.com
Page 174

Chiqui Esteban and Álvaro Valiño
Público
Madrid, Spain
infografistas.com
Page 157

Nicholas Felton
Megafone
New York, NY USA
feltron.com
Page 67

David Fierstein
David Fierstein Illustration, Animation
& Design
Felton, CA USA
davidiad.com
Page 47, 185

Brian Finn
Iaepetus Press
Bend, OR USA
iapetuspress.com
Page 165

Kimberly Fulton
University of Washington
Kirkland, WA USA
kjfulton@washington.edu
Page 181

Arno Ghelfi
l'atelier starno
San Francisco, CA USA
starno.com
Page 13, 50, 145

Arno Ghelfi and Katie Kleinsasser
Public Media Center
San Francisco, CA USA
publicmediacenter.org
Page 213

Janet Giampietro
Langton Cherubino Group
New York, NY USA
Langton
Page 113

Tonatiuh Arturo Gómez
AW Nazca Saatchi & Saatchi, Venezuela
Caracas, Miranda Venezuela
Page 221

Larry Gormley
History Shots
Westford, MA USA
historyshots.com
Page 128

Larry Gormley
History Shots
Westford, MA USA
historyshots.com
Page 162

Dan Greenwald and Kimberley Cloutier
White Rhino
Burlington, MA USA
Whiterhino.com
Page 128, 162

John Grimwade
Condé Nast Publications
New York, NY USA
johngrimwade.com
Page 98, 133

John Grimwade, Liana Zamora,
and Christine Picavet
Condé Nast Publications
New York, NY USA
johngrimwade.com
Page 80, 132

Peter Grundy and Tilly Northedge
Grundini
Middlesex, UK
grundini.com
Page 11, 105, 148, 223

Francheska Guerrero
Unfolding Terrain
Hagerstown, MD USA
unfoldingterrain.com
Page 94, 100, 227

Surabhi Gurukar
Apostrophe Design
Bangalore, Karnataka India
apostrophedesign.in
Page 97

Lane Hall
Wauwatosa, WI USA
lanehall@uwm.edu
Page 35

Jacob Halton
The Illinois Institute of Art
Chicago, IL USA
jacobhalton@gmail.com
jacobhalton.com
Page 187

Nathanaël Hamon
Slang
Berlin, Germany
slanginternational.org
Page 200

Simon Hancock
There
Sydney, Australia
there.com.au
Page 119

Kevin Hand
Jersey City, NJ USA
kevinhand.com
Page 20, 40, 194, 195

Colin Hayes
Colin Hayes Illustrator, Inc.
Everett, WA USA
colinhayes.com
Page 104, 139, 191, 215, 217

Bruce W. Herr II, Todd M. Holloway,
and Katy Borner
Bloomington, IN USA
scimaps.org/maps/wikipedia
Page 16–17

Nigel Holmes
Westport, CT USA
nigelholmes.com
Page 11, 30, 74. 75, 122, 178, 182–183

David Horton and Ian Koenig
Philographica, Inc.
Brookline, MA USA
philographica.com
Page 219

David Horton and Amy Lebow
Philographica, Inc.
Brookline, MA USA
philographica.com
Page 68

Erica Gregg Howe
Philographica, Inc.
philographica.com
Brookline, MA USA
Page 215

Erica Gregg Howe and Amy Lebow
Philographica, Inc.
Brookline, MA USA
philographica.com
Page 125, 223

Information Design Studio
Amsterdam, Netherlands
theworldasflatland.net
Page 134

Ian Lynam
Ian Lynam Creative Direction & Design
Tokyo, Japan
ianlynam.com
Page 61, 70, 87

Dermot MacCormack, Patricia McElroy
21xdesign
Broomall, PA USA
21xdesign.com
Page 157

Taylor Marks
XPLANE
St. Louis, MO USA
xplane.com
Page 12

Taylor Marks, Stephanie Meier, D. B. Dowd, Sarah Phares, Sarah Sisterson, Enrique VonRohr, and Amanda Wolff
Visual Communications Research Studio (VCRS) at Washington University
St. Louis, MO USA
Page 109

Rodrigo Maroja and Carlo Giovani
Carlo Giovani Studio
São Paulo, Brazil
carlogiovani.com
Page 166-167

Mark McGowan and David Goodsell
Exploratorium
San Francisco, CA USA
exploratorium.edu
Page 76

Stuart Medley
Lightship Visual
Duncraig, Australia
lightshipvisual.com
Page 110

Antonio Mena
Antonio Mena Design
Quito, Ecuador
Page 54, 114, 209

Will Miller
Firebelly Design
Chicago, IL USA
firebellydesign.com
Page 158

Daniel Müller and Joanne Haderer Müller
Haderer & Müller Biomedical Art, LLC
Melrose, MA USA
haderermuller.com
Page 10, 31, 90, 173, 186

Vu Nguyen
Biofusion Design
Seattle, WA USA
biofusiondesign.com
Page 180

Niall O'Kelly
Schwartz Brand Group
New York, NY USA
ms-ds.com
Page 213

A. Osterwalder, P. Bardesono, S. Wagner, A. Bromer and M. Drozdowski
i_d buero
Stuttgart, Germany
i-dbuero.de
Page 94

Karen Parry and Louis Jaffe
Black Graphics
San Francisco, CA USA
blackgraphics.com
Page 101

Stefanie Posavec
London, UK
stefpos@gmail.com
Page 153

Nivedita Ramesh
University of Washington
Seattle, WA USA
nivi@u.washington.edu
Page 176

Emmi Salonen
Emmi
London, UK
emmi.co.uk
Page 120

Adriano Sambugaro
Carlo Giovani Studio
São Paulo, Brazil
carlogiovani.com
Page 220

Jan Schwochow, Katharina Erfurth, Sebastian Piesker, Katrin Lamm, Juliana Köneke, Jaroslaw Kaschtalinski
Golden Section Graphics GmbH
Berlin, Germany
golden-section-graphics.com
Page 64-65, 149, 170, 189

Christopher Short
Christopher B. Short, LLC
Stroudsburg, PA USA
chrisshort.com
Page 60, 88

Jay Smith
Juicebox Designs
Nashville, TN USA
juiceboxdesigns.com
Page 116, 226

Dale Sprague, Joslynn Anderson
Canyon Creative
Las Vegas, NV USA
canyoncreative.com
Page 90, 205

Aviad Stark
Graphic Advance
Palisades Park, NJ USA
graphicadvance.com
Page 112, 139, 181

Shinnoske Sugisaki
Shinnoske, Inc.
Osaka, Japan
shinn.co.jp
Page 48, 62, 77

Russell Tate
Clovelly, Australia
russelltate.com
Page 118, 159

Kara Tennant
Carnegie Mellon University
Pittsburgh, PA USA
karatennant@gmail.com
karatennant.com
Page 152

Benjamin Thomas
Bento Graphics
Tokyo, Japan
bentographics.com
Page 105

Veronica Neira Torres
Granada, Nicaragua
ariesbeginner.deviantart.com
vero_nt88@hotmail.com
Page 48

David Van Essen, Charles Anderson,
Daniel Felleman
Produced with permission from Science
magazine
Page 24

Travis Vermilye
Travis Vermilye Medical & Biological
Illustration
Denver, CO USA
tvermilye.com
Page 190, 222

Amy Vest
Applied Biosystems Brand &
Creative Group
Foster City, CA USA
Page 147, 184

Juliana Vidigal, Reneta Steffen,
and Carlo Giovani
Carlo Giovani Studio
São Paulo, Brazil
carlogiovani.com
Page 21, 160–161, 164

Christine Walker
stressdesign
Syracuse, NY USA
stressdesign.com
Page 108

Dave Willis, Mischa Kostandov,
Dan Riskin, Jaime Peraire,
David H. Laidlaw, Sharon Swartz,
and Kenny Breuer
Engineers from Brown University and MIT
Providence, RI USA
fluids.engin.brown.edu
Page 151

Nancy Wu, Kim Rigewell, Lisa Nakamura
and Jeff Harrison
Rethink Communications
Vancouver, British Columbia Canada
rethinkcommunications.com
Page 225

Maziar Zand
M. Zand Studio
Tehran, Iran
mzand.com
Page 8, 46, 69, 88

Rose Zgodzinski
Information Graphics
Toronto, Ontario Canada
chartsmapsanddiagrams.com
Page 147